High School
Journalism

High School Journalism

A Practical Guide

JIM STREISEL

McFarland & Company, Inc., Publishers
Jefferson, North Carolina, and London

LIBRARY OF CONGRESS CATALOGUING-IN-PUBLICATION DATA

Streisel, Jim, 1971–
High school journalism : a practical guide /
Jim Streisel.
p.   cm.
Includes index.

ISBN-13: 978-0-7864-3060-4
(softcover : 50# alkaline paper) ∞

1. Journalism, High school.
I. Title.
LB3621.5.S77   2007   373.18'970973 — dc22   2007007509

British Library cataloguing data are available

Cover photograph © 2007 Shutterstock

Manufactured in the United States of America

*McFarland & Company, Inc., Publishers
Box 611, Jefferson, North Carolina 28640
www.mcfarlandpub.com*

For Stacia, Jared and Zach

Acknowledgments

A big thank-you to all of these people who made this book possible:

To Lisa Morris and Cathy Shoup, whose never-ending hard work and dedication force me to work harder in my own classes each day just to keep up. Both of you never fail to think of your students first; they are so lucky to have you as teachers and mentors.

To Bonnie Grimble, my department chairperson, who has always been a source of encouragement and professionalism.

To John Williams, my principal, whose understanding of what we do down in Room C147, even if it makes him uncomfortable, allows my students to grow and learn. The readers of Carmel High School appreciate your leeway.

To Mark Shoup and Tony Willis, the embodiment of what is good about scholastic journalism and professionalism. When I think about what I do in my classroom, I never fail to ask myself, "What would Mark and Tony do?" You may not be aware of it, but I am the teacher that I am today because of your example.

To the myriad journalism advisers who have offered me encouragement and inspiration throughout the years, I continue to learn from you. I can't possibly name you all; I hope you know who you are.

To my mom, dad and sisters, who have always encouraged my writing.

And last but certainly not least, to my wife, who is and always will be my rock and who always puts up with my projects, no matter how off-the-wall they may be.

Table of Contents

Introduction: Storytelling for a Sophisticated Audience

Meet Carl. Carl is a caveman. But he's not just any caveman. In fact, Carl's quite special. In his caveman society, he's a storyteller — call him the first journalist if you want because, really, that's what journalists are, right? They're storytellers.

They're just specific types of storytellers, instead of making up tales or writing stories about themselves, they tell the stories of others. Then they share those stories with a larger audience.

So Carl's a storyteller, the world's first journalist. His job is to record the events of his tribe or clan or whatever you call a group of cavemen and women. He records events like harvests and hunts. He previews upcoming harvests and hunts. He tells when and where food is plentiful or when others in the tribe are heroic or die.

In other words, he does exactly what today's journalists do. His messages may look a little different, but they serve the same function.

And that's an important point. When you really get down to

it — when you scrape away the technology, the modern-day advancements, all of that — the one element that human beings have had in common from day one to day one trillion and one is stories. As simple as that. Stories.

We humans like stories. Our lives are full of stories. Events happen to us. They happen to people near us. And we remember those events. We record them. We take pictures of them. We write about them in our diaries.

But more importantly, we share them.

The act of sharing stories is one of the most important parts of the storytelling tradition. Think about it. You're at lunch with your friends and someone starts telling a story. "You won't believe what happened today in Mr. Smith's class."

And then you're off, listening to or telling the story about how Mr. Smith "totally got Ashley in trouble today" or how "Chris just bombed his test in math" or "You won't believe how Mark asked Karen to the Homecoming dance."

And on and on and on.

Because once the storytelling starts there's really no end. Pretty soon, someone else has got a story to share just like the one you just told but better, and then someone else chimes in with, "Oh yeah? Think that's good? Well, you should've been there when..."

When you pare them down to their essentials, our lives aren't material possessions. They're not clothes or cars or X-Box 360s. They're stories. Stories built on stories. Stories that, woven together, create the tapestry of our lives. Stories that involve action, reaction, interaction, emotion. If only someone — some sort of professional storyteller — could help us make sense of it all. If only there were some medium where the myriad stories of our lives could reach a wider audience to help us validate our own experiences, to help us

think, to help us understand, to clarify, to let us cheer and mourn together. If only such a person, a place, existed. If only ...

Meet Carl.

Carl's job isn't easy. No one said it would be. It takes a special kind of person to be a professional storyteller, a journalist. It takes someone who understands the tools of information gathering. Someone who knows what information is relevant and what is not. Someone who is innately curious about the world.

But above all, it takes someone who understands his audience.

Audience

An audience is merely the person or group of people for whom a message is intended. But understanding that audience and, specifically, how that audience accesses information, isn't as easy as it seems. Let's say you're asking your 93-year-old grandmother for money so you can buy a new CD or a shirt or a DVD. How do ask her? How do you speak (besides louder)? How do you present yourself to her? Now turn the tables. Say you're asking for money from your parents. The message is the same, but does the presentation change? What about asking your friends for money? Again, same message, different approach.

Journalism is no different. At this moment I am writing this chapter as a full-fledged member of the so-called "X-generation." I am a child of the '80s. I was 10 when MTV began (and it actually played music videos). As a child, I learned how to use some of the first computers. I grew up with the Internet. The list goes on and on. Fast forward to your generation. Take what I learned in my life and increase it by a power of 10. Of 100. Of 1,000. At no point in our existence have human beings had so many ways to access information. Think cell phones. Think Web messaging. Think voice mail. Think conference calls. Think pagers. Think PDAs. The list is endless.

And it only gets more overwhelming.

Now, where does a yearbook or a newspaper or a school magazine fit into that group of information sources? It's probably not on many students' lists of priorities. But, saying that, don't fall into the same trap that many of your elders do. "Well," they say, "those kids are just stupid. They don't know how to read. Kids today," they say, "are not as smart as we were when we were their age."

Guess what? Your elders are wrong. Terribly, horribly wrong. If anything, kids today are smarter. And if not smarter, they're certainly more sophisticated. Information bombards you from every angle, and, unlike many from the older generations, you are able to weed through that steady stream of data to find what you want to know. You have abilities in information gathering that are astounding. So the problem is not that you don't know how to get information. The problem is that many of you — and many of your readers — don't know how to get information that you need to know. In today's information age, it's too easy to bypass news that doesn't directly affect you. Don't care about the lead story on CNN? Click here for a new link about fashion. Don't want to see this show about the war in Iraq? Change the channel.

Carl knew his audience much the same way that you should know your audience. For example, he knew that his audience couldn't read. He knew they lived in caves. He knew what they valued — good hunts and meat and furs — and he presented his information in such a way that his audience could easily access and understand it. To put it simply, he drew pictures on cave walls.

Your job is not so different than Carl's. What do you know about your audience? You could do a poll or a survey, but you really don't need to. Just take a look around. Or, better yet, look at yourself. What do you read? How do you read? Do you read? What catches your eye? What makes you stop and take notice?

You'll probably come to some conclusions. Chances are you'll determine that most of your peers say they don't like to read. Chances are, that's only half right. It's not that they don't like to read, they just don't have time to read. If you keep going, you'll probably notice that your peers, respond to visual stimulation — things like photos and graphics and colors.

These are pretty basic criteria and you could go further if you wanted, but it's a start. Your readers are visual people. Need more proof? Think about the kinds of magazines you or your friends buy. What do they look like? How do they feel? Where do you look first in these publications? What do you read? What do you skip?

Granted, many of the publications that students read aren't chock-full of earth-shattering information. I mean, how important can proper mascara coverage be? Or how pressing is the need to know which bikinis are in style this summer? But beyond the content (we'll get to that later), just take a look at the presentation of this information. These publications know their audience. They know what you like. They know how you read. They know how to present information. In fact, you pay good money for these magazines. You reach into your wallets and pull out hard-earned cash to purchase these periodicals. On the other hand, in the case of many school newspapers, you give your product away for free, and no one reads it. Why? Because many high school publications don't know their audience. They keep writing stories that stylistically would have been applicable in 1963. But it's not 1963 anymore. It's not 1973 or 1993. And just like fashions change (take a look at your parents' high school yearbooks if you don't believe me), people change, particularly in the way they read and access information.

Your publications need to change along with your audience. But as you already know, despite the change in how we read, everything still starts with good stories.

People

In his book *Somebody Told Me*, a collection of some of his best newspaper stories, Pulitzer Prize winner Rick Bragg tells the tale of Margueritte Thurston, a tiny old lady who owns a 70-acre orange, tangerine and grapefruit tree grove in Florida. Her property stands in the middle of progress and is worth a fortune — appraised between $2 million and $4.2 million. But Margueritte won't sell. She likes the trees too much, the history, the nature that seems to be disappearing from so many other places in Florida. The grove, she says, is her home. And nobody can take that from her.

Later in the article, when Bragg mentions that Margueritte won't let a photographer take her picture and that she "bristles" when he asks her age, Margueritte says, "This is a story about the grove. This isn't a story about people."

She couldn't be more wrong.

For as much as Margueritte knows about fruit trees (and for all I know she still remains there — an island amid an ocean of progress), she doesn't know a lick about journalism. But despite what Margueritte said, Rick Bragg knew the secret about journalism, he's known it for a long time, and now you will, too.

Simply, every story, if it's worth covering, involves people. In some way, somebody is affected by every event that occurs, at least the ones worth covering. If events didn't have an impact, why cover them? Why waste the space, the newsprint, the time?

Remember this: Topics are not stories. Topics lead to stories, but they are not stories. In Bragg's case, the grove was a topic. Or to broaden the scope, the topic was about progress, or the lack thereof. The story, on the other hand, was about Margueritte Thurston, a little old lady who refused to budge.

For your publications, topics range from tattooing to tests, from homecoming to heartache, from soccer to school spirit. You know your school environment. Pick an event, any event, dances, club meetings, big games, driver ed, you name it — those are all topics. Journalists don't write about topics.

They write stories.

And the thing about stories, as opposed to topics, is that they are nearly inexhaustible. Everyone has a story to tell. CBS news correspondent Steve Hartman knows this. He's even made a career of it. In his segment called, simply, "Everybody Has a Story," Hartman throws a dart at a map of the United States. He then travels to the city upon which the dart has fallen and gets out a local phone book. Then, randomly, he selects a name from that phone book and calls the number. Whoever answers becomes the subject of his story.

The idea is this — topics run out. Each yearbook from the dawn of time (perhaps even in Carl's yearbook), has covered pretty much the same topics. Don't believe me? Take a look. There's prom. There's the football team. There's the car wash, the school play, the student council elections. Each year. Every year. Ad nauseum. For the most part, topics do not change.

But people do.

Take another look at that yearbook. Look closely at the faces. While the events that occur year after year after year change little, the people who participate in those activities change a lot. They get older. They graduate. New people take their places.

Don't ever let me catch you saying that there's nothing to write about. See all those people in your yearbook? See them surrounding you each day in the halls? In the cafeteria? The truth is, there's too much to write about. The problem should be not in "What are we going to cover?" but in "What do we have to leave out?" The former means you aren't digging below the surface. You can't see the trees for the forest (to badly switch that cliché around). The latter means you're looking at people, at individual faces. Too much to cover? The latter is a good problem to have.

The Purpose of Stories

All of this talk about audience and people is well and good, but it doesn't answer the primary question that you should have at this point, which is this: What is the purpose of storytelling in the first place? A person like me can discuss the primary purposes of journalism — to inform, educate and entertain. A person like me can divide that information into categories — what readers want to know and what they need to know. But that doesn't really get to the heart of the issue.

Why does storytelling really matter? Why will it matter for our student readers? What's the point?

And the answer to these questions is really the whole point of journalism. And here is the answer: Stories can provide experiences, and those experiences are the only way that we can change, challenge or reinforce existing attitudes and behaviors.

Put it this way. Let's say you're pro-choice (or pick any other hot topic of the day — gay marriage, religion in schools, politics, etc.) and you're sitting in a room with someone who is pro-life. You begin to argue. Back and forth you go, debating point after point, making counterpoints, trying to gain the upper hand. Sound familiar? But let me ask you, if you've ever been in an argument like this, have you ever won? Even once has the person you were arguing with slapped his forehead and said, "By George, you're absolutely right. I'm an idiot"?

Probably not. In fact, what you probably ended up doing in a situation like this is merely defending your position even further, entrenching yourself even deeper into your beliefs. You may also have made the other person angry (this is also the reason my mother always said, when dating, don't talk about religion or politics). But did you change that person's mind? Did you make him or her see the world differently? Absolutely not.

But let's say, for the sake of argument, that you are staunchly pro-life and then something happens in your life that hits right to the quick of that issue. In other words, it's not just an argument but an actual experience that deals with the issue. Maybe you're faced with a personal decision or one of your close friends is. Maybe it's a family member. Would it change your mind then? Maybe not.

But it might.

At the very least, that experience will challenge your beliefs in a way that no argument can. That experience may force you to see the world in a way that you hadn't considered. And at the end of that experience, your views will either be reinforced or changed. At the very least, your views will be challenged in a way that they've never been challenged before.

So what does that have to do with

storytelling, I can hear you asking? Everything. Have you ever seen a movie that made you cry? Have you read a book that made you laugh? Have you seen something on TV that made you angry? Or scared? Or nervous? That's the inherent power of the arts. They can safely transport you to another place, another time. They can make you see the world in a way that you've never seen it before. They can help you to experience something, given your own narrow opportunities, that you may never get to experience any way else. They can take you to the moon and back. Or they can transport you to the deserts of Africa. They can put you in a courtroom or in a jail cell or in the death chamber. They can make you see the world through the eyes of a 10 year old with a physical deformity or a 75 year old dealing with the death of a wife or a husband.

And they can, in some instances, make you change your mind about the world around you. I'm not saying they will change your mind. But they might. At minimum, just as if those were your own experiences, they will challenge those beliefs.

Journalism, in this respect, is no different than the rest of the arts. The only difference is that the stories we tell, the places we write about, the situations we bring up, are real. And in many ways, that makes those stories even more poignant and powerful.

A trio of reporters for the *St. Petersburg Times*—Monique Fields, Dong-Phuong Nguyen and Pulitzer Prize–winning Thomas French—wrote a lengthy series of articles for the paper titled "13: Life on the Edge of Everything." In it, the reporters chronicled the lives of several middle school students as they faced various trials and tribulations during their seventh-grade year. The story relied heavily on detailed observations of these kids'

experiences, from overheard phone calls to classroom visits to time spent at parties, meetings and other typical events.

And what was the point? I think French put it best in his June 8, 2003, column that accompanied the series:

During the year we worked on the project, Phuong and Monique and I were struck by the creativity and strength of the students. The transition they were making away from childhood was painful and difficult, yet they were moving forward. Their lives were full of upheaval and melodrama, yes, but these were the signs of a profound and necessary transformation. To us, the kids were heroic.

In the end, I learned a great deal about my sons, especially Nat. I discovered the things Nat was struggling with were completely normal; having spent so much time with others his age, it was easier to see what an astonishing kid he was, even on days when he was withdrawn and sullen. I appreciated him all the more; I understood why, so often, he needed to push me away and figure things out on his own.

And French was not alone. If people took the time to read the story that they had written — if they saw these kids and lived their lives for a while — it might have challenged them to see their own world a little differently. The audience for *the St. Petersburg Times* is not students, of course. Demographically, they're skewed toward the adult side of the spectrum. So we must keep that audience in mind when we consider the effect of the story. But who would those readers have been specifically? Like French, parents of teenagers, for one. But also those whose kids were about to become teenagers. I'll bet teachers read it, too. And other adults, perhaps grandparents.

And what questions would those readers have after reading? Would the story challenge them to see teenagers in a different light? Would they be more understanding? Less so? Would the story help those readers to relive their own teenage years perhaps? Would they see in the people the authors chose to spotlight a little bit of themselves or their friends?

And, inevitably, could those "mental experiences" make them change the way they perceive the world and the people who live in it?

Maybe.

Which is a better answer than no.

When Harper Lee published her novel *To Kill a Mockingbird* in 1966, it challenged the way the world looked at racial stereotypes. It might have changed a few minds. It might have prompted a few people to take a stand and make a difference in the world when, before, they might have merely sat back and let the world pass them by. Why? Not because Lee was preachy. Not because she told the book's readers to make a difference in the world. No, all Harper Lee did was tell the story of a kind lawyer in the south, Atticus Finch, a man who was asked to do the unthinkable — defend an innocent black man in the 1930s. I still remember the first time I heard that verdict from the all-white jury — "Guilty" — and, like Atticus's son, Jem, how angry I was. Even today, even though I have read the book a hundred times since that first time, I get the same reaction at that part. Did the book change my beliefs? Maybe. Maybe not. But it certainly gave me something to think about. It challenged me. It stirred me. I have never lived in the South. I did not live in the 1930s (or even the 1960s). I have never really faced the issue of racism firsthand. But because I read Lee's story, I was there. For a short time, Lee transported me to a different time and a different place. And I came out on the other side a changed person.

Well-told stories can create experiences for readers, and those experiences can alter behavior, as educator Rick Du-Four writes in his book *Professional Learning Communities at Work* (1998):

> *Our attitudes are the result of our experience, and our experience is a product of our behavior. New experiences are needed for us to change our attitudes, and new experiences usually require us to use different behaviors. Thus, the effort to change attitude must begin with the effort to alter behavior in ways that result in new experiences.*

No doubt, Lee knew this concept quite well when, early on in her novel, Atticus told his daughter, Scout, "You never really understand a person until you consider things from his point of view...until you climb into his skin and walk around in it." Stories allow us to do that very thing.

And if you tell a good story, if you share that message with readers, if your words stir those readers to think and challenge themselves and their beliefs, then you've done your job as a journalist. Good writing and storytelling has power, after all. People remember it. They hold those stories close to them. In many ways, well told stories become part of their readers, part of a shared experience among many readers.

Again, Rick Bragg, in his autobiography *All Over But the Shoutin'*, knows this. In the prologue to his book, Bragg tells of a story he was covering the night his grandmother died. He was interviewing the mother of a little boy who had been shot and killed by a stray bullet as the boy stood in the doorway to his home, "his book satchel in his hand, like a little man going to work."

> *She told me how the boy looked up at her after the bullet hit, wide-eyed, wondering. And as she talked, her two surviving children rode tight circles around the couch on their bicycles, because she was afraid to let*

them play outside in the killing ground of the project courtyard. As I left, shaking her limp hand, she thanked me. I usually just nod my head politely and move on, struck anew every time by the graciousness of people in such a soul-killing time. But this time, I had to ask why. Why thank me for scribbling down her hopeless story for the benefit of people who live so far and safely away from this place where the gunfire twinkles like lightning bugs after dark? She answered by pulling out a scrapbook of her baby's death, cut from the local newspaper. "People remembers it," she said. "People forgets it if it ain't wrote down."

I reckon so.

Yeah. Me, too.

Summary

Every story you write must focus on people. Every story you tell must show how news, how events, affect people. Every story must have a "face" on it. Most of all, every story you write must have impact in some way. Every story must challenge your readers to think, to respond, to react.

As a local television journalist said in her 2004 speech to the Indiana High School Press Association, "Good writers can tell a story. Great writers can lend perspective." Once you understand these concepts, we can do business. Until then, your publications will suffer.

Certainly, these are enormous tasks. So how can you incorporate all of this knowledge? How will you apply these storytelling skills? What are those skills? What tools will you need? How can you develop those tools, not only in writing but in design and alternative coverage?

Where should you start?

All are valid questions, and each answer has its own story. Each aspect of storytelling is unique, and each aspect is as important as the others in terms of the storytelling process. But if you're willing to risk a few bumps along the way, if you're ready to face a few obstacles, then the end will be worth it. After all, the journey of a thousand miles begins with one step.

So come along for the journey. Carl's coming. You should, too. In the end, you'll be glad you did.

STUDY GUIDE

Terms and Concepts

Audience— the person or group of people for whom a message is intended.

Story v. topic— Topics are things or events. Stories are about the people who are affected by those things or events. Good journalism focuses on stories, not topics.

Try This

1. Have everyone in the class bring in his favorite magazines from home. Start an "idea file" in the classroom. Whenever you're stuck for ideas, go to the idea file. See if you can get some inspiration from what you find there.

2. Take those magazines and see if you can guess what kind of audience reads them. How can you tell? What clues help

you to determine the magazines' demographics?

3. From your favorite magazine, find one article that you enjoy and clip it out in its entirety (that includes everything that goes with the article, not just the words in the story). Be prepared to discuss what information you accessed. Did you read it all? Only some of it? Which parts? If you didn't finish, why not? Where did you stop reading?

4. Evaluating your own publications: Take a recent copy of your school's newspaper, magazine or yearbook (you can make photocopies if you don't want to mess up the originals) and do the following steps:

   a. With a highlighter pen, highlight everything you actually read in the publication. Stop highlighting when you're done reading or if you've moved on. Highlight everything you access including titles and headlines, stories, cutlines, photos, alternative coverage (also called infographics or sidebars), etc. See Fig. 1.

   b. On a separate sheet of paper, write the following words: "headlines/titles/summary decks," "stories," "cutlines," "photos" and "alternative coverage." See Fig. 1.

   c. Count the number of each of these items that appear in your publication and then count the number of items your read in their entirety.

   d. Evaluate. What do these results tell you about how you read? What do

Figure 1

they tell you about how your peers read? What do they read? What do they avoid? Of the items on your sheet, what element takes up the most physical space? How many people read that element in its entirety? What is the most well read element in your publication?

Information Gathering

What Are the Stories and How Do You Find Them?

Before you write, before you design, before you take photos, before you do anything, your first step is to determine what exactly you need to cover, or else, what's the point? As a result, you get a series of questions: What is the news? What do we want our readers to think about? What do my readers need to know? What do they want to know?

So, three steps:

1. Figure out what news topics you need to cover.

2. Find the faces within those topics to help readers relate to those newsworthy events.

3. Gather relevant information to be able to write and package your stories for readers.

This section on information gathering will explore these steps in detail. In Section II, we'll discuss putting that information together into an organized story, but for now let's talk about the raw materials of news, the bare bones of storytelling.

CHAPTER 1

Broccoli

What Is News?

Raise your hand if you like broccoli. Go on, raise it high. (Looking, looking...) Don't be shy. Just signify if you like broccoli. OK. One, two, three ... about five of you. Sound about right? That's usually the case in most groups of young people. A small percentage of the larger population that likes broccoli. Don't believe it? Try it for yourself.

But what about the rest of you? What's the deal? You'd admit, wouldn't you, that broccoli's good for you? It's got all kinds of important vitamins and minerals. It's a good source of iron. There are even connections between eating broccoli and reducing your risk of some cancers, or diabetes.

So why, nonbroccoli eaters, do you avoid the leafy green goodness of broccoli? Tell you what. Try this. How many of you would eat broccoli if it were offered to you with a generous coating of melted cheese? How about then? Would you eat it? Raise your hands. Raise 'em high. Eight, nine, ten.... Okay. So what you're saying is that more people are likely to eat broccoli if it's covered with melted cheese. In other words, you're still getting the goodness of broccoli, but you're making it more palatable by packaging the vegetable in something

that more people enjoy. Hmmm ... I think we're on to something here.

Let's carry this analogy away from the dinner plate for a moment and translate it into journalistic terms. Your publications

are full of broccoli. Not literally, of course; that would be messy and would smell bad by next Tuesday (not to mention what the school toilets would look like). Figuratively, though, your publications are full of broccoli. You fill your papers and yearbooks and magazines with information that readers need to know. Like broccoli, it's good for them. It may not always taste great, but it's chock full of news that they should access. But also like broccoli, only a few people actually do, in fact, ingest that information. There are some, of course (just as there are some who will eat broccoli in any of its forms), who will read that information because they don't care how that information is presented. These are the same people who stay at home on Friday nights, sit in front of a warm fire and crack open the phone book for enjoyment. Or perhaps, as a hobby, they read legal contracts. Or dictionaries. But most readers—the majority of your readers—see "broccoli" and simply turn the page.

Fine, you say, what does that have to do with me? I'm not the one avoiding the information. I've put it out there for them to see. I've done my job. Go bother someone else.

Wrong answer. This has everything to

A WORD ABOUT "NEWSPAPERS"

Most high school newspapers are really newsmagazines in broadsheet clothing. Don't fight it. Work with a new outlook.

The truth is, you don't publish every day. The truth is, you don't publish every other day. The truth is, most of you don't even publish every week. The truth is, most of you publish about once a month (give or take).

The truth is, professional magazines exist in the world that outscoop you.

Why fight it?

Yes, yes. You look like a newspaper. You run on a broadsheet. You use that nasty black newsprint that rubs off on your new white sweatshirt on distribution day. I understand. But let me ask this: If I dress up like Jessica Simpson—the bustierre, the pouty lips, the Daisy Duke shorts, all of it—and walk into the room, does that mean I'm Jessica Simpson?

The point is, to merely look like a publication doesn't mean that you are that publication. Not at heart, at least. But don't get discouraged. You can still look like a newspaper, just stop pretending that you are a newspaper. Because you're not. Not really.

Unless, of course, you publish every day. Or even every other day. The true definition of "newspaper" has to do with timeliness. Chances are, your local professional paper comes out every day (maybe a little less frequently if you live in a rural area, but not much less). Professional newspapers publish more frequently because they can. Because they have full-time staffs devoted to publishing that often. Because they have the money and the ad revenues to do it. My guess is you don't have those kinds of resources.

So what do you do? Simple. Change your philosophy. Become a newsmagazine. Maybe not in appearance, but in the way you cover events.

And how do magazines cover events? What makes them unique?

1. They publish less frequently.
2. They focus on the hard-hitting news questions of how and why.
3. They write stories about people, not things.

do with you. If you consider yourself a journalist, at least, this should be what it's all about. Remember, in journalism, unlike many of the other classes that you're presently taking, the work you do affects other people. No longer should you only concern yourself with, well, yourself. In journalism, you need to think about others. In particular, your peers. The people with whom you attend school daily. The people in your math class. The people not in your math class. The guy at your bus stop.

Your readers.

See, there are two types of information in journalism — information that readers want to know and information that readers need to know. It's easy to provide the former. After all, your readers want to know it. Let's say your administration decides to hold a lottery, and the random students picked in that lottery will get a new car. It doesn't matter if you print that story in reverse with invisible ink, your students will find a way to access that information. They want to know.

But what about the other? The information that your student readers need to know? Let's say your school has a new dress code policy or maybe the rules of your state's standardized tests have changed. What about then? I doubt that you'll have readers beating down your door for that information, but does it make that information any less valid? Any less important? On the contrary, that information often tends to be the most important information for readers.

The problem is that it reads like plain broccoli; most people see it and move on. Look at it this way. If you write a story and it gets published in your paper or yearbook or magazine, you've only done half of your job. For those mathematicians out there (and you know who you are), half is 50 percent. In most school settings, 50 percent is a failing grade. I don't care if you

spent weeks researching and interviewing and writing and rewriting. It doesn't matter if you taped your eyelids to your forehead each night so that you could stay awake to edit your article. If you've not thought of your readers and how they access information — if all you've produced is piles and piles of broccoli, in other words — you've failed. I'll say it again, with emphasis. Failing to think of your readers is to fail in journalism.

No pressure there, huh?

So What Exactly Is Broccoli?

What's the information readers need to know? We'll talk about what "cheese" is in Chapter 3, but for our purposes, we need to know what broccoli is before we learn how to make it palatable. After all, if we can't determine what makes news then we haven't done our job, cheese on top or not.

So, again, what is broccoli?

Broccoli — news — is simply one or a combination of the following factors:

- **Timeliness or timelessness**
- **Proximity**
- **Prominence**
- **Conflict**
- **Impact/consequence**
- **Human interest**

Timeliness or Timelessness

Time is an essential ingredient in good newswriting and storytelling. Events are either happening, soon to happen or happen continually. Your job as a reporter is to determine the type of story that you have. Newspaper writers tend to focus more on the timely stories—they focus on the events that happen close to publication dates. Yearbook writers, on the other hand, look at the timeless tales, since their stories, unlike those in the newspaper, must stand the test of time. Magazines fall somewhere in the middle.

That's not to say that newspapers can't run timeless articles or that yearbooks can't also be timely. On the contrary, some of the best articles in your publications may be out of the "usual" strain. But knowing what kind of story you have will determine where it goes in your publication. Is it news? A feature? Speaking specifically of newspapers, the timelier articles tend to be more newsworthy. Thinking always of readers, the closer an event is to publication, the more readers care (or should care) about it. We will discuss styles of writing later in this book, but suffice it to say for now that **news and feature are not styles of writing (see Chapter 6). Rather, what those terms refer to is time. News stories tend to be more timely while features lean toward being timeless.**

Proximity

Location of events is key to newsworthiness. The closer something happens to your readers, the more they should care about it. For example, the news may be that a school in your state has adopted a new attendance policy that allows seniors to call themselves in sick at the attendance office. That's newsworthy. It's interesting. Right?

Now imagine that that same event happened, not just in your state, but in your own school. Which story is more newsworthy? Which would more readers care to peruse?

But again, that's not to say that news that happens only in your own backyard should make it to print. No, what good journalists need to do is learn how to localize news events. Even if they happen miles away, most (if not all) stories can be made more proximal. You just have to ask the right questions, questions that, inevitably, your readers should ask.

Let's say the story is that a high school golfer in (insert name of state here other than your own) has been kicked off the team

---

CLUBBING YOU OVER THE HEAD

Don't use "news" and "feature" when referring to types of stories. Think "timely" and "timeless" instead.

Timely	Timeless
Definition: Information that has a definite time angle and must run in a certain issue of your publication (i.e., when readers access the information they can take immediate action).	Definition: Information that could run in any issue of your publication.
Example: Testing procedures for next week's schoolwide standardized state exam.	Example: An investigative report on fire safety in the average home in your community.
Purpose: To get important breaking information out quickly.	Purpose: To give readers information to think about.
Where it goes in your paper: Generally on the front page.	Where it goes in your paper: Anywhere, really, but most likely a little deeper in your publication. Consider, however, anchoring your front page with a timeless, in-depth story.

for using illegal clubs. Just ask the right questions. How could you localize this story? Could this happen at your own school? Why? Why not? What are the rules governing club use in golf? What are the rules to prevent cheating in other sports? Do some students get around those rules? How?

See what I mean? Even events that don't happen next door have meaning. It's up to you to provide that "closeness," that proximity, to your readers.

Prominence

Let's face it. Certain people at your school are more important than others. It's a fact of life. As a whole, we care more about these "important" people than we do the "unimportant" people. Why else do we spend so many hours watching music, movie and television awards programs? Why else do we pay money to see professional sporting events? Why do some people keep autograph books filled with signatures of celebrities?

Simply, prominent people are more newsworthy. If events affect prominent people in your school, then readers are more likely to care about those events. Likewise, your readers are more likely to listen to the words of prominent people than they are to listen to those who hold less prominence.

OBJECTIVITY: AN IMPOSSIBILITY

You've heard it too often: Keep opinions out of your writing. But how? As you see here, unbiased reporting can't be done.

Terms to know

Objective: without bias or prejudice; detached.
Subjective: personal; opinionated.

Journalists should strive to remain as objective as they can in their writing. They should talk to sources from all sides of an issue. They should research. They should make relevant observations.

But true objectivity is a myth. Journalism itself is riddled with subjectivity. Here's why.
1. Writers decide which sources get quoted, how much they say in a story and where in the story those sources appear.
2. Designers and editors decide which stories get placed, how long those stories are and where in the publication those stories are located.

INTERPRETATION: A PROBABILITY

Just because journalism is subjective doesn't mean you should write dry, uninteresting prose.

Terms to know

Interpretation: providing explanation, meaning.
Analysis: providing opinion based on information.

There is a time and place for both of the terms listed in today's journalism. Interpretation is fine for most journalistic stories, whether timely or timeless. In other words, journalists take the information supplied and help readers to understand its impact or significance.

On the other hand, reporters should reserve analysis for a newspaper or magazine's op-ed pages since this type of writing purposely includes a writer's opinions.

Your school is full of prominent people. Your principal is prominent, as is the rest of the administration. Teachers are prominent. School nurses. Counselors. Media specialists. All are prominent people and all make good sources for stories (more on this later).

But put yourself into the heads of your readers for a moment. Who do you listen to most? Your teachers? Your parents? Your principal? I doubt it. Certainly you should listen to these people. They are wise. They have lived. They have experience and fancy degrees from expensive universities. But if you're like most readers who have a choice, the words from these people go in one ear and out the other.

That leaves one group. Students. Your peers. Take a look around. Which students at your school are more prominent than others? There are the obvious ones—student body president, class senators, team captains. But there are others as well. Seniors, for example, have prominence for the underclassmen. Smart students have earned prominence. Class clowns (in some cases) have prominence. You need to identify the people, or types of people, that your student population looks up to. Quote these people and your readability increases.

Conflict

When people or events or ideologies are at odds, that's newsworthy. There are obvious conflicts—war, protests, sporting events between rivals, fights in the halls. But there are some less obvious ones (or, perhaps, less noticeable ones), too—debates over new school board policies, weighing students' rights to free speech with the school's right to limit that speech.

Your job as a journalist is to find where those conflicts lie and illuminate them for your readers. In his Pulitzer-Prize–winning story, *New York Times* reporter Ron Suskind writes about Cedric Jennings, a good kid from the worst school in Washington, D.C. Suskind shares obvious conflicts—Cedric, because he is smart, becomes the brunt of other students' taunting and threats—and also deeper-seated conflicts—Cedric struggles to achieve top grades, but because he is from a bad school his education does not stand up to the education of minority students from other, better schools. Over the course of the article, the reader begins to understand Cedric's struggles and realizes that Cedric represents a much larger problem that isn't so easily fixed.

Impact and Consequence

When events happen, they mean something. That's what makes them newsworthy. Events that you choose to cover should have some significance for the students in your school. But sometimes that significance isn't always obvious. That's where you come in. It is your job to share with your readers the significance of certain events.

You must answer (or, better yet, have sources answer) the two most important journalistic questions—how and why. Certainly who, what, when and where are important questions to answer. But of the five W's and an H, the two most important are the last two always listed. I say again, how and why? Thinking like a reader, how does this event affect me? Why should I care? Why is this important? How can I do something about this? These are the questions you should ask yourself as a journalist every time you write a story. Readers will care more if you make the news mean something to them. And the more they care, the more they will read.

RAISING THE ISSUES

Publications should help readers to determine what to think about

With the exception of editorials, columns and reviews, newsworthy items should drive a publication's content. However, the news isn't just a random collection of facts, statistics and numbers. If it were, anyone could do it — just fill in the blanks and, voila, your publication is done. You should leave your opinions (and the opinions of the rest of your staff) out of the content of your publication.

In other words, don't tell readers what to think. It's not your job. Half the time, they won't listen to you anyway. It is your job, however, to give readers something to think about.

That's a big difference. With the former, your stories are rife with opinion and conjecture. Often first and second person as well as unattributed claims creep their ugly heads into this type of writing. With the latter, the goal is to get readers to say, "Hmmmm, I never thought of it that way before." Or even, "I never even thought to think of that before."

See the difference?

With what to think about, journalists must take newsworthy events and make them make sense for readers in a way that, perhaps, they've not thought of before. If a hurricane hits the coast of Virginia and you live in Iowa, does it affect you? Not directly, of course. But a good reporter is able to help readers make a relevant connection. Using the same example, could lessons learned from a disastrous hurricane be comparable to tornadoes in your area? Could readers learn how to make themselves more prepared in the event of a natural disaster? Were there schools in Virginia that were affected by the hurricane? Is there anything your school can do to help?

Think like readers. What questions will they have? Or perhaps more important, what questions should they have?

Open that line of communication in your publications and you will reap the benefits of better readership.

Human Interest

Sometimes stories fit none of the categories above. They are simply interesting for the sake of being interesting. These are the human interest stories. Perhaps you have a student at your school who is eight feet tall. Or maybe a freshman has decided to take the SAT and scored a perfect 2,400. Could be a kid likes to dress up like Superman on the weekends. Or maybe someone's got so many body piercings that her ears whistle when she sticks her head out of a car window.

You get the idea. These kinds of stories are in their own category. They're not really broccoli because most readers will read these stories no matter how you present them. However, they should still be a part of your publication. Not the only part, mind you, but part. Actually, a smattering of readable human interest pieces can do wonders for the rest of your publication as a whole. To carry on the analogy, they are cheese for your whole publication. They make the entire work more palatable.

The Point

Take a hint, young journalists. You must have a point to make when writing your stories or else you're not doing your job. I'll say it again — have a point when writing. With no point, you are merely a Chatty Cathy doll, an inanimate toy where you are the one pulling the strings to see what random thoughts emerge from your pen or word processor. And your readers, who have no time for such nonsense, will give you the worst "tongue lashing" you can possibly have as a journalist — they won't read what you've written.

Don't get me wrong. Saying, "Have a point," is not the same as saying, "Be subjective." On the contrary, you should be as objective as you can when telling stories. But being objective doesn't mean being boring either. Good journalists can and should tell readers, not what to think, but what to think about. That's a big difference. With the former (what to think), you're running into the realm of columns and editorials and reviews. With the latter (what to think about), you're presenting information and viewpoints and interviews that make a reader step back and say one of two things: "I never thought of (insert topic here) that way before" or "I never even thought to think of that (insert topic here) before."

Make sense? Maybe not, so here's an example that might help. Let's say your school has adopted a new dress code for the school year and you've been assigned to write the story covering the changes (no pun intended). The boring journalist will write something like this:

This school has adopted a new dress code for the 2007-08 school year. No longer will students be allowed to wear hats of any kind or shirts that reveal bare midriffs.

"We think this is a good policy," Princi-
pal John Hawkins said. "But as with any new policy, this will take some time for students to get used to."

The policy came as a result of many students wearing inappropriate clothing last year, according to Hawkins. It requires students to wear "tuckable" shirts and no hats. In addition, boys are no longer allowed to wear pants that sag so low that their underwear shows.

"I think the policy stinks," sophomore Jeff Dawson said.

Junior Michelle Reed said, "I don't like the new rules, but I can see where the administration came from."

Certainly the story is newsworthy. It's a policy that will affect most students in your population. But does this story say anything beyond outlining the policy alterations and the new language in the rulebook? Look at the quotes. Do they actually say anything? Do they make you care one way or the other?

So the story's not bad journalistically, except for the fact that no one will care about the story and no one will read it. Not to mention that, since most high school papers don't come out more frequently than once every two weeks or so (or even less frequently), the information is actually old news. But if getting your readers to actually access the information you provide is not important to you or your staff then read no further.

The good journalist, however, will start the procedure by asking some preliminary questions. Things like, "Is there a correlation between proper dress and student academic success?" Or, "How difficult is it for students to buy contemporary fashions in light of the new dress code?" The good journalist will then focus on one of those questions and explore it, finding a "face" to illustrate both (or more than both) sides of the issue. Having a point will also help narrow the focus of the reporter's questions when interviewing. It will help him to determine what types of observations would be most relevant.

So if I'm the reporter and I have chosen to explore the question of contemporary fashion versus dress code, I could start by finding a student who no longer has anything in her closet that will meet the new dress code requirements. I could go to her house and have her go through the contents of her closet with me. I could ask her questions about how she plans to cope. Will she go out and buy new clothes that do meet the requirements? Will she just wear her old clothes anyway, despite the new policy? And what about other relevant sources? I can talk to those who made the policy, finding out what went into the decision. But what about the stores? Are places like The Limited and Express losing business because of schools' dress code policies? Will schools' dress code policies affect the sales market? Have they ever affected it historically?

So your story might look something like this:

When senior Jessica Green went back-to-school shopping last June, almost three months before this school year began, she thought she would get a jump on the competition. She spent more than $300 on several outfits, including almost a dozen midriff-revealing shirts.

Just a week ago, she found out that her pre-planning was all for naught.

"I heard about the new policy and my heart jumped in my throat," Green said. "I mean, almost everything I bought doesn't meet the new requirements."

Green is not alone. Many students must reevaluate their wardrobes because of a new policy just passed at last week's school board meeting. Now the dress code rules state that students must wear "tuckable" shirts. "That's,

like, everything I own," junior Mary Skelding said. Skelding, like Green, shopped early to avoid back-to-school store crowding. In addition to shirts, students can no longer wear hats and they can't don pants that reveal undergarments.

"We had to do it," Principal John Hawkins said. "I know there will be some dissention, but students' clothes can certainly be a distraction to the learning environment, and we want to provide the best environment possible."

But this explanation doesn't help Green.

"I don't know what I'm going to do with all of these clothes," Green said. "I can't take them back because it's been more than 90 days since I bought them. I guess I'll just have to buy something else and wear these on the weekends."

See what can happen if you have a point? No longer is the story just about dress code. It's about what the dress code means, or can mean, to students.

Looks Can Deceive

So here's the story: A student on my newspaper staff looks at the front page of our publication — the one that's scheduled to go to press in, like, an hour — and she says, "Who wants to read about that?" She's pointing at the screen, her face looking like she's just bitten into something sour.

The editor, a nice young man who can't stand the sight of his own blood (another story entirely, but *funny*) looks up and says, innocently enough, "Why?"

The girl is incredulous. "Because she's riding a lawnmower in the street," she says, still pointing, as if that answers the whole question. "Why is this story about a girl riding a lawnmower on the front page of the paper?"

The editor cringes. He's pretty proud of the page. I can tell he doesn't want to rock the boat any further. He stays quiet.

"Kids don't want to read about that," the girl says. "They want to read about sex and drugs and parties."

At this point, I decide to step in. "Did you read the story?" I say quietly.

"Well, no," she says casting her eyes down. But then her finger regains its previous prone position. "But she's on a freaking lawnmower in the street. What's she doing?"

"Learning to drive," I say.

"But you can't learn to drive on a lawnmower."

"Are you sure?"

"Pretty sure."

"Hmmm," I say. I like that word, "Hmmmm." It catches students off guard, as if to say, "Hmmmm, you may have a point," or, "Hmmmm, you may want to think about that," or, "Hmmmm, you're a big moron." It says all of these and more.

The girl looks more carefully at the story. She starts to read. It's a good story, about a sophomore girl who, for a lot of reasons, has chosen not to take the traditional driver education course to learn to drive. First of all, a busy, 4.0 student, she doesn't have enough time to devote to a class that teaches her to drive. Second, she and her family don't want to shell out the hundreds of dollars it costs to take driver ed from one of only three accredited driver education schools in the area. Third, the lawnmower girl did her homework and found out that the only benefit of taking an approved driver ed course is that teens can get their licenses six months before those teens who opt not to take the course. Six months. For hundreds of dollars, not to mention the countless hours of class time and driving time.

So the story wasn't about a girl on a lawnmower. It was about more than that.

It was about the system and how one girl decided not to be a part of the system. It was about options and choices that students can make even if they thought they didn't have those options. It focused on a girl riding a lawnmower to avoid taking driver ed, but she represented a whole group of readers who may be dealing with similar situations. And not just driving situations. Driving was the focus, but the story could be about any situation where students felt they were being monopolized.

After a minute or two, the girl steps back from the page. She shakes her head. "I see it, but I still don't like it," she says.

"Fair enough," I say. "But you don't have to like it." I look at the page for a second. There's the girl, riding high in the saddle of her lawnmower, regular traffic whizzing by her. There's the title and summary deck, "Cutting Out of Driver Ed: Sophomore Replaces Class with Riding Lawnmower."

I look back at the newspaper girl. "The thing is," I say, "it made you have a reaction, right? I mean, like it or not, you saw this story and you took notice. Maybe, just maybe, it made you read at least part of the story. And maybe, if you read, you learned a little something. Just maybe.

"A minute ago you said that students want to read about sex and drugs and parties. I agree. But those aren't the only stories out there. I mean, we'll run stories like that as long as they have something new to bring to the discussion, but, honestly, how many of your peers don't already know about those topics? What can we say in the newspaper that approaches those topics in a new and interesting way?"

I point back to the screen. "Now how many of our readers know about this?"

"I guess," she says, but I can tell she doesn't really mean it. The girl shakes her head and walks away.

Granted, the story wasn't Pulitzer-

Prize–winning stuff. Most of the stories that we write from issue to issue aren't. But that doesn't make the story any less important. It's easy to tell readers what they want to know. It's not so easy to tell them what they need to know. As journalists, we have a job to provide both kinds of information.

Here's the bottom line: Good journalism takes time and effort. You have to have a point and you have to make all of the information in your story—from research to interviewing to observation—relevant to that point. As a reporter, you must know why you're writing a particular story. What do you want readers to think about? Why should they care? How does, or should, the news affect them?

Know the answers to these questions and you'll be on your way to telling better stories in no time.

STUDY GUIDE

Terms and Concepts

Timeliness—An element of news referring to events that happen close to publication dates.

Timelessness—An element of news referring to events that have global themes and can be run in almost any issue of a publication.

Proximity—An element of news referring to events that happen close in location to readers.

Prominence—An element of news referring to events that affect people with more perceived "importance."

Impact/consequence—An element of news referring to how events affect a publication's readers.

Human interest—An element of news referring to events that are interesting for the sake of being interesting.

Interpretation—Providing explanation, meaning. Appropriate for "objective" news stories.

Analysis—Providing opinion based on information. Appropriate for "subjective" stories like reviews, editorials and columns.

Finding the "News" at Your School

Newspaper

Step 1: Jot down a list of all of the publication dates for this year's newspaper.

Step 2: Write a list of timely events that will occur during the year (i.e., Homecoming, prom, Valentine's Day, scheduling, etc.)

Step 3: Write a separate list of timeless events and topics.

Step 4: Use the list for future reference for ideas and planning throughout the year.

Yearbook

Step 1: Jot down a list of all of the proofing dates for your publication (this may come from the yearbook plant).

Step 2: Write a list of timely events that will occur during the year for events that will occur within those proofing dates.

Step 3: Write a separate list of timeless events and topics that could be incorporated throughout the book.

Step 4: Use the list for future reference for ideas and planning throughout the year.

Example: First semester Issue dates	Timely events (must run in specific issues)	Timeless events (can run in any issue)
Sept. 10	State academic testing Freshman Class elections	Censorship
		Students who volunteer for Habitat for Humanity
Sept. 30	Homecoming	
		Students enrolled in peer facilitating classes
Oct. 15	Halloween Fall sports tournaments Presidential election	
		Males enrolled in "traditionally" female classes (and vice versa)
Nov. 12	Thanksgiving	
		Student First Amendment rights
Dec. 2	Student council blood drive Care-to-Share program	How businesses market to teens

CHAPTER 2

Pepperoni Pizza
Where Are the Stories?

If I've heard it once, I've heard it a thousand times: "There's nothing to write about." Man, it's like being trapped in a locked, padded room while the same old song (one that you hate) plays over and over and over again. "This school's boring," you say. "Nothing's happening. What can I possibly write about?"

If it will help you to understand my and thousands of other advisers' pain, say those words while whining like a 4-year-old child. Now say it again and again and again. You get the idea.

But rather than wince away from the needling, simpering voices, I will take this opportunity to do battle with those words. I will, once and for all, quell the growing tide of nagging phrases and blood-curdling pleas of "Why, oh why, hated adviser of mine, did you give me such a terrible, un-newsworthy topic?

What can I possibly write about (insert name of hated thing here)?"

Yes, I will take up arms and rage into the fracas. But first, allow me to choose my weapon. It must be a stout weapon to fight such an annoying verbal assault. The weapon must be sharp. The weapon must be strong. It must, perhaps, contain some sort of magic to counteract the evil words of those throngs of disheartened pupils.

Or I could just choose pizza.

You heard right, pizza. That gooey, cheesy, pepperoni-laden Italian pie. Thick crust or thin, it doesn't matter. Take your pick. Deep dish. Stuffed crust. Whatever. You may choose any one topping you like, too. Olives, sardines, mushrooms, extra crunchy peanut butter. No matter. Of course, for the purposes of example, we'll use pepperoni. It's my favorite (and it may be your favorite, too). But if pepperoni's not your first choice (vegetarians, I'm looking in your direction), just insert your favorite in-

25

MAD LIB JOURNALISM

These were fun when you were, like, 8. But your readers aren't 8 anymore.
Try the exercise below. Do your stories sound like this? If so, you need to
find the angles behind the topics.

It's _____ time again. And that means that _____
        (name of event)   (number)

students at _____ High School will be ready for the
                (name of school)

festivities.

This year's activities include_____, _____
                     (activity)   (activity)

and _____ .
     (activity)

_____ is one of the students involved in planning _____
    (name)   (name of event)

He said, "_____
               (generic quote about event)

_____."

The dates of _____ are _____
           (name of event)   (dates)

---

gredient wherever the dreaded "P"-word appears from here on out.

And here we go.

Imagine that you're about to eat a pizza. You're looking at it with one longing eye as you read this with the other. Imagine, too, that this is the best pizza in town. It's got the best cheese, the best crust. It's piping hot, and it's just sitting there, ready to be eaten. But hold off for just one more minute, just long enough to take a really good look at that pizza. Now there's a pizza place near where I live that boasts a pie that has "edge-to-edge" toppings. The pepperoni stretches from one extreme side to the other. You can't even see the crust underneath for the amount of toppings. The pizza is just laden with pepperoni.

The thing is, I can't eat the whole thing. Not by myself, at least. I don't want to end up with a stomach ache, and, more importantly, I don't want to gain 20 pounds at one sitting. So I can only afford to eat a little bit. Just one small part of the larger pie. I can save the rest for later if I want, but I don't have to because in a lot of ways, one small taste is enough. The rest of the pizza will taste pretty much the same as that first bite. Sure, there will be some small variations, but for the most part the whole pizza tastes exactly the same.

Which brings me to my point (and as you know by now, you must have a point when writing). Imagine this pizza represents your topic. It doesn't matter what that topic is. Need some help? Look at an old issue of a yearbook, or maybe last year's newspapers. There they all are, the

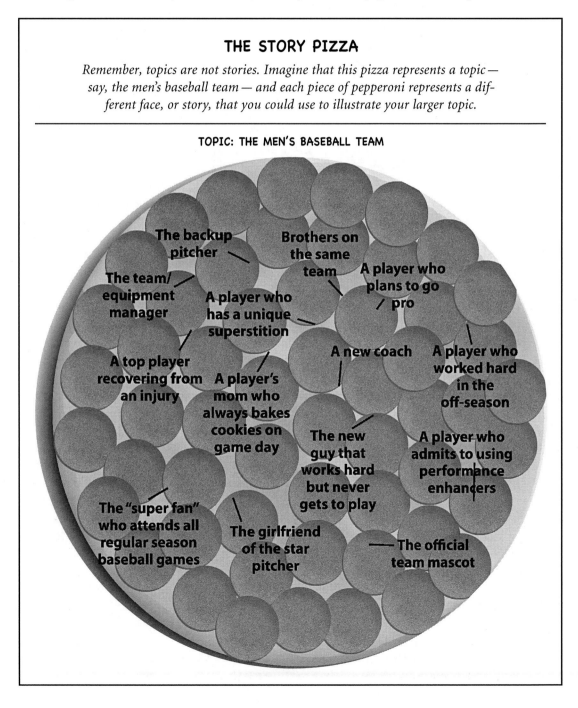

THE STORY PIZZA

Remember, topics are not stories. Imagine that this pizza represents a topic — say, the men's baseball team — and each piece of pepperoni represents a different face, or story, that you could use to illustrate your larger topic.

TOPIC: THE MEN'S BASEBALL TEAM

The backup pitcher

Brothers on the same team

A player who plans to go pro

The team/equipment manager

A player who has a unique superstition

A new coach

A player who worked hard in the off-season

A top player recovering from an injury

A player's mom who always bakes cookies on game day

The new guy that works hard but never gets to play

A player who admits to using performance enhancers

The "super fan" who attends all regular season baseball games

The girlfriend of the star pitcher

The official team mascot

"boring" topics. Homecoming. Prom. The soccer team. Tattoos. The archery club. Same old, same old. Day after day. Month after month. Year after year.

What have we learned? Simple, topics do not change, people do. So from year to year, the topics remain static. I admit, in some ways this can be a little boring. If all you're writing is a story that outlines the events each year, then, yes, it is boring. As a matter of fact, if that's all you plan to do, then I can make your job so much easier. Here's how:

Step 1: Grab a copy of last year's newspaper or yearbook and open to the appropriate page (Homecoming, baseball preseason, prom, etc.)

Step 2: Cross out the old names and dates.

Step 3: Replace those crossed out words with current names and dates.

Step 4: Recirculate the publication.

Step 5: Repeat.

But if you care about your readers (and your own sanity), you can try a different approach, one that takes a little more effort. And it all starts with people.

Take a look at the faces in each of those stories or photo essays. They're different, aren't they? Sure, they compete in the same events, but they do them differently. They bring to those events a whole different set of life experiences.

Think of that pizza again. You remember it, right? How could you forget the pizza, what with it sitting there so tantalizingly delicious right next to you as you read. Before you eat, though, think of the entire pizza as a topic. You've just ordered the "Prom Special" or the "Math Department Surprise," or something along those lines.

Now pay attention to this part because this is the key to the whole pizza analogy: Each piece of pepperoni represents a different story that relates to the larger topic. In other words, just like if you take one bite of the pizza you pretty much get the idea of what the rest of the pie will taste like, focusing your story on one particular piece of pepperoni (one person's story) also will give your readers a pretty good "taste" of the larger topic. And the thing about pepperoni (i.e., stories within a topic) is that there are a lot of them. Remember edge-to-edge toppings?

Let's say you're writing about Homecoming. How many people are involved in your school's Homecoming festivities? My guess is that most, if not all, have some connection to the celebration. Of course, some folks have more prominent roles than others (remember prominence from Chapter 1). There's the Homecoming queen, the star quarterback, the float building chairperson. But these aren't the only people who have Homecoming stories to tell. What about the kid whose family donated the little footballs that cheerleaders always seem to throw into the stands? Or perhaps the girl who works on the decorations for the dance? Then there's the guy who donates his convertible for the parade. The freshman who paints his entire body in gold glitter paint. The football player who doesn't get to play because he's injured. And on and on and on.

Now here's the trick. You don't have to cover all of these people. If you did, your publication would be a million pages long and would cost an arm and a leg to produce.

No, the trick is, you only need to find one of these stories to tell.

One.

That's the magic number.

One.

Remember it.

One.

I'll say it again.

One.

For each year, for each time your staff tackles the same topics, remember the number.

One.

That's one face. One person. One experience to illustrate the larger topic.

One.

And what do you do with all of the rest of those stories? Save 'em until next year. Or the year after that. Or the next issue. Or the issue after that. See, the irony of the statement, "There's nothing to write about," is that, in fact, there's far too much to write about. The real trick of journalism is not searching for a source but, instead, narrowing down the plethora of potential sources to just, you guessed it...

...one.

Some people call this piece of pepperoni — this "story" within the larger topic — an angle. **The angle is simply the way you choose to focus this particular story to get your point across.** An angle depends on the people you use to illustrate your focus, to help readers to know what to think about, as we discussed in the previous chapter.

But if it helps you to think of the angle as pepperoni — and it seems so much more appealing to me — then so be it.

MAD LIB V. PEPPERONI PIZZA

Two stories, both the same length. One focuses on an event. Insert different names, different dates, and it's the same year after year. The other focuses on one group of people. One event. One moment. Which is more successful?

Playing in the near-freezing weather, the Lions stopped a late fourth-quarter drive to preserve a 14–7 victory over Jefferson in the state championship game. The Lions finished the season with a 14–0–1 record, the best mark in the school's history.

"The kids surpassed all of our expectations," Head Coach Ernest Buckner said. "More than a few times, they could have given up, but each time, they reached down deep and found the character to win."

"We sure were excited," quarterback and senior Mike Calumet said. "It was an amazing accomplishment for all of us. We worked really hard all season to make this a reality. We all dug down deep and found the strength to win."

The season opened with a 20–17 win over Roosevelt, followed by consecutive wins over Glenview, 14–10; Kennedy, 28–24; and Taft, 17–7.

Twenty minutes after the game had ended, they remained on the frozen turf of Remington Field, players and their girlfriends, coaches and parents, hugging one another, slapping backs and strutting up and down the field.

They pinpointed where Jeff Reymer scored on a crucial third-down fingertip catch and where Ron Vaught planted his helmet in the ribs of Jefferson's all-state quarterback Patrick Whaley, knocking the football loose to stop a late fourth-quarter drive and preserve the 14–7 win.

Long after most of the fans had escaped to their cars, they braved the 25-mile-per-hour winds and near-zero wind chill, refusing to surrender the moment and thumbing their noses at Mother Nature as only state champions can do.

"I wanted the moment to last forever," Bill Gammon, offensive guard and senior, said. "I doubt that I'll ever have as big a thrill as winning the state championship."

Brainstorming

It's easy to tell young reporters to find "faces" behind their stories. It's also easy to read excellent examples of writing, if you know where to go to find them. But where does that leave you? By now you know the elements of news. You know what topics to write about. And now you understand that putting a face on a story—finding someone who is affected by the news, in other words—is the key to getting readers to relate to that newsworthy topic.

But where do those ideas come from in the first place?

What follows is a plan that will help you to find the story ideas—and faces—that you need to tell readers important information and, more importantly, to give them something to think about.

The key is in brainstorming.

Brainstorming. Now there's a word you've heard before. "OK, kids. Today we're going to do some brainstorming." Or, "Let's brainstorm some ideas," your editor might say. A good concept, brainstorming. I mean, we can all agree that the ultimate goal of a brainstorming session is to generate a lot of ideas. So why is it that when you ask people to brainstorm they all look at you with blank stares and groans?

It's because most people don't brainstorm correctly.

"Brainstorm" has become one of those words like "nice" in the English language. It's been used so much that it doesn't mean much anymore. It's such a ubiquitous word, too. It's a noun: "That brainstorm really wore me out." It's an adjective: "Let's get this brainstorm session over with." It's a verb: "If we brainstorm for a minute, I'm sure we'll have all of the answers we need." It's gotten to the point that people just have no concept of a right and wrong way to brainstorm. The word means so much,

it's so overused, that, in fact, it means nothing.

Let's put a stop to that right now. Follow these steps to find out how.

Elect a Brainstorming Leader

For most staffs this decision is made pretty easily. The brainstorm leader can be your editor in chief or your page or section editor. This allows these people in leadership positions to practice using their leadership skills as they guide the brainstorm group through the process.

But the leader doesn't have to be an editor on staff. Actually, allowing other staff members to lead discussions and brainstorm sessions may help to give some of those staff members a better feeling of belonging and empowerment.

The job of the leader is pretty easy, too. As leader, you should stand up front (or sit somewhere in a prominent location) and be prepared to clearly and legibly write down ideas as they come. And just because someone's the group leader doesn't mean he or she is off the hook for generating ideas. While this person is the "leader," he or she should also be a contributing member to the brainstorm process being conducted.

Everyone's Ideas Count

The first concept to remember in brainstorming is that everyone should have an equal say in the process. Easy to say, not so easy to put into practice because every group of young people seems to have its own dynamic. You've got the brown-noser kid to your left who always wants to contribute regardless of whether his ideas are valid. You've got the quiet kid to your right (or maybe it's you) who would rather be at home sleeping than paying attention to some silly "brainstorm session." And then you've got the other ones in between.

FREEWRITING 101

Like brainstorming, lots of people say they know how to freewrite, but few people do it correctly. Here's what you should be doing:

---

1. Have a blank sheet of paper and a pen or pencil.
2. With the topic at the top of your page, write constantly for the designated amount of time (30 seconds or a minute or five minutes).
3. Don't stop writing. Once you've placed pen (or pencil) to paper, you can't stop. You also can't go back. If you can think of nothing to write, write "I can think of nothing to write" (or whatever else) over and over until you can think of something else to write.
4. Don't worry about grammar or spelling or punctuation. Nobody's grading you on your freewrite. The only person who needs to read what you've written is you.

The ones who may not feel like their ideas are any good or the ones who don't take the process seriously and try to turn everything into a joke.

But remember, everyone should have a say in the brainstorm process. You can't ignore people just as you can't focus all of your energy on the one or two people who seem to be actively contributing. Why? Because everyone involved in the project (the newspaper, the yearbook, the magazine) should feel like they have an equal say as to what gets included in the publication. Even if their ideas ultimately don't get picked, they have as much a chance of having them discussed as anyone else. And why is that important? Because if you don't validate these kids' ideas, after a while they'll give up on you entirely. And there's nothing worse than having a staff half-full of people who don't feel like they're part of the process.

Getting Started

The first step in the brainstorming process is to start with a topic. Remember, topics are not stories (it's the stories that you'll be trying to generate in these brainstorm session), but you've got to start

somewhere. Sometimes you may even need to step back to brainstorm the topics, too. Whatever. For our purposes, we'll assume we know the topic. Let's say it's "prom." That's your "pepperoni pizza," if you will. We know we want to cover the prom in our publication, but we don't know how. Here's what you do:

Step one: The leader should put the word "prom" at the top (or the center) of a large workspace — maybe a chalkboard or a large sheet of paper.

Step two: The leader should instruct the group to write ideas in a notebook for one to three minutes focusing on the word "prom" (see alternative coverage about freewriting for more information).

Step three: Give the group members a few seconds to go through their lists and mark their top two or three ideas.

Step four: Go around the group in a circle twice, having each group member share one idea from his list each time it's his turn. The leader should write each idea down on the workspace, and everyone in the group has the option of passing his turn only once.

One important note: Do not discuss any of these ideas as they are being placed on the large work space. Discussion about these topics will come later. Remember, at this stage you're just generating ideas and you're trying to give everyone an equal chance to contribute.

Narrowing the List

At this point, you should have a pretty good list. If you want, you can add more rounds to the circle, having people share four or even five ideas. Or you could take a few of the subtopics that you brought up and do a whole new brainstorm. It all depends on your group and the ideas it brings up. One thing is true, though, and that's that your final list should incorporate actual angles to the original topic. If the topic is "prom" and your list includes words like "tuxedo rentals," "the dance" and "dinner," you need to keep working. Those words and phrases aren't stories yet; they're merely subtopics within the larger topic of prom. And if your list still includes these subtopics, don't despair. Chances are your main topic was too broad anyway and these subtopics have allowed you to narrow the focus even further.

In the end, though, look for faces and people to crop up in your list. If your list includes phrases like "the prom queen candidate whose sister was a prom queen," or "a kid without a driver's license who can't drive his date to prom," or "a girl who makes her own dress," then you're in pretty good shape.

The Final Step

Once you've gone this far and you have a pretty extensive list on the board, now is the time for discussion. Up to this point you've remained pretty quiet, and that's a key concept. Everyone in the brainstorm session needs to feel equally important to everyone else; everyone's ideas are

valid. Sometimes your best ideas come from the quietest students, and sometimes the "stupid" ideas can be the catalyst to lead to brilliant ones.

But now that the ideas are there, the group leader should facilitate the discussion by posing a series of questions:

What seems to be the most newsworthy angle?

What angle affects the most readers?

What stories have we already covered in past issues and years?

Narrow your list to the top two or three and don't agonize over your decisions. The idea of brainstorming is that by the time you get to your final list you should have lots of great ideas, most of them equally as great as the others. But you simply don't have time to cover them all. You only have time and space for, you guessed it...

One.

But do save the lists you made for later. Why reinvent the wheel? The stories may be just as valid next year or the year after only they'll include different faces. Like computers, brainstorming is just a tool. You use it right, and you reap the benefits. You use it wrong, and you're no better off than when you started. Understanding the concept of brainstorming is one thing, but you've got to practice it yourself to get better.

Summary

The problem with journalism isn't that there's nothing to write about, it's that there's far too much. Like a pepperoni pizza, we don't need to eat the whole thing to understand what the pizza tastes like. If readers are faced with stories that are too broad or that try to cover too much, chances are they'll simply avoid reading altogether. The problem that most staffs face is how to narrow the topics down to just a few angles that could then be presented to readers.

Proper brainstorming is a big key to finding story ideas. Make sure when you brainstorm that everyone gets an equal say in the process. Additionally, make sure your ideas begin to focus on the people that are affected by the topic. Once you have that list of angles, you're ready to begin gathering more information.

STUDY GUIDE

Terms and Concepts

Topic — a general term that refers to events or things.

Story and angle — Topics are things or events. Stories are about the people who are affected by those things or events. Good journalism focuses on stories, not topics.

Brainstorming — a process that generates lots of ideas in a short time.

Freewriting — a method that can be used during brainstorming to generate lots of ideas.

Here's Your Chance to Try Brainstorming

1. Start with a topic.
2. Find ideas to correspond to that topic. You're looking for "faces" here. Who is affected by this topic?

And Here's an Example

Topic: Prom

Story ideas:

The student who can't afford to go.

The kid with no date.

The student whose mom will help chaperone.

The girl who's up for prom queen.

The girl who's up for prom queen whose older sister was also prom queen.

The kid who refuses to go to prom.

The students who choose to forgo dining at an expensive restaurant and choose, instead, to eat at home.

The girl who can't seem to find "just the right dress."

The girl who made her own dress.

The freshman who got asked to go to the prom by a senior.

The kids who go as friends rather than as "dates."

The boy who helped organize the prizes for the school's official "after-prom" event.

The student whose older brother or sister died in a car accident during prom.

The kid who knows there's pressure to have sex on prom night but who sticks with his decision not to.

CHAPTER 3

Gold Coins

What Is the Role of Observation?

Do this. Get a blank notebook and a pen, just something to write on and to write with. Now go home. Go to your bedroom. Close the door. Find a comfy spot, take a deep breath and look.

Look around you. What do you see? What do your hear? Smell? Feel? Be specific. Do you have CDs? What are their titles? Do you have a desk? What's on it exactly? Books? What condition are they in? Is music playing? What song? What are the lyrics? What about outside? What's the view?

Is there a dog frolicking in the backyard? What's his name? How does he bark? Do you have any pictures? Who's in them? What are they doing? What are their names?

Now write it all down. Spend 10 minutes or 20 or 30. Longer, if you want. Just get it all down. No detail is too minute. Everything is valid. You cannot be too specific here.

When you're done, close your note-book and take a break. In about an hour, open up that notebook and see what you've written. Now ask yourself, what do the observations that I've made say about me? If you've done the exercise correctly, they should say a lot. They should, for example, let an outsider know some-

thing about your musical tastes. Are you into punk or rock? Pop or jazz? Is your room yellow? Maybe you're perky. Dark brown? Subdued. Do you have pictures of family and friends throughout? You're per-

THE HUNT FOR GOLD COINS

Remember first that you need to have a story to tell and a face that will connect readers to it. But once you have that, you've got to grab your readers' attention and then keep it throughout the story.

What are Gold Coins?
Most often, gold coins take the form of details, description and dialogue.

- **Details**
  Is your main source a fan of music? What are the specific titles in his music library? What's the CD in his car right now? What kind of car is it? Does your source have a dog? What's that dog's name? How old is it?

- **Description**
  What color are your source's eyes? How tall is she? What mannerisms does she display as you interview her?

- **Dialogue**
  What does your source say when she's not answering your questions? How does she respond to the people around her? What do they say back?

How do I organize gold coins? How many should I have?
That's up to you. Just remember that not all stories are best told chronologically. A good rule of thumb: the longer the story, the more gold coins it should contain. Another rule: Your two most important gold coins are the ones at the beginning (your lead) and at the end.

What about the information in between the gold coins?
This is the path of the story. The information in between gold coins brings out the point of the story, what you want readers to think about. These "spaces" in between the narrative contain relevant facts, quotes from expert sources and solid transitions. The gold coins keep readers on the path. The gold coins keep readers' eyes on the path so that they'll be more likely to access the important information there.

Why have gold coins?
Without gold coins, readers have no way of entering your stories. Without gold coins, your stories are merely collections of facts and data and quotes. Readers—particularly your visual readers—can't connect with those things. Gold coins provide a "face" for the story and a way to help readers to relate to the information that lies within.

sonable. Are your clothes hanging neatly in the closet or are they thrown haphazardly on the floor? Can you see the floor?

Get the idea?

Information gathering is the key to good journalism. And there are three elements to solid information gathering — observation, interviewing and research. When most people think of journalism, they think of the latter two (interviewing and research). They think of a reporter with a notebook asking questions to a source. Or they picture that same reporter in front of a computer screen sifting through scads of data. Certainly, these two forms of information gathering are important; as a matter of fact, they constitute two-thirds of good reporting. But that leaves one-third unaccounted for. And for your visual readers, it's probably the most important third — observation.

In this chapter, we'll discuss that first element of information gathering, mainly because observation is the technique that's most often overlooked (pun absolutely intended) by high school journalists. To be a good journalist, you have to hone your skills in all aspects of the field, and the process might as well start with opening up your senses to the world around you.

Gold Coins

Pretend, for a moment, that Carl (you remember Carl the Caveman) is a nature lover. He enjoys taking walks outside, away from his cave. He likes exploring new paths and experiencing new scenery.

On this particular bright, sunny day, Carl has found himself with a dilemma. In front of him is a meadow, and beyond the meadow is the beginning of a wooded area. Carl likes woods. He likes the trees and the shade and the sounds. Taking a walk in the woods is not the problem. The problem is that, carving long, curved gashes into the thicket, there are several paths. Each one is unique. Each one promises its own adventure and satisfaction.

So which path to choose?

Carl moves close to investigate. Nothing stands out on the first two paths. Nothing seems out of the ordinary. Nothing shows him the difference between the paths — one's just as good, or bad, as the other.

But as he passes the third path, something catches his eye.

It glints softly in the bright sunshine. Carl moves closer. The gleam doesn't move. As he bends down onto the rough grass, Carl sees the source of the light.

A gold coin. Or, in Carl's case (since his culture hasn't invented money yet), a shiny trinket. In other words, something valuable.

Now the choice of which path to follow is easier. Carl picks up the coin, pockets it and heads into the forest.

But he walks this path differently than he's walked trails before. Before today, Carl would let his eyes and his mind wander, scoping the scenery, listening to the birds (or approaching dinosaurs), whistling happy tunes. But today, his eyes remain riveted on the path before him. After all, he saw one gold coin, chances are, he might find another.

He walks a few more steps and, lo and behold, another gold coin. He places it in his pocket next to the first coin and resumes walking.

The walk down the trail continues like this, Carl moving methodically, purposely, his eyes only on the ground in front of him. The trail, meanwhile, doesn't fail to do its part, providing shiny gold coins at regular intervals. When Carl gets to the end of the path, his pockets are full of valuable trinkets and he smiles; the choice to follow this particular path was worth the trouble.

GOLD COINS IN ACTION

Need to see it to believe it? Check out the story below and notice how gold coins help to keep readers on the path of the story.

Gold Coin #1

Introduces readers to Jessica Green, one of many students who is or will be affected by the school's new dress code policy.

When senior Jessica Green went back-to-school shopping last June, almost three months before this school year began, she thought she would get a jump on the competition. She spent more than $300 on several outfits, including almost a dozen midriff-revealing shirts.

Just a week ago, she found out that her planning was all for naught.

"I heard about the new policy and my heart jumped in my throat," Green said. "I mean, almost everything I bought doesn't meet the new requirements."

The Point

Illuminates the main idea of the story, what the reporter wants readers to think about.

Green is not alone. Many students must reevaluate their wardrobes because of a new policy just passed at last week's school board meeting. Now the dress code rules state that students must wear "tuckable" shirts.

The Path

This is the meat of the story. Shares secondary source (Skelding) as well as expert source (Hawkins). Outlines the specifics of the new policy.

"That's, like, everything I own," junior Mary Skelding said. Skelding, like Green, shopped early to avoid back-to-school store crowding. In addition to shirts, students can no longer wear hats and they can't don pants that reveal undergarments.

"We had to do it," Principal John Hawkins said. "I know there will be some dissention, but students' clothes can certainly be a distraction to the learning environment, and we want to provide the best environment possible."

Gold Coin #2

Brings the readers back to Green. Lets them know that this policy affects people just like them.

But this explanation doesn't help Green.

"I don't know what I'm going to do with all of these clothes," Green said. "I can't take them back because it's been more than 90 days since I bought them. I guess I'll just have to buy something else and wear these on the weekends."

Fast forward. Pretend you're a high school student (for some this is a stretch) and some industrious, young journalism student has handed you the latest copy of the school newspaper. In front of you are choices, paths, if you want to call them that. Only they're not paths into the woods, they're stories, and you must decide what, if any, stories you will read.

The problem is, each story looks pretty much like the one before it. Nothing stands out. Nothing catches your eye. And unlike Carl, who likes to walk down wooded paths for the sheer enjoyment of it, you (if you're like many teens) don't like to read. You don't have time for it. Something else is more interesting. Like sleeping. Like writing love notes to your girlfriend/boyfriend where all of the I's are dotted with tiny hearts. Like watching paint dry. And what do you, typical reader, end up reading?

Nothing.

Unless...

Occasionally, a piece of writing does catch your eye. There's something about it. Something unusual. Something captivating.

Something that seems to glint in the bright sun.

A gold coin.

When young readers find one of these, then it's off to the races. You can't stop them from finding more. They hunt those gold coins like prospectors in 1849. And along the way, they learn a little something.

Show, Don't Tell

If you read just about any book about writing—fiction, nonfiction and everything in between—you'll see the advice of "show, don't tell" crop up almost every time. And journalistic writing is no different. Actions and images speak louder than words almost every time. It is this ability to show and not tell that is the basis for gold coins in the stories you craft.

So what exactly are gold coins in writing? Remember cheese on the broccoli way back in Chapter 1? In a lot of ways, gold coins are the same as cheese. Cheese, you'll remember, makes the broccoli more palatable. Cheese tastes good and it helps to take the edge off of the, for many, distasteful flavor (albeit goodness) of the green veggie. Cheese helps readers to relate to stories. For most, it's the "face" that a writer puts on the news that helps readers to relate.

Gold coins serve a similar purpose. They're just more specific.

We discussed your readers at the beginning, too. We said that your readers are visual people. They like their information presented to them visually. They expect their information (at least the stuff they choose to access) to be visual.

This idea of being visual relates to writing as much as it relates to design and photography. I'll say it again in a slightly different format: You must write visually for your visual readers if you want them to actually access what you've written. You must show them the information they need to know and not just tell them about it.

The Three D's

In general, gold coins constitute three D's—detail, description and dialogue. There are other types of gold coins—storytelling quotes, for example, or interesting or shocking facts—but we'll discuss those in the next two chapters. For our purposes, we'll explore the first three—the three D's, I like to call them—because these three are most closely related to the information gathering technique of observation.

Description

What color is your source's shirt? Is there music playing? How loud is it? Does the source wear glasses? What's the weather like outside? Does the source wear perfume? How tall is he?

Description, the first D, involves paying attention to your surroundings. Interviewing, as you probably already know, utilizes your sense of hearing; you ask a question and you listen as the source answers. **Description, on the other hand, involves using the rest of your senses to tell a story.** If it's Christmastime, did you notice if there's a Christmas tree in the person's living room? Were there presents underneath the tree? How many? How were they wrapped?

So often, reporters spend much of their time worrying about their interview — their questions, their notebooks, their tape recorders, their pens — that they spend little, if any, time looking at the world that surrounds their source. But just like answers to questions, a person's possessions, the way he looks, the way he smells, say something about the source as well.

Let's say you walked into a source's house at Christmastime and you noticed that there wasn't a Christmas tree. Would that tell you something about your source? You'd have to ask to be sure, but it might.

And what if you walked into an interview and noticed that the source had hundreds of swimming trophies displayed prominently around the room? Or you noticed that the source's folders were really ripped and torn up with wadded up papers falling out?

What if the source was reading a book? A newspaper? A comic book? What if the teacher you're talking to had a picture of him (or her) sitting on the back of a Harley Davidson motorcycle?

As a journalist, you have to learn to notice the world around you and that involves more than just using your interviewing skills. Your other senses — smell, sight, hearing, taste and touch — count, too. Now just because you notice something doesn't always mean it's relevant (and we'll discuss relevance later in this chapter), but before we talk relevance you have to first practice getting the information. Like just about anything else in life, learning to describe takes time and practice.

Detail

So you've practiced using description and you've gotten to this point:

An old man sits quietly in a bar smoking a cigarette and drinking a beer. He's watching a TV that hangs above the stained counter.

Not bad. At least you're starting to pay attention. Your descriptions are getting better.

But it's not enough.

There's an adage that we journalists like to use: "If there's a dog barking in the background, I want to know that dog's name." I'm pretty sure the intent of that sentence had much the same intent that police who investigate crime scenes would use — everything is evidence; leave no stone unturned. In other words, if a journalist is doing a good job and being as objective as he can, then he should try to get as much information as he can.

While this is true, I will venture another reason behind "finding out the dog's name." And that reason is this: Readers like details.

Details are simply specific words that help to further describe something.

OBSERVATION IN ACTION

For this piece of writing, the reporter just spent about half an hour in his school's media center computer lab. It's not a story yet (it has no point — see page 42), but notice the use of the three D's — description, details and dialogue.

10:31 a.m.

"I know her password now," the girl whispers to her friend. Her long red hair, tied back with a blue rubber band in a ponytail that descends to the middle of her back, swishes over her left shoulder as she conspires with her partner.

The library computer lab is empty except for these two girls tucked neatly away in the back corner. The remaining 20 or so computer screens in the room stare back with blue backgrounds and a message:

CHS Media Center
Students and Patrons
To use the INTERNET,
You and your parents must have
signed the Carmel Clay
Schools Acceptable Use Policy.
Copies available in Activities Office.

"How do you know her password?" her friend says. She looks over her shoulder, glancing about the room, checking for eavesdroppers. The black girl wears a white, hooded windbreaker, a direct violation of this school's "No coats" policy.

"I don't know," the redhead replies. "I just guessed." She points to the screen, which has just popped up an error message. "Shoot," the redhead says. "I thought I knew her password."

At the top left-hand corner of each of the girl's keyboards is a space for them to put their student IDs, showing they have signed the appropriate permission forms, the same forms to which the blue screens refer. Both spaces on both of the girl's keyboards are conspicuously blank.

10:45 a.m.

Muted laughter fills the room as four photojournalism students enter the lab to work on an assignment. They heave their heavy backpacks from their adolescent shoulders and get to work. The assignment: to find photojournalistic Internet sites.

Three of them sit in a row, two boys flanking a pretty, thin, blonde-haired girl with tight black pants and a short-sleeved blue sweater. The third boy, a redhead with bleary eyes, a fleece vest and baggy khaki pants, sits in the row in front of the other three, his seat still a good vantage point to see the blonde. Almost simultaneously they arrive at Yahoo.com to begin their search.

"Aw, crap," the lone boy in the front row says as he frantically slams his finger on the mouse button.

"Having some trouble, John?" Tyler Kirsh, a bespectacled sophomore in a long-sleeved Abercrombie and Fitch T-shirt, says.

"I'm always havin' trouble, man," John says.

The room is quiet for a long moment before the blonde speaks. "Why do I suck?" she says, glancing at her screen and then at Kirsh's. She can't find the right website. Kirsh looks over and points to her screen, asking for her to follow his finger with her mouse.

"Click here on the 'How to take better pictures' link," Kirsh says. The blonde does as she's instructed and a large yellow and white Kodak emblem fills her screen.

"Thanks, Tyler," she says. "What about you, Tim?" She looks to her left to see how the plaid-shirted boy there is progressing. Tim doesn't respond. Instead he just moves his mouse and clicks, meandering in some other area of cyberspace.

"Tim's lost in his own world," Kirsh replies laughing.

Finally, Tim hits something. He looks over at the other two, oblivious to their conversation about him. "Go to the 'Playground,'" he says.

Kirsh brushes him off. "I don't wanna go to the playground," he says. Then Kirsh looks up to the boy in front of him. "Hey, John," he says. "You do that website and I'll do this one, and we can copy each other. What do you think?"

John pauses for a moment. "OK," he says finally.

The students continue to work, moving from Web site to Web site jotting down notes. Kirsh figures out how to print and his pages come spilling out of the Hewlett-Packard laser printer in the back of the room.

Often, those details include specific names of items, words on pages, etc.

Here are some images:

- *Facial tissue v. Kleenex.*
- *A rap CD v. Limp Bizkit's "Chocolate Starfish and the Hot Dog Flavored Water."*
- *A poisonous snake v. a black mamba.*
- *An expensive watch v. a Rolex.*
- *A soda v. Diet Coke.*
- *A thick book v. Steinbeck's The Grapes of Wrath.*

Get the idea?

The old man in the bar is good. It incorporates some description (the first D), but it lacks an ability to really bring us in to the scene. That's where details come in.

Try the same scene this way:

A 72 year old wearing a worn John Deere cap sits quietly in Mickey's Pub, a half-smoked Winston dangling from his lips and a half-empty Budweiser in front of him. "Monday Night Football" airs on mute on the old Sony above the counter.

See how the second example brings you in? Details can do that for readers. If our big concern is that we need to show rather than tell, often these details can show more than a more general description.

Consider this description:

A light-brown dog with shaggy hair that stands about three feet high and weighs nearly 80 pounds.

And this:

A golden retriever.

It's the same dog, but which one can you picture better in your head? This example actually brings up the other benefit of details (besides their ability to show better than tell)—conciseness. The first example contained 17 words; the second used three. Which one was a more efficient use of space?

In journalism, space is at a premium. We have a finite amount of room to fit the news that our readers need to know. On the other hand, in order for our readers to actually access that information, we have to incorporate gold coins, which take more space. Specific details can help you find a happy medium.

Dialogue

A quote happens when you ask a source a question and that source answers

---

OBSERVATIONS AREN'T YET STORIES

They're just random words on a page. But they're a start. Look at how the observations from pages 40 and 41 could lead to some pretty decent story ideas.

---

1. The problems with how students choose to use their study hall time. Is this schoolwide program a waste of time?

2. The rules governing Internet usage. Who makes the rules? Why are they there in the first place?

3. Inadequate technology and software throughout the school. Should the school be more consistent in the way it sets up labs? What should be available? Who will pay for it?

4. How collaborative learning works or doesn't work within the school. Can some students just get by without trying very hard?

5. How schools monitor student computer usage. What is and is not acceptable and how will the school know what you're doing in the first place?

6. How the Internet helps or hinders the research process. Does the Internet have all the answers or are there other alternatives?

7. Dress code and how students get around the rules. How difficult is it for faculty to monitor and enforce?

8. How adept students are at using available technology. Are teachers able to keep up?

---

your question. Dialogue, on the other hand, is the words that a source says to other people and what those other people say back to the source. That's why we'll discuss getting good quotes in the next chapter (interviewing) and we'll discuss listening for dialogue here. Like description and detail, getting dialogue in your stories is just another form of observation.

In your English classes, you've probably learned the three basic ways you can find out about a character:

1. By what the character says and does.
2. By what others say about the character.
3. By what the author tells us about the character.

These three guidelines apply to journalistic writing as well. If we want our readers to see and understand the people we're writing about, we need to provide information that will help them under-stand. The way a person speaks to others and the way those people speak back to him can say an awful lot about who that person is.

Let's say you're writing a story about a student who volunteers at a nursing home (larger topic: Why do students volunteer their time with no pay? What benefit do they receive?). You want to show readers how this person really cares about these elderly people and how he's really made some valuable connections. So you go to the nursing home on an evening when your source will be working (a good start, by the way) and you follow your source, notebook or tape recorder or both in hand, throughout the night.

Along the way, you notice some things. First, you watch how the elderly people start gravitating toward your source from the moment he walks in the door. They all have smiles on their faces (description). After a few pleasantries, your source joins two old men with thick glasses at a table with a Monopoly game on it. One of the old men hands your source the top hat piece (details) and a wad of Monopoly money.

And then comes the dialogue.

"You trying to shortchange me again, Joe?" your source says with a smile.

Joe smiles back, "Nah," he says, "I just figured you didn't need to pay as much as me for medications."

"Don't let him fool ya," the other man says. "He's got more money than Donald Trump stored away somewhere for Christmas presents."

Your source looks at the other old man and says, "Hey, Bernie, speaking of Christmas, you still need me to get something for your granddaughter?"

"Ayah," Bernie says. "That'd be great. I just can't get out to the stores the way I used to."

And thus, dialogue is born.

From that short exchange, we readers learned quite a bit about the source's relationship with these people at the nursing home. In particular, the dialogue lets us understand quite a bit more about the source's relationship with Bernie and Joe.

Specifically, we learned that the source was on a first-name basis with these two gentlemen. We also could see a little humorous give-and-take among the three of them. These three are close. We can see that because we can not only see them, but also we can hear them.

Notice how the reporter didn't have to ask a single question. Instead, he simply put himself in the right place at the right time and he paid attention to his surroundings. He watched for description and details and he listened for good dialogue.

These three D's working together made for a much better story.

A Word of Caution

Take heed, young reporters. Hundreds of words full of nothing but observation do not yet constitute a journalistic story. Observations in and of themselves aren't relevant. They give nothing for readers to think about yet. That's where you come in. Look at it this way. If I want to play the piano and I learn how to play the scales with my left hand, I may have something that sounds OK. But who wants to hear an entire concert played with just the left hand on the bottom notes of the piano? But add something—the right hand and the foot pedal, or add more instruments—and now we're getting somewhere.

Observation is just one tool of many that you will need in your journalistic toolbox to help you become a better writer. And like with most big tasks, you need more than one tool to get the job done.

Summary

Providing relevant observations is essential to writing readable stories for your visual audience. Reporters should remember the three D's—description, detail and dialogue—when they gather information for their articles.

The next two chapters will focus on the other two types of information gathering techniques—interviewing and research. In Section III, then, we'll discuss how to blend those three techniques together into a well-written journalistic story.

STUDY GUIDE

Terms and Concepts

Gold coins —Places in writing where readers stop and take notice. These are often areas of detail, description and dialogue.

Description —A reporter's ability to use his senses— sight, smell, touch, hearing and taste — to provide information for a story.

Detail —Specific words that help to further describe something. Often this means using proper names for elements rather than just physical descriptions.

Dialogue —The words that a source says to other people and what those other people say back to the source.

Practicing the Information Gathering Technique of Observation

For this activity, you need a notebook, something to write with and 30 minutes of time.

Step 1: Find someplace to become a fly on the wall. In other words, find a spot where you have a lot to look at and a comfortable place to sit, preferably a place where people converge. Maybe it's a seat in the library, or perhaps you could go to a local park or coffee shop.

Step 2: For 30 minutes, jot down as many observations as you can while you sit in this location. Be aware of all of your senses— the way things smell, their sounds, the way things feel to the touch — not just the way they look. Listen for any snippets of dialogue that you may hear along the way. No detail is too small.

Step 3: Take your notes and try to put them in some sort of coherent essay (see example on Page 40 "Observation in Action").

Step 4: Look through your essay and try to determine if any story ideas emerge (see example on Page 42 "Observations Are Not Yet Stories").

Step 5: Save these notes for later use when you're looking for story ideas.

CHAPTER 4

Interviews

Inquisition or Conversation?

A friend of mine from college, Jason, used to get all the girls. Mind you, he wasn't the most attractive guy in the world. He was a little short, and he wore a bit too much cologne. But, man, could he attract the ladies.

Every night his room in our fraternity house was crawling with them. If we had a party and you were looking to meet, you always knew you could go up to Jason's room and maybe pick up on some of his cast-offs; after all, there were too many of them for Jason to handle by himself. If you asked Jason, he'd just shrug his shoulders (which were a tad wiry) and just dismiss his obvious mastery of the females. So I took it

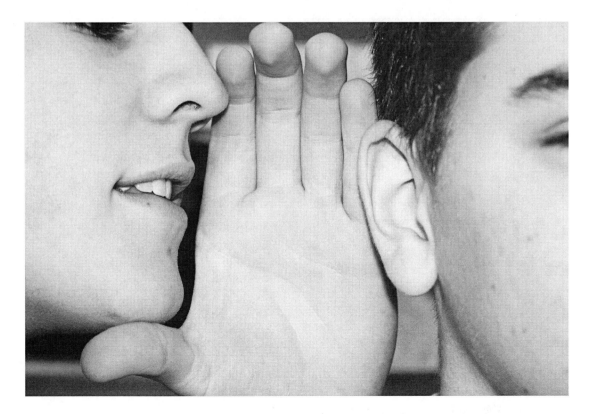

upon myself to ask his quarry. And do you know what they said, almost to a woman?

"He's a really good listener."

That's it. His mastery had nothing to do with looks or clothes or the car he drove (I think it was an '85 Chevette). It had nothing to do with money (he was always asking me for cash) or prestige (he rarely got involved in anything other than fraternity flag football matches). None of that. What set Jason apart from all of us was a simple ability that everyone can perfect to some degree.

Listening.

Notice I didn't say "hearing" or "pretending to listen." There's a big difference. Go ahead and ask any woman. To listen — to truly listen — means you actually have to understand the words that are coming out of someone's mouth. You have to respond — a laugh, a nod, an occasional "mmm-hmm" — and you have to ask questions in response to their words that show that you listened. You need to be empathetic and, sometimes, even conspiratorial. You need to give eye contact. You have to at least appear interested, and, above all, the person talking to you needs to know that she (or he) can trust that you'll keep this information in the highest regard.

Listening.

In journalism, we call it interviewing.

They're not very different, listening and interviewing. With interviewing, the only difference is that you're jotting down (or tape recording) the information that the person says to you. But all the rest? The same.

AVOID "COACH QUOTES"

Beware of quotes that state the obvious or, at their worst, say absolutely nothing at all. And guess what? Coaches aren't the only ones who provide these gems. Don't use them.

Avoid

"I'm just out there to give 110 percent."
(Let's hope this isn't from a member of the Math Club.)

"All that matters is the score at the end of the game."
(Really? I had no idea.)

"The problem is that they scored more points than we did. But next time, I'm sure we'll come out strong."
(Duh.)

"I'm just really proud of the effort the kids put forth."
(What would be interesting is if he said, "I think these kids are just big losers.")

Paraphrase

"The meeting will be on Thursday at 3 p.m."

"We have 47 members in our club."

"The starting line-up will be John Smith, Jason Blakely, Fred Martin..."

Ask a follow-up question

"I'm just really disappointed."
(Why? What specifically are you disappointed with?)

"It wasn't fair."
(Why not? Who's to blame?)

"It was an amazing experience."
(Why? Describe it for me.)

A Conversation

When I teach journalism to my classes, I rarely use the term "interviewing" when we discuss the information gathering technique. Maybe it's because when I think of interviewing I think of Spanish inquisition-type scenarios or, at the very least, my own uncomfortable job interviews where I sweated in uncomfortable cheap suits and squirmed under a myriad of difficult, and often vague, questions. Instead, I like the term "conversation" better.

Conversation is a much less intimidating word. It's far less antagonistic. You have conversations with your friends every day, after all. You sit at the dinner table and have a conversation with your family. The word "conversation" seems to bring to mind some evidence of comfort, of give-and-take, of equality, of "we're both in this thing together."

The journalistic "conversation" should take on this tone. The only difference is, a journalistic conversation is one in which the other person (your source) does most of the talking. And you? Like Jason, you do the listening.

In many ways, the conversation scenario plays out like this.

Let's say there's this girl (or boy) that you've been pining over for a long time. If you had your chance, this person looks like someone you could spend the rest of your life with. The only problem is, the object of your affection has a boyfriend (or girlfriend). Bummer. So you bide your time. You befriend this person because you're nice and your parents raised you well (even if you have ulterior motives).

And then one day, out of the blue, it happens. The inevitable break up. And the object of your affection comes to talk to you. Are you excited? Are you interested? Do you want this person to know she (or he) can trust you? Do you let this person do most of the talking? Do you ask more questions from time to time to keep her (him) talking?

Yes. Yes. Of course. Yep. Absolutely (because the more attention and time she gives you the better).

In a weird sort of way, you should approach every interview/conversation with this scenario in mind. Pretend the person you're interviewing is that special someone. Give that person the same attention you would give to the object of your affection (within tasteful reason). Respond just as intently as you would if the object of your affection were talking to you.

In other words, listen.

Don't get me wrong. Interviewing isn't quite as easy as it sounds. Good journalists still have some hoops to jump through to do it right. But it just all starts with an ability to listen. Once you have that skill down, you're ready for the rest. Until then, keep practicing. But if you're ready to move on, then here we go.

Step One: Prepare

Research

All journalists prepare, from the lowliest beat reporter to the fanciest professional journalist. All of them get ready for their interviews in much the same way, and you should, too. It all starts with research. We'll discuss the ins and outs of research in more depth in Chapter 5, but for now, you should understand how important it is to find out as much as you can about a topic before you go off talking to people. After all, there's nothing a source likes worse than a young reporter coming up and asking, "So, what is it that you do?"

Try to use the resources available to

INTERVIEWING NO-NO'S

Tell me if you haven't tried these techniques before.
NOW STOP IT. Here's why.

What's wrong	Why it's wrong
List of question in a staff member's mailbox.	Leaves no room for follow-up questions. Impersonal.
E-mailing questions to sources.	See above.
Walking up to someone and saying, "Hey, man, you got a quote?"	A quote? About what? Who are you? Why are your talking to me? Why should I waste my time with you?
Writing your list of questions on several sheets of paper with spaces left in between for answers.	What about follow-up questions? What if you run out of room? What if the interview doesn't follow the "script" of your questions?

---

you to give you some background into the story you're writing. If it's a story about the basketball team, what was the team's record last year? Who are the starters this year? Who are the seniors? Who is the team's main competition this year? If it's a story about your school's dress code policy, what is the policy exactly? What other schools in the area have policies like this?

Research doesn't always have to be via the Internet and it doesn't always need to be extensive. Sometimes your best research may mean just reading the articles from past issues (or from previous years) to see what's already been written about the topic. Or you may jump on your school's Web site (if you have one) and find out some of the basics. The bottom line, at least in terms of interviewing, is that you need to conduct enough research so that you can speak intelligently and knowledgably in front of your source. As a journalist, you have a responsibility to convey clear, articulate stories to your readers. Chances are, if you don't understand something, your readers won't either.

List of Questions

In particular, research can help you approach the next stage — preparing questions — with greater ease. After all, many of your questions may stem directly from the preliminary research that you have conducted. Again, all journalists prepare questions. Most importantly, that list helps to keep you and your source focused. As nervous as you may be conducting and interview, remember that you are the one running the show. You asked the source for his or her time and so it is your responsibility to come prepared. A list of good questions will facilitate this.

First and foremost, your questions should all be written (legibly) on one page (if possible). Why? Because a typical interview doesn't always follow a strict format. Your list of questions is not a script that must be followed; rather, it's a guideline. You may find during the course of the interview that you skip around your list as the source's answers dictate. So while you're running the show, the source is in the driver's seat. In addition, keeping the questions on one page will help to prevent annoying pauses in the conversation while you (the interviewer) frantically try to flip through the pages of your notebook looking for that one pertinent question that you were sure you wrote down, if only you could find it. Your hands will be full enough as it is, as you'll see when we discuss materials; don't let your list of questions detract from your professionalism.

Your list of questions is much like a bread crumb trail through a maze. You have a starting point and an ending point, but you have no idea what side trails you'll go on during this journey with your source. Sometimes the source will lead you down "good" paths — places where there is a story and the source provides lots of details. But almost as often, you'll wander down some "dead ends" — places that the source really doesn't know about or doesn't want to talk about. Or, even worse, the source talks and talks but about a subject that is completely off the original topic — interesting, yes, but not relevant. As the interviewer, it's your job to keep that interview flowing smoothly, and your list of questions, like the bread crumb trail, will keep you on the right path.

As for the list itself, you need to keep one basic rule in mind — ask questions that cannot be answered with a simple "yes" or "no." Your questions should solicit answers that you can then use in your story. Your questions should lead to quotes that should stand alone. In other words, the question you asked should be obvious by the answer from the source. The quotes should hold up on their own merit. If you ever find yourself writing "When asked about..." before putting the source's answer ("Yes.") then you're in trouble. Avoid questions that start with "are," "did," "will," "can," "should," "would." Instead, try starting with "how" or "why." These latter question words will solicit much better responses. Bad answers, after all, often come from bad questions.

That's not to say that every question you ever ask will be a how or why question. In fact, as you conduct your interview, you may find yourself asking several "concrete" questions as follow-ups, but don't plan for them. Or you may ask some of my favorite questions — questions that ask a source to describe or explain something. "Describe for me a typical afternoon in your office," you might ask. Or, "Explain for me the difference of the class you're taking now to the class you took at your other school." See how those questions will force the source to speak?

Another tip is to avoid two-part questions. If you've ever watched a politician speak, you'll know why. Reporters in the audience will ask the politician a two-part question and, many times, the politician will only answer one of the questions — most likely the easier question that he doesn't mind answering rather than the tougher question which might cause difficulty or controversy.

Finally, you can't prepare for everything. Your list of questions is a guideline, a starting point. The rest is up to you. Your questions are there for support, but most of the work comes from you listening to the answers and asking pertinent follow-up questions that may or may not be on your list.

Set Up the Interview

It's common professional courtesy to set up an appointment with your source(s). Many people will tell you how they dislike it when a reporter catches them off guard, when he storms in and demands an interview right then and there. First of all, it's rude, and secondly, the source may not be able to provide you with as much information or time as he would have had you set up an appointment.

You should always set up a meeting

A SAMPLE LIST OF QUESTIONS

Even the professionals generate a list of questions for their sources. It shows that you're prepared. Use this example from a story about a marketing class project as a guide for your own questions.

---

1. Please spell your name and provide your title as it is pertinent to this story.

   Accuracy is important. It leads to credibility. Spell all names correctly

2. Do you believe that people of all ages can enjoy Santa's Secret Shop and Gifts Unlimited?

   The filter question. Usually answered "yes" or "no," it tests your angle. Reporters should be 95 percent sure of the answer.

3. What other differences are there between Santa's Secret Shop and Gifts Unlimited other than the age targets? How are these differences significant?

   Questions 3 to 14 are open-ended questions. Most of them ask "how" or "why." These types of questions, rather than "yes" and "no" questions, will result in better storytelling quotes.

4. How are these programs funded from year to year?

5. Why is the increase for profit on merchandise 35 percent?

   This question indicates that the reporter conducted some background research.

6. How do you think the prices of these shops compare to other places where students could shop? Why?

7. Who decides which marketing class will run the different shops?

8. How do elementary and junior high students organize opportunities to visit the shops?

9. How do the underclass (junior) marketing students assist the seniors in running the shops?

   Like Question 5, Question 9 indicates research. This reporter already knew that the shop primarily uses seniors.

10. How do the marketing students help kids choose the gifts they want to buy?

11. Describe for me the typical experience that a young shopper would have if he visited the shops.

    This is not really a question but an opportunity for the source to open up and provide some storytelling information. Questions like this should be followed up with several detail questions to fill in any "holes."

12. What changes, if any, have been made this year or are planned to be made?

13. How will these changes affect customers?

14. As a teacher, what skills do you hope your students gain from this experience? In other words, why is this a valuable experience?

15. Is there anything that I haven't asked that you think readers should know?

    It's important to phrase this question in terms of the audience. It reminds the source that people will actually read this information. Leave the door open for follow-up (nobody's perfect), but a subsequent interview doesn't need to be face-to-face.

16. May I get in touch with you if I have additional questions? What is the most convenient way to do this for you?

time with your source. And you should make sure you set it up in a location that is convenient for the source, not for you. You should interview on the source's "turf," in other words. Why? Because sources can be just as nervous as reporters during interviews. Even administrators and teachers get nervous. After all, as a reporter, you represent your school's publication. The words you write (including the quotes from your sources) have the potential to be read by the entire school population. Your source wants to look good (or, to be fair and balanced, at least accurate), and he or she trusts you to be as accurate as you can. Sources feel more comfortable in their own environments. You should go there.

Besides, when you interview in the source's environment, the byproduct of that is that you put yourself in a location where you might be able to pick up on some relevant observations (see Chapter 3). Does the principal have a picture of his family on the desk? Does the counselor have one of those cutesy motivational posters on the wall? Does the soccer player have dozens of trophies on his shelves? These "gold coins" may be just what you need to make your story come alive.

In addition to setting up the time and location of the interview, you should also give your source a general idea of the angle of your story — what you're trying to get readers to think about (see Chapter 1). This will help the source to focus on possible questions before the interview or, in some cases, even prepare some information for you before you arrive.

STORYTELLING QUOTES

Good quotes should stand alone. Check out these examples from professional journalists. Ask yourself, what questions did these reporters ask to get these responses?

"A lot of [the soldiers] are young and scared to be going over," says Rachael Mays of the Sleeping Dragon tattoo parlor. "They come in for their meat tags. You know, dog tags for the skin. Their name, rank, serial number, religion, blood type and gasmask size. They want 'em in case they're blown in half. Then at least some part of them can come back to their folks."
— *from Rick Reilly's "Why the Preparation for War on Iraq Really Hits Home in Jacksonville, N.C."*

"You know, I made a promise when [my son] was born. I said if anything ever happened to him, they wouldn't find me in some nightclub or some drug house. If the police had to come, I'd be right here at home."
— *from Mitch Albom's "A Son Dies and a Mother Struggles On"*

"The ferrets must have a mouth full o' teeth. No filing of the teeth; no clipping. No dope for you or the ferrets. You must be sober, and the ferrets must be hungry — though any ferret'll eat yer eyes out even if he isn't hungry."
— *from Donald R. Katz's "The King of the Ferret Leggers"*

"Well, if you're grown-up, you'd have a car, and whenever you felt like it, you could get into your car and drive somewhere and get candy."
— *from Susan Orlean's "The American Man at Age Ten"*

Face-to-Face Is Best

One final note before we move on. If at all possible, conduct your interviews face-to-face. It's the accepted practice of most professional journalists, but beyond that, the face-to-face interview is much more personal. It allows the source to meet you and you to meet him. It gives you an opportunity to get valuable observations. And it ensures that you'll have the ability to ask follow-up questions.

Phone interviews are OK only if they can't be avoided. For example, you are trying to write a story comparing your school's dress code policy to one at a neighboring school. You're not allowed to leave the building to get the other school administrator's quotes. Using a phone in this instance is acceptable. But that's only if you have no other choice. E-mail, too, but be sure to use the words "via e-mail" when you give attribution to those quotes. That's because readers need to know that the source had time to plan and measure his responses, as opposed to the responses you might get "off the cuff" from an interview in person.

Step Two: Pre-Interview Checklist

So you've done your research. You've prepared your list of questions. You've arranged a convenient meeting time and location with your source. Now it's time to just get down to business and do it. But there are still just a few more important tips to remember before you arrive.

Attire

The first thing you need to remember is to dress appropriately for the interview. That doesn't mean you need to wear a three-piece suit or a fancy dress. On the contrary, unless you happened to be interviewing people at the prom you'd probably look and feel a little (OK, a lot) out of place. Dressing appropriately means taking a few minutes to make sure your look is both professional and clean. Every time you step out of your publication room you are representing that publication. And every publication wants to keep its reputation held in high regard.

So, ladies, really short skirts and midriff-revealing shirts probably won't cut it.

Gentlemen, pull your pants up and avoid wearing T-shirts with borderline profane words on them. Comb your hair. Brush your teeth. Wash your face.

Just look respectable. You're not going to church. It's not a funeral. It's not a wedding. It's an interview. But there's still a dress code to follow. Certainly you can wear a T-shirt and jeans to your interview, but make sure they're nice. Just think about the interview as a trip to Grandma's house. You know, Grandma? That nice old lady who bakes you cookies and sends you $20 for each birthday? What would you want her to see you wearing? Wear that to your interview.

Materials

This is an easy one. Here's your list of items to bring:

1. Your list of questions.
2. A notepad.
3. At least two writing utensils.
4. A tape recorder (optional).

The questions: As we have already discussed, you need these to keep you focused on the angle of your story. They should be typed (or neatly written) so you don't have to try to decipher your handwriting while in the middle of the interview. Also, try to keep all of your questions on one page.

The notepad: Even if you use a tape recorder, you should still keep a notepad. Remember, technology can break. The tape recorder may free you up to listen a little better, but you can still jot down good storytelling quotes (for later verification) and any pertinent observations that you notice during the course of the interview. If you choose not to tape record, the notepad is vital for getting down all of the information that you need for your story. Find one that best suits your interviewing style. What's easiest for you to write on? Some reporters prefer large notepads while others opt for the smaller steno-type pads.

The writing utensils: Seems like a no brainer, but you'd be surprised at the number of interviews I get asked to do where the student journalist has neglected to bring something to write with. I even had a source come back and tell me that the reporter actually wrote down the responses on her hand. What kind of confidence and trust are you building if the interviewee's first impression of you is that you can't even be responsible enough to bring all of your important materials? How confident will I be in your ability to quote me accurately in a story if I need to lend you a pen? Also, bring at least two utensils. Pencil leads can break and ink pens can run dry when you least expect it.

A tape recorder: I mention this as optional equipment. Some reporters swear by them. They claim that a recorder ensures that they'll get all the quotes as accurate as possible and that they free up their hands for other things in the interview, like writing down observations. And granted, there are several nice digital recorders on the market that make fast-forwarding and rewinding pretty simple.

On the other hand, those who choose not to use recorders argue that the machines seem too impersonal, that they and their sources are extremely conscious of

---

WHO SHOULD YOU INTERVIEW?

The sources you talk to should play a relevant part in how you tell your story. Try to get these three types of sources into every story you write. Here's why.

The main "face"	Generally, this should be a student source, since student readers will relate better to their peers. This is the person who the news affects. Most often, this person is introduced in the lead of the story.
The secondary source	Often, this person is also a student. This person verifies the information presented by the main "face" by saying that the news affects more than one person, that it affects others, too. On the other hand, this source may be a person who contradicts the main source, who presents an alternate view of the angle.
The "expert"	Not always an adult, but often so, this source provides credibility to your story. For example, if the main source makes a claim that stress from too much homework led to his insomnia, then the expert source (say, a counselor or a doctor) might indicate that from his experience many other students also suffer the same or similar fates from stress.

the metallic object sitting between them, and, as a result, they don't necessarily get the same "personal" effect as they would without the recorder. In addition, these people would argue, taping an interview—especially an exceptionally boring interview—means that you'll end up having to listen to the interview twice, once while you conduct it and the other while you listen to it again.

The choice to use a tape recorder is yours to make. Just do what you feel comfortable with.

Arrive Early

I'm not talking, like, an hour early, but at least five minutes early is nice. First, it shows your source that you are reliable and punctual (hence, professional). Second, it gives you an opportunity to calm your nerves and prepare your materials. Finally, arriving early gives you time to jot down any good observations while you wait. Are there other people also waiting to see your source? Does the source have a secretary? What kinds of magazines are on the tables?

Step Three: The Interview

OK. You're in the door. Your materials are ready. You're ready. The source is ready. It's time to begin.

Start with the List, Then Move Beyond

Remember, you're running the show, so start with your list of questions. Allow the source time to answer and do your best to jot pertinent information down. But be careful to listen and ask follow-up questions. An interview is not a race. The first

one done doesn't earn some sort of door prize. On the contrary, the interview is done when either you have all the information you need to tell your story to your readers or the interviewee says the interview is done (after all, you're doing your work on his time).

During the course of the interview, don't be afraid to ask follow-up questions. Don't forget to get details (And what did you say? And then what did he say? What time was it again? What color was the car? What year?). If you don't understand something, chances are your readers won't understand it either.

Let's say you're interviewing a bank employee about the ins and outs of getting a car loan. Do you know how interest works? Do you know what principal is? Do you know what residual value is? What's a lease? How does that work? What's a cosigner? Does everyone need one? Granted, some of this can be (should be) done during the research phase, but you might try bouncing your understanding of the concept off of your source to make sure you've got it right. No source wants to look bad or inaccurate. Of course they'll take time to make sure you get it right because if you get it right, then your readers will, too.

Your list of questions is there to help you, you'll recall, but it is not a script to follow word-for-word. Use your list as a starting point, but then move beyond to find the real stories.

Actions Speak Louder Than Words

The way you present yourself in an interview can also do wonders to improve your credibility with the source. And one of the best ways to achieve this is through eye contact. When you speak to you source, you should look the person directly in the eye. And when you listen, same thing. There are times when you will have to look down (at your list of questions, at your notebook to write), but you should take some time to look up.

My sister has a degree in court stenography. That's the person in the courtroom who writes down every single word that everybody says in a courtroom. Every single word. You're not a court stenographer. Don't pretend to be one. Everything your source says is not important. You need to learn to listen for the "gems." Those are the tidbits you'll write down. But don't write down every single word. First of all, the interview will drag on incessantly, and second, the last thing a source wants to see the entire time is the top of your head.

Remember, too, that looking up from your notebook from time to time also allows you an opportunity to observe your source. This is why face-to-face interviews are best. How is the source sitting? Does he smile when he speaks? Cry? Does he lean back in his chair? Does he fiddle with a paper clip the entire time? You may not end up using all of these little details, but sometimes they can really help to connect readers with the sources.

What Are You Listening For?

Here's the key to the interview. Yes, you're looking for quotes. But what kind? How can you tell a good quote from a bad one?

First, you're listening for good storytelling quotes—quotes that only the source could tell in his or her own words. You'll find some examples of these in this chapter. These are quotes that are rich in detail and description. Of feeling and emotion. Quotes that, by their very nature, make readers think about the topic or angle at hand.

Second, you're looking for quotes that

express opinions. As a journalist, you have to remain objective. Your job is to tell readers what to think about, not what to think. But that doesn't mean your sources can't share their opinions. In fact, you should encourage your sources to share those opinions. Conflict is a huge element of news, after all. If there were no conflicting viewpoints, would it even be news? Your job is to find those people who have differing views on a subject and allow them a chance to speak. By sharing both (or all, if there are more than two) of those views in your story, you will have done your job while at the same time inserting the passion and emotion of those sources into your stories.

Step Four: Wrapping It Up

You're almost done. The end is in sight. You're going to make it. But just a few more steps before you're completely out the door and on your way back to the publication room.

Final Questions

Your second-to-last question should always be this: Is there anything else that I haven't asked that you think readers should know?

Notice the phrasing there. Not "what I should know" and not simply "Is there anything else?" Rather, the word "readers" appears quite deliberately. By asking the question this way, you're reminding the source that you're a reporter and that the words you write will be read by however many hundreds or thousands of readers you have for your newspaper or yearbook or magazine.

Not only that, but that question can often lead to a great storytelling quote, perhaps one that you might consider ending your entire story with. After all, your source has gone through the entire interview with you. By now, he or she should have a pretty good idea what you're trying to get out of the interview, and if you haven't asked the question already, this is the time for the source to sum it all up.

Finally, the true purpose of the question is, in fact, to make sure that you've covered all of your bases. No matter how much research you've done, no matter how complete you think your questions are, you may have still missed something. Asking this question may catch that mistake.

Verify Your Quotes

This is a must and it's often overlooked by many young journalists. At the end of the interview, go back through your notes and check with your source to make sure that every fact and direct quote is accurate. It's also important to put those direct quotes in context. You might phrase it like this, "When I asked you X, you said, 'X.' Is that correct?" If it is, put a little star by it or have the source initial it. Whatever. Just find some way of indicating that this quote or this fact is both accurate and verified. Going through this step will also save you some potential headaches later, especially if the source, for whatever reason, claims that he never said what you wrote down that he said.

And if you tape recorded the interview, be sure to hold on to the tape for a while. The longer the better. You just never know how much time may elapse before a source decides to come forward to indicate a problem.

Leave the Door Open

It's possible — heck, it's pretty likely — that you may have missed a few pieces of information here and there during the interview. No problem. Just ask the source if it's OK to contact him or her again if you do, in fact, have additional questions. For these follow-up interviews, too, it's also fine to conduct them over the phone or even via e-mail. You should follow the source's lead, though, and do whatever's most convenient for him or her.

Say Thank You

The bottom line is this: The relationship between a source and a reporter and, consequently, a source and a publication is vital. Anything you can do to maintain a strong impression of professionalism is important. This applies to how you conduct yourself before, during and even after the interview.

Once you've left an interview, it's important that you take a few moments to thank the source for his or her time. This doesn't need to be anything drastic or lavish, just a simple note that says something like this:

Dear Mr. Smith,
Thanks so much for taking the time to speak with me about the dress code. The information you gave me was very useful for the story I'm writing. I look forward to speaking with you again.
Sincerely,
Your name.

You can use your own stationery for this, or, as with many staffs, official thank-you cards and envelopes may be available. Whichever the case, make sure you do it and do it in a timely fashion. If it helps, think of Grandma again. Every year on your birthday she sends you a check for $20. If you want $20 next year, you'd better thank her for her generosity this year.

Step Five: Sifting Through the Info

Go Through Your Notes

With time and experience, you'll get better at interviewing, and that may mean that you develop some sort of shorthand when you write. After a day or two, what that also may mean is that you may look back at your notes and have absolutely no idea what you wrote down.

To avoid this, when the interview concludes, find a quiet spot and go through your notes. Double-check everything that you've written inside quotation marks. Clarify any abbreviations. Make notations in the margins to help make the words make better sense. If you prefer, you could start to organize the information. Looking back at the interview after it's done may give you some perspective on what just transpired. You may think of some immediate follow-up questions to ask later, or the source may have given you an idea for some additional research or another source to interview. If you've already conducted some research, now's the time to jot down the correlation of that research to what the source said. If there are relevant observations, the same rule applies.

The purpose of this step is so that you don't forget the context in which you got the information. It's important to be accurate, and accuracy is more than just getting the words right; it's making sure those words are relative and pertinent to the questions that you asked.

Follow-Up

Follow-ups are questions that you failed to ask that reveal themselves later. It's common to have them — even professional journalists can't think of everything in an interview — but it's your responsibility to find the answers. As I mentioned, you may think of some follow-up questions immediately after the interview. But you may think of more as you begin writing your story.

If you've done your interview correctly, you have already set up a procedure with your source in the case of additional questions. Follow whatever procedure your source has said is most convenient. Here it's OK to use the phone or e-mail. Or if the source has indicated that it's fine to stop back in, then do that. Either way, just like with the first interview, make sure you appear professional. Have your questions prepared. Have something on which to write (or record) the responses. Thank the source again (verbally this time is OK).

File Your Notes

Accuracy is the cornerstone of any publication. Every publication should strive to be as accurate and as objective as possible. Accuracy leads to credibility, after all, and credibility leads to trust. As a reporter you need to do your utmost to make sure your stories are as accurate as possible. That's why verifying your quotes at the end of an interview is so important.

Occasionally, you may have a source indicate that he or she never said something from a story that appeared in print. Or he might say that research you've printed is wrong. Reporters need to protect themselves by keeping everything. This means that good reporters should keep a file with all interview notes (or tapes) and hard copies of relevant research. Organization is the key. You never know when a source might be upset.

For example, when I advised our school magazine, a student of mine wrote a story about a girl who was clinically depressed but didn't know it. As a result, she self-medicated (with illegal drugs and alcohol) to the point where she became suicidal. To compound the problem, the girl was diabetic, and the drugs didn't help that condition either.

We printed the story in late winter, and it included quotes from the girl, the girl's mother and the girl's therapist (who couldn't speak about the girl specifically but who could discuss the larger issue of clinical depression as a relevant, credible expert source). The good news was that the girl finally discovered her clinical depression and got proper treatment. The reporter had a strong point (the thing she wanted readers to think about)— that there may be several other students at school who may also be clinically depressed and not know it and who may be going down the same path as the main source. The expert source provided information about the signs of depression and the steps students (and parents) could take to get help. The mom provided insight on her daughter's behavior both before and after the treatment.

In the story, the girl mentions that one of the factors that led to her depression was the divorce of her parents. She said that her father alienated her and that situation pushed her farther down the destructive path she was on. The father, meanwhile, had moved out of state and was unavailable for comment.

It wasn't until six months later that the staff got a call from the father. He was appalled. He said the story was false. The information, also false.

Luckily, the reporter who had written the story was still on staff. Even better, she went right to her cabinet and pulled out every single piece of information that she had collected for that story. Even six months later, she still had all of her information down to the most minute detail.

In the end, the story stood. The father had been contacted but he was unavailable, and that had already been included in the story. The daughter's quote about her father had been verified and documented. It was accurate. But more than that, the reporter had a solid premise for her story. Her point was valid; she knew and could clearly communicate what she wanted readers to think about. And that, above all, protected her and the publication.

What does this mean to you? Call it a scare tactic, but reporters must stay organized and they need to understand their responsibility as a journalist to be as fair and accurate as they can. You just never know when you'll be called to verify your words. As a reporter, you represent more than just yourself; you embody an entire publication and all the integrity that that publication stands for. Keeping good notes is an important part of that equation.

Summary

Good interviewing is one of the keys to good storytelling. Storytelling quotes can add personality, emotion and life to your articles and can help to effectively bring out for readers what you want them to think about by having faces respond to the very questions you pose in your story.

But reporters need to practice professionalism whenever they conduct interviews. This means planning through proper research and question creation to conducting themselves professionally and respectfully during the interview. Even afterwards, reporters have certain steps they must follow to ensure that their information is as credible and accurate as it can be.

Finally, the only way to become a good interviewer is to practice the skill. The more you interview, the better and more comfortable you will be with the process.

STUDY GUIDE

Terms and Concepts

Filter question — Usually answered "yes" or "no," this question tests your angle with a source to see if what you're writing about is accurate.

Coach quote — Quotes that state the obvious or, even worse, say nothing at all.

Follow-up question — A related question that proceeds one you have already asked a source. Often this type of question can provide more detail or insight into a source's answer.

Storytelling quote — Quotes that only the source could tell in his or her own words. Often these quotes share an opinion or are rich in detail and description.

Main source — the "face" on your story. Often a student, this is the person who is being affected by the news.

Secondary source — a person who either backs up the main source (and lends credibility) or who contradicts the main source (to lend conflict).

Expert source — Often an adult (but not always), this person lends credibility and relevance to your story.

Practicing the Information Gathering Technique of Interviewing

Step 1: Particularly if you've never interviewed before, try interviewing some-one in your class. The idea is to come up with enough information to write a focused story about one aspect of this source. In other words, don't write the "Student Trading Card" and only provide answers to questions that merely scratch the surface. Try to dig deeper and get detailed information about one moment/event in this person's life.* Good interviews should take a while, so reserve at least 30 minutes per interview (longer if necessary). You should go into the interview with a prepared list of questions (see Page 50).

Step 2: When you've concluded the interview, look back at your notes and jot down a list of relevant follow-up questions that you failed to ask.

Step 3: Conduct a second, follow-up interview.

Step 4: Write a one-source story that focuses on the information you gained from your interview(s).

Step 5 (optional): Using your completed story, think of possible secondary and expert sources you could talk to make this story newsworthy. Also, consider incorporating your observation skills (from Chapter 3) into the interview as well. What observations did you make with your source that are relevant to the story at hand? Did the source tell a story about a time when he had major surgery? Does he have a scar to prove it?

Note: For most interviews that you will conduct, you should know beforehand why you are writing the story and you should prepare focused questions accordingly. The inherent flaw in this assignment is that your list of questions will be rather vague since you will not know your focus until you find it during the interview. However, the benefit of this exercise is that it forces the interviewer to listen intently to the source and ask relevant follow-up questions in order to provide the detail and description necessary to write a focused story.

CHAPTER 5

Research

Is Data More Than a Four-Letter Word?

The world — your world — is full of numbers. The number of students in your school. The number of clubs. The number of school lunches sold in a day. The number of steps it takes to walk from science class to your girlfriend's locker. The number of minutes you can spend with your girlfriend before you have to leave so you don't exceed the allotted number of tardies to class. The number of minutes of detention you'll have to serve if you are tardy again.

And on and on. Numbers are everywhere. You can't avoid them. They are a necessary part of life. Ask any mathematician, any scientist, and they'll tell you how important numbers are in understanding our world.

Problem is, numbers by themselves don't say a whole lot. They're not very readable, especially when they're taken out of context. For example, let me give you this number: 5. It's by no means a terrible numeral. But what does it mean?

What if I told you that 5 was the percentage of "foreign material" that the FDA allows breakfast cereal manufacturers to include in their products (i.e., bug parts, fecal matter, etc. — in other words, anything not considered "cereal")? Would it mean more to you? What if I told you that, if you ate a bowl of cereal each day for a year, using that 5 percent as a base, you would ingest the equivalent of over 20 insects? And in a lifetime, you might as well be digging into an anthill or a beehive with a knife and fork?

You see, numbers—and any data, for that matter—don't mean much unless you can relate them to readers somehow. And researching that data is an integral part in the information gathering process. And data doesn't just include numbers, either. What were the names of the seniors who graduated from the championship women's basketball team last year? Where did they go to school? What's your school's policy on cell phone usage? See what I mean? Each of these questions results in some sort of fact, some sort of statistic. How you use that data, though, is up to you.

The Purpose of Research

Say you're writing a story about perceptions of students' emotional attachment to your school. You know, like school spirit. You've been hearing some grumblings lately, and some students and faculty are hinting that their lack of connection is due to the fact that the school is too large and impersonal. They say they don't feel connected because they just feel like cogs in a machine. They don't feel like an integral part of the school "family."

Certainly interviews and observations are important in the information gathering process for this story, as you learned in the previous two chapters. You can find a main face—maybe someone who felt more connected at his or her middle school but now is not nearly as involved at the high school—and a few secondary sources—maybe one student who, like the main face, doesn't feel connected either (to lend credibility) and another student who does feel connected (to provide balance). You can observe these main and secondary sources doing whatever it is that makes them feel disconnected—getting on the bus right after school and heading straight home, for example. You can incorporate "expert" sources—the principal who discusses what the school is doing to make people feel more connected, a counselor who can discuss what problems he's encountered with "disconnected" students and what he suggests those students (and faculty) can do to help or to fit in better.

But if all you have are interviews and observations, your story is not yet complete. Who's to say that the sources you chose aren't the only one or two people in the entire school who feel that way? Do other students feel that way, too? How do you know? What's to indicate that the principal isn't just saying that new pro-

---

JUST THE FACTS

Headline: "A Thief Dines Out, Hoping Later To Eat In"

Author: Rick Bragg, *The New York Times*, May 19, 1994

Point: The prison system doesn't always work to punish criminals. Sometimes people prefer life in prison to life on the streets.

Face: Gangaram Mahes, a "serial diner" who eats in expensive restaurants and then does not pay so that he will be arrested and then returned to Riker's Island.

Relevant research: "It costs taxpayers $162 a day to feed, clothe and house Mr. Mahes at Rikers Island. His 90-day sentence will cost them $14,580, to punish him for refusing to pay the $51.31 check. In five years he has cost them more than $250,000."

grams are in the works to help "make the big school seem smaller"? Do those programs really exist? What are they? Have they been successful? And are these perceived problems focused solely on your school, or do other similar schools have the same problems? What have they done to combat these problems? Have those approaches been successful?

Enter research. **What research does is provide statistical evidence to support the information that you're providing for readers, information that is brought up by your sources. In a word, research provides credibility to your story.** It provides readers with empirical evidence to support or refute the claims of your sources.

Let's say that you discover that each counselor at your school is responsible for an average of 415 students and that at a much smaller school in your area, the counselors only have a case load of 200. Or perhaps you find class size averages are at 30 students per class this year versus 20 students per class five years ago. Maybe you find out that, of the 1,000 students who were involved in sports in varsity athletics in middle school, only 500 are involved in the high school. Do these numbers neces-

sarily support or refute the main point (what you want readers to think about) which is the question of whether students feel less connected to their school? No. They're just numbers. But they definitely provide hard evidence that gives your story credibility; this, in turn, may mean that your readers will lend more credence to your story and perhaps think about that thesis even more.

Research can provide relevance to your story, a sense of timeliness and immediacy that your article might otherwise be lacking. Maybe your article was spurred on by a recent article published in the local professional press that included credible survey statistics correlating student dropout rates and school size. Your story, therefore, is a localization of that national news. By including those survey results, you let your readers know that this is a current issue in the news and, hence, something new that they should consider in terms of their own school environment.

Research can help lead to more and better questions. For our example story about students' emotional attachment to your school, let's say you want to interview the school counselor. Which is the

---

JUST THE FACTS

Title: "The Return of Laura Marks"

Author: Kevin Bushweller, *Teacher Magazine*, November/December 2001

Point: Teachers are often the victims of violent assaults from students, which, in turn, causes many of them never to return to the classroom.

Face: Laura Marks, a health teacher at a school in New York City, who was assaulted by a senior who was unable to graduate because she had failed Marks' class.

Relevant research: "Between 1994 and 1998, an estimated 668,400 violent crimes were committed against faculty members at public and private schools. That translates into 31 violent crimes for every 1,000 teachers per year, according to Indictors of School Crime and Safety 2000, a report released by the U.S. departments of Justice and Education."

better question? So, do you think students here feel disconnected? Or this recent study shows that 20 percent more students feel disconnected in larger schools than in smaller ones, is that the case here? Why? The second question relies heavily on research. It shows the source that you've done your homework. As a result, you'll end up with better, more relevant answers. The first question, on the other hand, is a blind shot in the dark. It's based on conjecture and hearsay. If you ask this question, you don't know what you're going to get as a response.

And a valuable side effect of using research to ask better questions is that you won't look like an idiot in front of your source. There's nothing worse than going up to the head coach of the state champion football team and asking, "So, what exactly is your job?"

When to Conduct Research

That last paragraph brings up the next segment of research — when should you conduct research as part of the information gathering process? I know this chapter is the third of the three chapters dealing with information gathering techniques, but in all reality, research should be conducted first in the process. And it should be first for a number of reasons.

First, conducting research before you go off to interview and observe can provide needed background that you may find useful during those other processes. If I'm writing a story about attendance, it might be helpful if I had some actual attendance numbers first. Or if I need to write about the future of technology at the school, I think it would be helpful if I knew exactly what technology the school had to begin with.

And this doesn't just apply to writers, either. Say I'm a photographer and I'm assigned to cover the football game. I think I would find it extremely helpful if I knew a few things, like who the star players are, whether those players like to run or throw, whether they tend to run or throw to the left or the right. In fact, if I wasn't already familiar with the game of football in general, I might even want to do a little research to find out about it. As a photogra-

---

JUST THE FACTS

Title: "Hope and Gory"

Author: Chuck Palahniuk, *Gear Magazine*, June 24, 2001

Point: Wrestlers compete, not for the glory of the sport (which is almost nonexistent), but rather for personal feelings of accomplishment, camaraderie and drive, despite emotional and obvious physical strains.

Face: Phil Lanzatella, among many other wrestlers, competing at the North Regional Olympic Trials for a spot on the Olympic wrestling team. Lanzatella, who wrestles with a repaired torn heart valve, knows "this is his last shot at the Olympics after decades of training and competition." In the end, he does not make the team.

Relevant research: "In the 28 years since the law that requires colleges offer equal sports opportunities for men and women, 462 schools have dropped their wrestling programs."

pher, the answers to those questions would help me to know where I should stand in order to be more likely to get a better picture.

Second, sometimes research leads to story ideas and angles. I might come across an article in the *New York Times* that highlights recent study results that show that more teenagers are suffering from severe depression. Or maybe the *Wall Street Journal* indicates that more students are pursuing advanced college degrees (masters and doctorates) than ever before. In both of those cases, could you use that research to find out if those trends are true at your school? Could you use those results to prepare questions for more local sources who can make that information more relevant for your readers?

Third, research can help writers to determine if a story really does exist, and it can lead to some hard-hitting stories that will certainly challenge your readership to think. This investigation can be especially useful for long-term projects.

For example, a student of mine was curious about how the administration was going to deal with new technology in the schools. Specifically, she wondered about so-called Blackberries, devices that multitasked as cell phones, e-mail machines and personal organizers. The dilemma behind her question was that the school board had just awarded a grant to a fifth-grade class that provided each of its students with a personal organizer. She knew, though, that the high school had a specific policy against cell phone usage during school, so, she wondered, since the school board seemingly endorsed the use of personal organizers with the grant, would the school relax its policy on Blackberries, since they could also be used as personal organizers in addition to their other functions?

What she found was that the school had no specific policy either endorsing or prohibiting Blackberry use. Once she had conducted her preliminary research, the reporter talked to each of the school's six administrators who kept referring her to other sources because none of them had an answer to her questions. In fact, the messages that the administrators gave her were so varied as to suggest that they had no idea how to deal with this new situation. In the end, as a result of her scrupulous research, the reporter ended up exposing a hole in administrative policies. And because of this research, she gave her readers quite a bit to think about that maybe they hadn't thought about before. This discussion of preliminary research should not suggest that the only time you should do research is at the beginning of the process. On the contrary, often interviews, observations and even other research can lead to more research questions. For example, what if, in the process of an interview, an expert source — say, a marketing teacher — tells you that teens see an average of 1,000 advertisements per day? You could take the person's word for it, of course, but it would probably be better for you to find this research for yourself to verify. Or, to use our example from the beginning, the principal mentions that the school already has several programs to promote school involvement and connection. Could you find out what those programs are? Could you find out how many participants those organizations include?

Research is an ongoing process. Good journalists tend to keep an ear toward that data and those numbers and statistics. But they also tend to look beyond the surface of those numbers to the underlying questions that truly affect their readers.

How to Conduct Research

When it comes to conducting research, the key word is relevance. The sheer

---

JUST THE FACTS

Title: "School Daze"

Author: Kathleen Schuckel, *Indianapolis Monthly Magazine*, September 2002

Point: Large schools don't always offer the best opportunities for students.

Face: Christopher Naidus (among others) who transferred to Carmel High School, the largest school in Indiana with 3,500-plus students, during his junior year. "Not a single person made an effort to talk to me," Naidus said.

Relevant research: "The federally funded National Longitudinal Study of Adolescent Health, released in April [2002], found that the optimal high-school size is 600 to 900 students. Children in smaller schools are less likely to use drugs or have sex, the study found. The reason? Staff and students often know each other well, which helps kids feel more connected."

---

amount of information that is at a student's fingertips today is astounding. To think that literally trillions of pieces of data are a computer keystroke away is a sobering thought. How can you possibly sift through all of that? You can't. And this is why relevance is so important.

Good research often starts with a solid research question. What is it that I want to find out specifically that will help advance the angle and theme of my story? Case in point, are you writing about technology or are you investigating what knowledge of technology do colleges in Indiana require their incoming freshmen to possess? Are you writing about standardized tests or are you trying to find out how your school's students performed on the latest SAT? Chapter 2 outlined the difference between topics and stories. Research is really no different. Topics are broad; unrefined research questions are equally broad. Stories are specific and focused, as are specific research questions.

Keep in mind, too, that the Internet isn't the only source of information in the world. Let's say you're trying to find out graduation destinations for your school's seniors over the past five years. You could go online, maybe to your school's Web site, to try to find that information. Or you could use a search engine to generate lists of data. Chances are you'll end up pretty frustrated. In this case, wouldn't it just be better to walk across the hall to your school's counseling center? My guess would be that the counselors probably have the exact information you need within arm's reach.

Credibility

While we're taking time to discuss the relevance of the research you find, it would be prudent for us to take a moment to chat about the credibility of that information. In particular, **you should always consider the source of your research.**

Let's say you're writing a story about the fact that many of today's high school students can earn their diplomas without working very hard, as *Time* magazine did in its 1999 collection of stories "A Week in the Life of a High School." In one of the stories, the *Time* reporter focuses on Minnie Phillips, an English teacher who teaches a pretty standard sophomore English class. Phillips is a good teacher who says that her hands are tied in terms of giving homework; she can't give it out because she estimates only about 15 percent will actually do it. The reporter decides to talk to an administrator about why this is allowed to happen. Why not let the students just fail the homework if they choose to, the reporter wonders? Why is this a bad thing?

The administrator, assistant principal Jon Clark, says that he doesn't want the students to fail because if they fail, they'll quit. "And we don't want that," he says. "We think [the students] are much safer in here than out on the streets."

But wait, the reporter thinks. Safe from what? The "streets" Clark mentions are suburban streets. Streets like many of the suburban streets around the country (which is one of the reasons *Time* chose the school it did). It's not like these kids live in war-torn Bosnia.

So the reporter considered the source — the assistant principal — and the reporter realized that of course an administrator would say something like "we don't want students to quit." What administrator wouldn't? And certainly the administrator had numbers that could easily be verified that supported the fact that the school's attendance rates were quite high.

But the reporter, because he took the time to consider the source, also knew that there was more to the story. And sure enough, he soon found his answer: money. The school recently earned a financial incentive (almost $150,000) for its high attendance rates, and it stood to gain the same amount of money each year that it continued its high attendance.

So what did that research do? Plenty. Most importantly it raised the biggest issue of the story, the very thing that the reporter wanted readers to think about — that fixing problems in schools isn't as easy as it seems. On the one hand, you've got good teachers like Minnie Phillips who want to challenge their students. On the other hand, you've got administrators who know

---

JUST THE FACTS

Headline: "Against all odds: In rough city school, top students struggle to learn — and escape"

Author: Ron Suskind, *Wall Street Journal*, May 26, 1994

Point: Good kids in bad schools find it difficult to escape their situation. Even if they get out, they find that, academically and socially, they lag far behind their peers from other, better schools.

Face: Cedric Jennings, a bright student in one of Washington, D.C.'s worst schools. Jennings wants to attend MIT, but he fears, despite extra work that he continually asks for from his teachers, that he won't have what it takes to succeed.

Relevant research: "Cedric is one of a handful of honor students at Ballou, where the dropout rate is well into the double digits and just 80 students out of more than 1,350 currently boast an average of B or better."

Also: "Some 836 sophomores enrolled last September — and 172 were gone by Thanksgiving. The junior class numbers only 399. The senior class, a paltry 240."

that those teachers want to challenge their students, but their hands are tied if they want to get more money for their schools, money that could be used for more technology, classroom supplies, even more teachers.

But none of this discourse would have happened in the story if the reporter hadn't considered the source of his information. Making sure that the research you have is credible is key.

And you can't have a conversation about credible sources without discussing the Internet. Here's your warning: **Be wary of the information you find online.** Today, if I wanted to, I could go online and create a Web site about brain surgery. I could simply call it brainsurgeryiseasy.com or imabrainexpert.com, or something like that. And on that site, I could give tips for doing your own brain surgery at home. I could list all of the parts of the brain and what those parts do. I could write essays about how the brain is capable of living in a jar next to your bed, residing peacefully in a mixture of shoe polish and mayonnaise.

And all of it would be a bunch of baloney. I know as much about brain surgery as I do about the climate on Rigel 7. Which is to say, absolutely nothing.

But I can make a Web site.

But, you're saying, I would never make such a foolish decision. I know what's true and what's not. I can delineate between credible information and information that isn't so credible.

Right. And monkeys might fly down from Rigel 7 right now and put your brain in a jar beside their beds.

The point is, **you must always be on the alert for false information.** You can avoid the problem in a couple of ways. First, **verify your online research.** If you find the information on one site, find it also on another. Or, better yet, take that research to an expert source and ask them if it looks credible. Second, **stay on sites that you know are credible.** News organizations generally have credible information. Or Web sites created by governmental organizations, like the Centers for Disease Control or the National Institutes of Health. Or you may check with your school's media center to see if your school subscribes to any online databases. Schools can pay for access to these databases which employ people to do the very thing you're trying to do—verify online information. Chances are, information from these databases is much more credible than the information you might find with a random search.

Finally, as you're conducting your research, **always look for the most timely information.** The advent of the Internet, while it does have its share of credibility issues, truly made up-to-the-minute information a reality. A decade or more ago, this wasn't the case. Researchers relied more on books and even magazines, which could quickly get out of date. Specifically in the case of books, because of how long the actual publishing process can take, the information contained inside might already be outdated by the time the book hits the shelves. What if you find survey results that say that 45 percent of your student population has tried alcohol in the past year and that 20 percent of students have binged on alcohol in the past two weeks? Sounds newsworthy, right? But what if I told you that those results were from 1985? Not newsworthy anymore, are they? And in terms of time, the Internet isn't always the answer. If I made a Web site in 1995 and I haven't posted anything since then, that information is still there (as long as I've paid my bills). Case in point, I ran a half marathon about eight years ago and counting. My race results are still there.

How to Incorporate Research

So you've got lots of good research. Reams of it. Scads of it. Now what do you do with it? The first thing you need to understand is that **you won't use it all.** In the research process of information gathering, like with interviewing and observation, you'll most likely end up with far more information than you can possibly use. And that's OK. As a matter of fact, it's an important part of information gathering to get more than you need. You need to make sure that you've covered all of your bases, for one. But once you start writing your story, you'll soon find that not all of the information gathering you've done is relevant.

Say you're doing a story about students who are trying to recover from athletic injuries. You have the following credible information from research:

- *The names of every player on every varsity sport that your school offers.*
- *A list of players who have been treated in your school's training room over the past six weeks.*
- *Information that outlines the proper technique for wrapping a bandage around an injured wrist.*
- *A diagram that shows the procedure for arthroscopic knee surgery.*
- *A chart that outlines players' performances (statistics) before an injury versus their performances after an injury.*

Which information do you use? All of it is certainly valid, and all of it is relevant in its own right. But some research is more valid than other research. When you write, you should only incorporate the information that is the most valid and relevant. Save the rest for another story. Or pitch it. But don't feel compelled to use it all.

Using the list of research above, the most valid, most relevant piece of research really depends on the specific focus of your story. If it's an article about athletic trainers and how difficult it can be to become one, then the information about wrist wrapping may be the most relevant. Or maybe you could use the list of the athletes who have been treated in the last six weeks to show how busy the trainers are. If the story's about how athletes struggle to come back after injuries, then the statistics about their performances pre- and post-injury would be best.

Whatever you end up using, though, remember that the last thing readers want to do is to read a string of research tied end to end like some long chain of data. Just because you have it doesn't mean that you need to use it. Research should only be used to enhance the point of your story, to lend it credibility; it is not the story itself. In fact, in Section III of this book, we'll take some time to discuss alternate ways to present research for our visual readers, ways that actually take much of the data and pull it out from the story to be placed alongside the actual article. But until then, keep your research credible, relevant and brief.

Polls and Surveys

I would be doing you a disservice if I failed to mention one last research technique that young reporters always seem to want to try: the survey or poll. If only I had a nickel every time a student suggested that he could conduct a survey to get the relevant research that he needed to accompany a story.

Those students are so naïve.

Polls and surveys are a lot more complicated than they seem. According to Dr. George H. Gallup (yes, the guy who conducts the Gallup Polls) in his pamphlet

"How to Conduct a High School Poll" (1996), students must consider several factors before they proceed. First and foremost is the sample size. According to Gallup, a sampling of 200 students out of 1,000 (20 percent) is appropriate to get a margin of error around 8 percentage points. But what if your school has 4,000 students (as mine does)? Will you have enough time to administer a survey to 800 students? And this doesn't even take into account the fact that your sample size must also represent the smaller variation within your larger sample — say, the number of males to females or freshmen, sophomores, juniors and seniors, for example.

In addition, surveys in most school settings must be approved by your school's administration before you can give them out. Administrators want to make sure that the information you're asking for doesn't disrupt the learning environment or, perhaps, ask for information that is illegal for students to disclose.

That's not to say that I haven't had students conduct surveys, and successful ones at that. I will admit that the information garnered from a well done survey can be invaluable, and it would certainly be quite relevant to whatever story it is accompanying. But for my money, surveys can be more trouble than they're worth. They take a lot of foresight and planning. And in reality, you can probably get just as relevant information elsewhere.

Summary

Research is the third component of information gathering. Like interviews with expert sources, research can lend credibility and relevance to your stories. You can conduct research at any point in the information gathering process, but doing so at the beginning can help reporters to narrow their focus and ask better questions. Be wary of research, though. Make sure the information you gather is from credible sources. Also, be sure that your research is as timely as possible.

STUDY GUIDE

Terms and Concepts

Credibility — Reliability. With research, readers need to know that the information, statistics, data, etc., that you provide can be trusted.

Relevance — Pertinence. Research must relate to the main point of the story (what the writer wants readers to think about).

Poll — A random sampling of people's preferences often open to any individual. Polls tend to be quick "snapshots" into people's thoughts that may or may not represent the larger group.

Survey — A more scientific determination of the situation or habits of individuals. Surveys tend to reflect the beliefs of a much larger group by usually trying to get responses from at least 20 percent of the total group(s) sampled.

Practicing the Information Gathering Technique of Research

1. *Incorporate research into an existing story.*

Using the story you wrote from Chapter 4, brainstorm a list of relevant, credible sources that would lend research to your story. Remember that it is this research that gives your story more relevance to other readers. Remember, too, that research doesn't just exist online. Think of some other places to access statistical information (i.e. the attendance office at school, the program of studies book, the athletics department, etc.).

2. *Start a story from research.*

Read through a current newspaper or magazine or peruse some online news sites (cnn.com, msnbc.com, etc.) and try to locate where current research appears. See if you can "localize" this research by brainstorming possible sources (main "face," secondary source, expert source).

Example: A recent $1 million study by the John S. and James L. Knight Foundation showed that, in terms of First Amendment rights, 97 percent of teachers and 99 percent of school principals said that, yes, people should be allowed to express unpopular views. Only 83 percent of students said yes. In addition, three in four students said flag burning is illegal (it's not) and about half said that the government can restrict any indecent material on the Internet (it can't).*

Or:

A study by the Nielsen Norman Group showed that teens (ages 13 to 17) as a group are not as adept at navigating the Web as adults. Given a series of online tasks, from making an appointment for a driving permit to discovering when Norah Jones would be in concert in California, teens completed the tasks 55 percent of the time while the adults completed them 66 percent of the time. The study attributed the students' poorer performance to immaturity and poor reading skills as well as teens' weak research skills and unwillingness to tough it out when sites posed design obstacles.

---

*Note: By the way, the study also showed that students who take part in media activities (i.e., newspaper, yearbook, TV production) are much more likely to support expression of unpopular views. Just some food for thought.

Writing

The Lifeblood of Your Publication

Take a pile of dog manure. Just big ol' steaming, stinking pile of it. Now put it in a box and wrap it up in beautiful, decorative paper. Put a gorgeous bow on top. Decorate it. Adorn it. Lavish it with attention. Spray perfume on it.

Guess what?

Inside that beautifully wrapped package is still just a big pile of crap. And that's the case with so many scholastic publications—they look great on the surface, but that's as far as it goes. When it comes right down to it, they're just window dressing something that's worthless.

Your publication is only as good as its writing. And the design? That will come later.

For now, let's take that information you gathered from Section I and learn how to turn it into something worth reading.

CHAPTER 6

The Fall
of the Pyramid
The Readable Narrative Style

OK. I admit, the title of this chapter is a bit sensational, a little over the top. Trust me, there are some journalistic heavyweights out there right now who are accusing me of destroying everything that is sacred about journalistic writing. And, in many respects, rightly so.

The real scoop is this: The inverted pyramid isn't actually dead, as the title implies, but in scholastic journalism, the need for the inverted pyramid has sort of overstayed its welcome.

What's the pyramid?

Before we proceed we have to discuss what exactly the inverted

pyramid is. The inverted pyramid (see diagram on page 74) is a style of journalistic writing which requires reporters to put the most important information in a story in the lead and then follow that lead with information that proceeds in decreasing order of importance. One rule of thumb to follow with the

most important

least important

inverted pyramid style of writing is to put as much of the "five W's and the H" (who, what, when, where, why and how) at the beginning of the story as you can.

I'm not violently opposed to the inverted pyramid by any stretch.

It does have its merits. For one, the inverted pyramid is a style that allows publications to provide information to time-pressed readers quickly and efficiently. If something happens the night before a publication comes out (i.e., the Chicago Cubs win the World Series, a bomb has exploded in Des Moines, Coca-Cola has filed for bankruptcy, etc.), the inverted pyramid provides an efficient, effective way of getting that information ("broccoli") out to readers who need to know it.

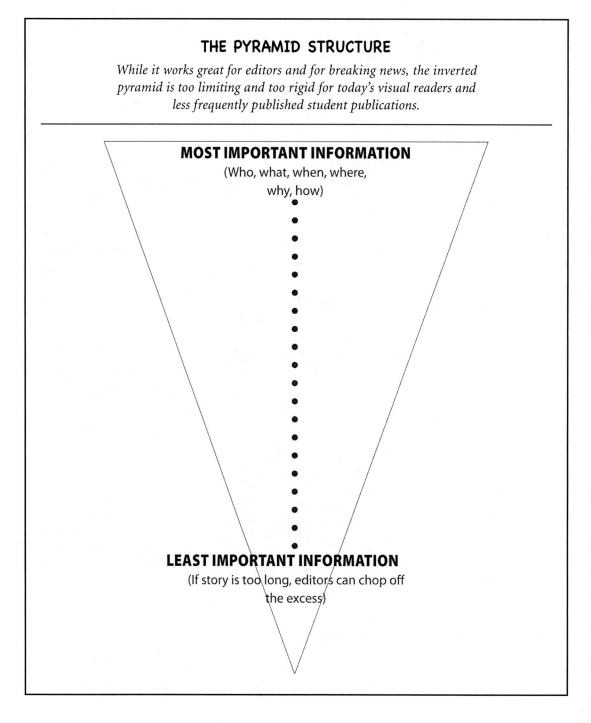

THE PYRAMID STRUCTURE

While it works great for editors and for breaking news, the inverted pyramid is too limiting and too rigid for today's visual readers and less frequently published student publications.

MOST IMPORTANT INFORMATION
(Who, what, when, where,
why, how)

LEAST IMPORTANT INFORMATION
(If story is too long, editors can chop off
the excess)

In addition, the inverted pyramid, particularly for new journalists, provides a more rigid framework for students. The inverted pyramid has a definite structure, almost a "formula," for writing.

But what are the downfalls? What are the inherent flaws in the inverted pyramid, particularly in the world of scholastic journalism?

For one, the nature of the pyramid — putting the most important information first — implies that readers may not read the rest of the story. And if you've learned anything about our young readers to this point (see the Introduction), it's that they don't want to read in the first place. The inverted pyramid isn't a very entertaining style of writing; its sole purpose is to get information out fast. But if our readers aren't reading in the first place, why would they bother with an inverted pyramid story? That type of writing just doesn't connect with younger readers. In addition, how many of our readers, if they do choose to start the story, will actually finish it? And knowing that most won't even start, let alone finish, a story, why are we taking up valuable space in our publications with inverted pyramid stories? Couldn't we use that space for something else that our readers will read?

Also, the purpose of the inverted pyramid is to release breaking information to readers quickly. This isn't a problem for daily newspapers that have staffs that stay on the clock until the wee hours of the morning to get that information out to subscribers within hours. But how often do scholastic publications publish? Every week? Every two weeks? Every month? Every year (i.e. yearbooks)? In addition, most high school publications don't have immediate turnaround like the professional press. A school paper that comes out on a Friday is usually, at the very latest, sent to the printer on Tuesday or Wednes-day. And that being said (unless you have a school Web site that can be updated by the minute), what can you publish that's written in the inverted pyramid — even if it happens moments before you send the paper to press on Wednesday — that readers don't already know by that Friday?

Finally, though the definition of the inverted pyramid indicates that it contains the five W's and the H, many inverted pyramid stories neglect two of those — specifically, the "why" and the "how," which, as you learned from Chapter 1, are perhaps the two most important questions you can answer for readers.

That being said, the only real people who benefit from the inverted pyramid style of writing in scholastic journalism are editors. Editors benefit from the style because, if a story is too long, it can be shortened by simply chopping off the end. Notice, however, that I didn't say readers benefit, at least not with high school publications. Certainly, readers benefit from the inverted pyramid in the daily professional press, but not when your publications come out less frequently.

Face it. In many cases even professional magazines outscoop high school newspapers. *Time* and *Newsweek* are published weekly. *Sports Illustrated* is weekly. And guess what? Those publications rarely use the inverted pyramid because of the very same reason outlined above — they don't contain breaking news.

So what does this all mean? Should we abandon the inverted pyramid? Should we just forget this style that's been used for generations? The answer is no, we should not. We should understand the inverted pyramid. We should even practice with it a bit. We should understand its merits. We should acknowledge how it asks reporters to find the true "meat" of a story (the who, what, when and where, in particular).

DON'T WRITE LIKE THIS

The inverted pyramid structure just doesn't work for high school journalists. Most of your stories will end up looking like this. Here's why that's not appropriate for your visual readers.

Homecoming is here once again.	Lead states the obvious.
Most students are looking forward to the activities planned for the week. The Senate has planned a week that kicks off with daily spirit activities.	Overgeneralization. How do you know "most" students look forward to events?
Students can dress up for each of the themed spirit days. The days are as follows: Monday, college T-shirt day; Tuesday, hippie day; Wednesday, pajamas day; Thursday, cartoon character day; Friday, spirit day.	Boring list.
Students will spend time building class floats which they will then enter in Friday's parade. Events will culminate with the football game against Springfield on Friday evening. At halftime, the Homecoming queen will be crowned.	More lists of boring data that readers probably already know.
"I can't wait for Homecoming," junior Jay Fleer said.	Random quote from a random student.
"I'm sure the Senate will do a great job this week," science teacher Fred Johnson said. "They always do."	Source is not relevant.

But then we should move on.

Look at it this way. In English class, you may have learned how to write the ubiquitous "five-paragraph essay." You know the one — introductory paragraph with a thesis, three supporting paragraphs and a concluding paragraph that restates the thesis. You learned that each paragraph should have at least five sentences. I've even taught with teachers who have turned the five-paragraph essay into a formula — like a math problem — where students simply fill in the blanks for their essay. These "templates" have blank spaces for transition words, for thesis statements, for supporting evidence, so you end up with a sort of Henry Ford assembly line of papers (see "Mad Lib Journalism" in Chapter 2).

Like the inverted pyramid, these formulaic approaches to writing have merit. In the case outlined, the approaches teach organization and transition. But the downfall is that they suck any sort of creativity out of the writing process. They turn the art of writing into an equation that has a right and a wrong way of doing things.

And how many of you would like to go home on a Friday or Saturday night to read a stack of five-paragraph essays? I

THE NARRATIVE STRUCTURE/THE PLOT LINE

Look familiar? It should. You probably learned about this structure — the plot line — in your English class when you learned about short stories. Guess what? Journalists can use it, too.

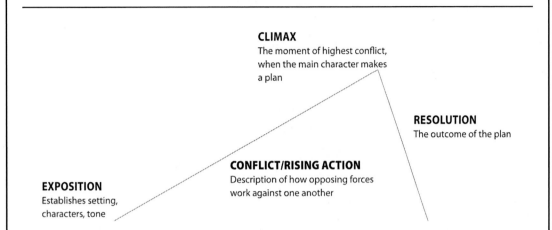

CLIMAX
The moment of highest conflict, when the main character makes a plan

RESOLUTION
The outcome of the plan

CONFLICT/RISING ACTION
Description of how opposing forces work against one another

EXPOSITION
Establishes setting, characters, tone

The key to the narrative structure is that stories have a beginning, middle and end. That's not to say that narrative stories must follow in chronological order. On the contrary, like the inverted pyramid, that would get monotonous. Certainly the narrative style has much room for flexibility.

One rule of thumb is to "start with the moment that's different" for your main source. Sometimes that means starting the story at one of the later conflicts or the climax and then working backwards to fill in the gaps of the story before concluding.

Authors know this technique quite well. In Jon Krakauer's *Into Thin Air* about Mount Everest, Krakauer's first chapter puts us with Krakauer at the top of the world's highest peak. Readers know from Page 1 that the book is not about the ascent of the mountain, but rather, the tragedy that befell the climbers on the way down.

Experiment with different organizational structures and use the ones that work best for the stories you are telling.

know a lot of teachers who dread the task, so why would students bother? The same holds true for the inverted pyramid. The style turns the art of journalistic writing into something that is cold and lifeless. It serves a purpose, of course, but understand that that purpose is best served somewhere else where the news gets distributed far more frequently than you or your publication are capable of doing.

Moving Beyond the Pyramid

So what do we do now?

In Section I (Chapters 1 to 5), we learned mainly about information gathering and reporting. We learned the definition of news and how to find the stories. We learned how to put a face on the news to make it more readable. We then learned how to gather relevant information for those stories by using our information-gathering techniques of interviewing, observation and research. These techniques, by the way, are no different if you publish weekly than if you publish monthly or yearly. Information gathering is information gathering in any discipline.

Let's assume, then, that you've accomplished your task of information gathering for the story you are working on. You have pages and pages of observation notes. You have tapes full of interviews. You have reams of research that are relevant to your point, what you want readers to think about.

WRITE LIKE THIS

The narrative or literary style is much more appropriate for your visual readers. Narrative stories do a better job of putting a face on the news; in other words, they show how the news affects readers.

Next to the unfinished class float in the middle of a colorful mountain of crepe paper, senator and freshman Eric Stevens throws another glue-laden wad onto a growing pile of mistakes.	Lead puts a "face" on the story.
"I don't think I'll ever get this right," Stevens says quietly. "And it needs to be done by tomorrow."	Storytelling quote.
Stevens isn't alone in his frustration. Many freshmen said that the pressure of the high school Homecoming takes away from the fun.	Transition to main point of the story. Tells readers what to think about (Homecoming isn't fun for everyone).
"My homework is piling up," Freshman Class President Ashley Jones said. "But I know I can't do my classwork because I'll be letting down too many people in my class."	Secondary, relevant source to back up main source.
For most freshman officers, this is their first glimpse of Homecoming festivities. And for many of them, according to class sponsor Rita Carson, the work is more than they can handle.	Relevant "expert" source. Reinforces the point.
"I've seen it before," Carson said. "These are highly motivated kids, and doing a bad job is not an option." But at the same time, she said, they don't know how to prioritize their lives.	
Stevens said he agreed.	
"I thought Homecoming was supposed to be fun," he said, his fingers coated in glue residue. "But now I'm not so sure."	Ends with good storytelling quote.

Now it's time to write. What do you do now?

By now you know that the inverted pyramid is not a viable option. For your purposes, it's not readable. So what does that leave?

Journalistic writers can learn quite a bit, at this point, from their contemporaries in the world of fiction. We're not writing fiction, of course, but we can learn something about a readable style of writing from these fiction writers. The only real difference between fiction and journalistic writing, after all, is that fiction writers make stories up and journalists write down stories about real people with real observations and real research. Both types of writing, though, include "characters" and character development. Both types include conflict and conflict resolution. Both types incorporate descriptions and details.

So why should the style of writing be any different?

Think about your favorite book for a minute, or even your favorite movie. Maybe it was a *Harry Potter* volume or perhaps some young adult fare. Maybe it was serious or funny or thought-provoking. Whatever the reason, the book or film stuck with you for some reason. Something about it — about its characters, its plot — became part of your life and wouldn't leave you.

Now think about your favorite journalistic story. What? Can't think of one? Why is that? After all, we know the news affects people, why hasn't it affected you? Am I to assume that nothing that's happened in the world has had an impact on you?

Of course it has. The problem isn't that news doesn't impact readers, it's that those who write about those events don't do a very good job of relating those events to your life. The how and the why are lacking a bit, especially in scholastic journalism, but even in the world of professional journalism, too.

But times are changing. And why? Because readers are changing. Readers demand more from their publications because they can afford to be more discerning. If it doesn't catch their eye, then they move on to something else. As a result, publications must either adapt to those changes or go the way of the dinosaur (or the pyramid, as the case may be).

Learn from the Fiction Writers

Here's another way of looking at journalistic writing. Pretend, for a moment, that the inverted pyramid style does not exist, and all you have in front of you are your raw materials — your observations, your interviews and your research — and you need to tell your story, the one you've worked so hard on, to others. How do you do it?

Remember a few things first. **One, you need to grab your readers' attention from the very beginning**, the first sentence, the first paragraph. You need to hook them and hook them early. If not, they'll move on to something else and it doesn't matter if your story's 1,000 or 100,000 words long, they won't read the rest.

Two, you need to make your point clear to your readers. They need to know early on why you're telling them this story. If not, like with the lead, they will become confused or bored and will, ultimately, move on.

Three, you need to keep your readers interested throughout the story. They need to be able to relate to your sources (characters). They need to be able to see and feel the conflicts that those sources are

HOOK 'EM

The beginning of your story is the most important part.
Check out the following examples of good leads.

The room seems normal enough. A queen-sized bed with modern, black metal posts and a white, textured, down comforter. Jungle-green carpeting to match the flowered and striped wallpaper stretches wall to wall. Other than the decor, though, the room is mysteriously empty.

But it wasn't always that way.

> *–about a girl who accidentally burned her house down when she fell asleep with candles still burning.*

As sophomore Dan Cassidy sat drinking, thinking of what his mother had done to him, anger built rapidly inside and turned to rage.

> *–about a boy whose alcohol abuse led him to beat up his mother and, later, to find redemption and a second chance.*

They sit on the couch with an old episode of "Love Boat" muted on the television in front of them. His hand rests upon her knee, and they are comfortable with each other. Under the circumstances, they feel they have no choice.

> *–about a high school couple pressed into marriage after an unplanned pregnancy.*

The red is first in line but now goes to the end. The green goes into the middle. The blue takes a spot close to the end. The rainbow one will remain in the center for the moment. Then she makes a decision and moves the blue, which she transfers to the opposite end.

Her concentration level is high and repeats for most of her class period. Pencil organization, after all, is important to senior Kylene Webber.

> *–about a girl with Down's syndrome.*

---

facing. They need to care about these situations somehow. They need to know how the newsworthy situation affects those sources. Because if they don't? You guessed it, they move on.

And four, you need to leave the reader satisfied but somehow wanting more. At times you might leave your readers with more questions than they have answers. You want them to leave with a "taste in their mouths," whatever that taste might be. You want them to go find out more for themselves.

And why not? Good books do this. Good movies, too. Recently I read Dan Brown's *The Da Vinci Code*. I didn't believe it, of course, it's a work of fiction, with fictional characters and fictional conflicts.

But some of it is based on actual religious fact and theory. The book spends some time discussing topics like missing biblical books and strange religious societies and theories about female roles in biblical times. And although the book was made up, it led me to explore these other topics on my own. I went to my local bookstore and to my surprise found several nonfiction titles dealing with these very same issues. It might have spurred me to talk with a local priest or other church leader. Again, did I believe *The Da Vinci Code*? Of course not. It's a work of fiction. But good works of fiction can get readers to think and, more importantly, they can give those readers something to think about. *The Da Vinci Code* got me thinking about issues I knew nothing about because it intrigued me enough to want to find out more on my own. Dan Brown created compelling characters and conflicts that transported me for a short time into their world.

Good journalistic writing should do the same thing. The only difference is, instead of making information up (sources, conflicts, etc.) like Dan Brown did, we write the same information objectively. Instead of a character, we have a living, breathing source. Instead of made up plot points, we have sources dealing with real-world conflicts. Instead of dramatic dialogue, we have storytelling quotes.

Put another way, the tools for fiction writers and journalists are slightly different, but the results should be the same. There is no reason why journalistic writing can't have the same impact as fictional writing. And in many ways, one might think that journalistic writing could have more of an impact; after all, the stories are true, not made up.

The Narrative Style

In journalism, there's a name for this type of non-inverted–pyramid style of writing: literary journalism. I like the term "narrative journalism," too. Both indicate that journalistic stories follow a more "fictional" style of writing, for lack of a better term. Both indicate actual stories rather than just articles or lists of information. Both indicate that the stories follow a very different format than the traditional inverted pyramid style, one that includes, like many works of fiction, character development, conflicts and conflict resolution, setting, etc.

For you die-hard journalists out there, many will say that these literary or narrative styles define "feature" writing. Not

true. As mentioned in Chapter 1, "feature" is not a style of writing. Rather, the terms "news" and "feature" deal with time. News stories tend to be more timely while features tend to be more timeless. The style of writing is irrelevant.

So to begin, let's take our four concerns from above and address them one at a time using specific examples.

Grab Readers' Attention in the Lead

The lead — the beginning sentence or paragraph in your story — is widely considered to be the most important part of your story. And here, those inverted pyramid story folks wouldn't disagree. It's the most important part of that style of story, too. But it's in the content of that lead sentence or paragraph where pyramid folks and narrative folks differ.

The inverted pyramid suggests that a writer should put as many of the five W's and the H in the lead as possible. Consider the following:

Lakeview High School students have seemingly bucked the national trend regarding the growing number of obese students in the United States. Those statistics — released last month from the National Institutes of Health — indicate that teen obesity is on the rise. But according to school nurse Julie Barker, Lakeview's numbers have, in fact, decreased in the last four years, perhaps, she says, because of the school's new mandatory exercise program.

The lead is by no means a bad one. It certainly contains the elements of news. It's timely. It affects the entire student population, so it has impact and prominence. The local side of the story gives it proximity. It has an expert source.

But how many student readers will truly access this information? Think, honestly, about how many students in your school would have chosen to read any further. How many wouldn't have even gotten past the word "statistics?"

Why? Why aren't they reading this story?

Because, quite simply, they don't care.

So what do you do? Simple. Find a "face," and then put that face in the moment that makes him or her newsworthy. Remember that the news affects people (preferably your readers) in some way or it wouldn't be news. Remember, too, from Chapter 4, that the main source in your story is a student (again, preferably) who is affected by this news. For your lead, you need to introduce readers to that main source in a moment that illustrates his or her relevance to the newsworthy event.

So the inverted pyramid lead from above — rewritten as a narrative lead — might look more like this:

When he stepped on his bathroom scale last week, senior Josh Mayer smiled. Once considered overweight by his doctor, Mayer now falls into the "acceptable" weight range. He said he attributes much of his success to Lakeview's mandatory exercise program.

"I watch what I eat now, too," Mayer said. "But I don't know that I would have even started to care if it hadn't been for the school's program."

In this lead, readers meet the main source first in order to be able to relate to the newsworthy information that will follow. That reporter hopes that giving the "human" side of a news story will help your readers instantly to connect with the piece and will entice them to want to read more.

But that's not always as easy as it sounds. Leads are tricky. Your readers are fickle, as you know, and they're tough to win over. Not only that, they don't have time. So you have to do your best to grab a reader's attention as early as possible.

There are some techniques that might help. One technique is, again, pulled from the world of fiction, and it is this: Start with the moment that's different.

Here's the scenario the way the author could have started it:

FOUR STEPS TO A SOLID LEAD

Follow these procedures when introducing your story. Failure to do say may mean that your audience won't bother to read the rest of your article.

Step 1: Introduce the main character (either a name or a description) — the face on your story. This is generally a student source, since your readers will relate better to their peers.

Step 2: Establish the problem or conflict — the thing that makes that main character newsworthy. After all, if there were no conflict, the story wouldn't be newsworthy.

Step 3: Describe the setting — where this event is taking place. Especially if the setting is relevant, readers will want to see it. This is where good observation comes into play.

Step 4: The tone — Is this a serious piece? Lighthearted? Sentimental? A story about the death of a teacher should not have the same style as a piece about student bands.

So you've got this young girl who lives in the South — in Alabama to be exact — during the Depression. She's got an older brother, and they've both befriended a kid who has just moved into town. Her father is a single parent and a lawyer. She's about to go to her first year of school. The rumor is that a man lives next door who never comes outside except at night, and he terrorizes the people of this small Alabama town. The girl's father has been asked to defend a black man for the alleged rape of a white woman.

Or you could write the lead the way Harper Lee, the author of *To Kill a Mockingbird*, chose to:

When he was nearly thirteen, my brother Jem got his arm badly broken at the elbow.

Often, a good lead will lead to more questions than it provides answers. But it is in this questioning that we entice readers to proceed. We pique their curiosity. We make them want to find out the answers. And as they proceed (i.e. read more of the story), they find out answers only to be enticed again with more questions.

With *To Kill a Mockingbird*, Lee chose to provide readers with the moment that was different, and that led to questions. "Who's Jem?" they might ask. And, perhaps more importantly, "Why did he get his arm broken? Why 'badly'? What did he do? Did someone do it to him?" It's just enough to get readers to find out more. Up to that point, Jem's arm had been fine; Lee didn't choose to start there. Instead, she chose to start with the event outside of the norm.

In the world of children's literature — picture books, young adult novels, etc — where the audience's attention span is even shorter than the typical high schooler, the rule of thumb is to hook readers in the first sentence. The world of journalism is no different. In that first sentence, just as if you were writing for children, you should provide four crucial elements:

1. Main character (either a name or a description): the "face" on your story.
2. The problem or conflict: the thing that makes that main character newsworthy.
3. The setting: where this event is taking place.
4. The tone: Is this a serious piece? Lighthearted? Sentimental?

Check out this example from *St. Petersburg Times* reporter Sue Landry's story titled "He Wanted You To Know":

Cigarette smoke hangs in the air in the room where Brian Lee Curtis lies dying of lung cancer.

That one sentence contains all of the elements. Don't believe me? Look again. And more important, it raises intriguing questions for readers. Who is Brian Lee Curtis? How did he get lung cancer? Why is there cigarette smoke in this dying man's room, particularly a man's who dying of lung cancer?

Remember, of course, that these are just guidelines and you can bend or even break them sometimes, but not without good reason. I would also argue, in many cases, that you can at least expand that guideline of the first sentence to your first paragraph, but, again, only if it's necessary. The bottom line is that your lead needs to establish your face, the conflict and, most importantly, questions that will make your readers want to find out more.

And leads shouldn't be long, either. One of my favorite leads consists of only five short words:

The CAT scan results lied.

In those five words, I'm hooked. You need to try to hook your readers, too.

Make Your Point Clear

Grabbing a reader's attention is a start, but it's not everything. Once you've got those readers hooked, you need to keep them on the line (to continue with the bad metaphor). And the way to do that is to let readers know early on why you're telling them this story. The point that we've discussed so much up until now becomes crucial in the stories that you write, and it should be made clear soon after the lead.

Look at it this way. Pretend there's this attractive girl (or boy, depending on your preferences) that you've always secretly had a crush on. It's taken you weeks to gather the nerve to talk to this person. You don't want to sound like an idiot, and so you've planned exactly what you would do to try to get this person's attention, something that would make you seem cool and debonair or cute and sentimental. And finally you have your chance. One day after school you see the object of your affection standing alone outside waiting for a ride from someone. It doesn't matter who the ride is from, all that matters is that you have an opportunity to be alone with this person. This is it. Your weeks of planning have finally paid off. So you casually work your way up to the person and, maybe, you offer a cheesy line (i.e., your lead): "Well, I'm here. What are your other two wishes?" Or perhaps: "If I were to rewrite the alphabet, I'd put U and I together." Or maybe you do something creative, like a double back handspring or an interpretive dance. Whatever it is, the technique works and it makes the attractive girl (or boy) smile. She (or he) even offers a cautious, "Hi."

You've got her (or him)!

Now what?

This is exactly the position that writers find themselves in with every story they write. "OK," their readers say, "you've got my attention. Now, what did you want to say?"

And you'd better say it quickly or, like that attractive girl (or boy), they will eventually lose patience and walk off (and possibly think you're some kind of weirdo).

In Section I, we discussed how important it is to have a point when you're telling a story. You need to be able to communicate what you want readers to think about. The best time to incorporate that point is right after your lead. So grab my attention and then let me know why you grabbed my attention. It is in this transition from gold coin lead to the rest of the story that you give your readers a purpose for reading. And it should be in this transition that you successfully advance your story from talking about one face (your main source) to the larger audience.

The lead and transition from Tom Hallman Jr.'s April 1996 story for *The Oregonian* illustrates this concept perfectly:

Donalda Purrell adds with her fingers and can't make change for $20.

Lenetta Bell can't give directions to her home or read the children's book Green Eggs and Ham.

Amber Hancock can't read a thermometer and doesn't understand what it means when the grocery store sells something at 3 pounds for a dollar.

The three are mentally retarded — adults whose minds are trapped in childhood. Yet they have children of their own, youngsters who will be smarter than their mothers by the time they turn 9.

These women and their children are what happens when theories and good intention collide with reality. They are what people failed to anticipate in the 1970s when mentally retarded men and women were moved out of institutions and into mainstream society.

See what happened there? The lead grabbed the readers' attention by forcing them to ask questions. Who are these women? Why can't they do these simple tasks? And then came the hammer blow: These are mentally retarded women who have children of their own. This is, of course, the point. This is the angle that Hallman wanted readers to think about. And often, that point will lead to more questions—How was this allowed to happen? What will happen to those kids? Are these women fit to care for the basic needs of these children? What will happen as these children get older? Where are the fathers? How can this be monitored and helped?—many of which will be answered in the story itself and many—Is this happening in my community? Do children like this go to my school?—that are still left to the reader to explore.

But remember, when writing your own stories, this point needs to be clearly stated and it needs to be stated early on in the piece. First, it gives readers purpose in continuing on with the story. Second, it allows you as a writer to make sure that everything you write from that point on—research, observations, interviews—is relevant to that main point.

Keep Your Readers Interested

One thing I've seen far too often when I teach these journalistic techniques is the story that effectively grabs my attention and then, just as effectively, makes its point clear and then...

Nothing.

In many of these cases, it's almost like the writer has worked so hard on the lead and transition that he hasn't left himself enough time, or he doesn't have enough

energy, to continue, and so the story falls back into the typical inverted pyramid style.

Sometimes this may be because reporters have too much information (there's no such thing) and they feel compelled to put it all in the story. When you write you have to make choices, and those choices should go directly back to these related questions: How is this information advancing the angle of this story? Why is this relevant to the point?

Professional reporters, good ones at least, make good choices about that all the time. I can't tell you the number of times I've been interviewed by a professional journalist only to find my quotes either nonexistent or seriously truncated in the final piece. Do I get mad? Of course not. That reporter was simply doing his or her job, which involved finding as much information as he or she could. But all good journalists make choices in the end. Maybe my quotes were said better by someone who was a little more relevant. Or maybe my information was used to verify some research the reporter did. Maybe there was a choice among several faces on the story, and the reporter went with the one that illustrated the story the best. Whatever the reason, just because you have the information doesn't mean you need to use it.

Now I say this to student journalists and they look at me like I've just urinated on the drapery. Why would you take the time to interview and research and observe if you're not going to use it? And my response: If you're panning for gold, you're going to find a lot of dirt in the process.

To be successful as a journalist means you need to find out as much as you can about a subject so that you can communicate the story intelligently and clearly to readers so that they can understand. In his book *Under the Banner of Heaven* about fundamentalist Mormons, Jon Krakauer spent a lot of time — years, probably — researching his topic. He read lots of books. He interviewed lots of people. He spent countless hours observing the people he was writing about. Did he use it all? Absolutely not. I'm just guessing, mind you, but I'd bet Krakauer, on a book that size, probably has enough information left over to write at least another book, if not more. But he didn't choose to include it all. He made choices, choices that, ultimately, advanced his story and brought out the larger issues that he wanted readers to think about. He thought about his readers — he thought like a reader — and provided information throughout the story that would keep readers interested until the very end.

Another point to keep in mind as you progress through your story is that you can't forget about the "face" that you established in the lead. Remember that the face, the main source, lets readers understand how the news may affect them and why they should care — if it affects this main source, then it could affect me or someone I know the same way, your readers might say. This isn't just true at the beginning; it's true in the middle and at the end. It's almost like you're reminding readers from time to time that this news has an impact on real people. And that's important to remember, especially when you're discussing big issues. By bringing your "face" back into the story, you're keeping your readers grounded in reality.

In Rick Reilly's February 2003 *Time* magazine article ("Why the preparation for war really hits home in Jacksonville, N.C."), he shows the Iraq war's effects on Jacksonville, a small town whose main business is the military base. His larger point (what he wants readers to think about) is that the war doesn't just affect soldiers and their immediate families; it affects everyone — store owners, religious leaders, even the local prostitutes — and

these "others" care just as much about those soldiers as everyone else. Jacksonville is merely a microcosm of what was (and is) happening all over the United States. Flower shops, car dealerships and grocery stores — who count on those soldiers for business — are shutting down while for churches and wedding planners and prostitutes, business is on the upswing, at least until the soldiers who are flocking to those places are shipped out.

But throughout the story, Reilly never forgets about that face — the people in Jacksonville — that helped him connect with readers in the first place. While the subject matter affects all readers in *Time* magazine's extensive national audience, Reilly keeps his focus on the people of Jacksonville. He comes back to them frequently throughout the story. He lets readers see them and care for them and laugh with them and cry with them.

And he never forgets about them.

As you progress through your stories, you can't forget about your main sources either. Frequently coming back to those main sources will keep your readers interested to the end.

End with a Bang

If the most important part of the story is the lead, then, at least in the narrative style, the second most important part is the end. Notice how this is quite a bit different from the inverted pyramid style story, where the end is the least important part.

Let's go back to the date analogy to make this make more sense. So you've made a good first impression. You've gotten the person's attention (the lead) and then you've managed to pique that person's interest (the transition and the point). You've even gone on a date and managed not to screw up pretty well (the body of the story).

But where to end? I mean, if the date was good, you want to end it on a high note, right? You want to make that person want another date. But how?

Now I can't really help you with your social life, but I can certainly help you with your storytelling. Like a good date, you want your audience wanting more. You want them to leave your story thinking that it was well worth their time. But at the same time, you want them to have a few questions of their own.

The one thing about audiences and stories is that they like some kind of clo-sure. Life, as you know, doesn't have a neat beginning and end. It's constantly evolving and changing; one event leads directly into another. But a good writer can take those evolving moments and provide some structure and relevance to them. And a good way to do that is to **try to tie your lead into your ending somehow.**

If, in your lead, you described a soccer player getting her knee taped up before a game, you might consider coming back to an ending "scene" at the conclusion — perhaps the girl running out onto the field or maybe her talking as she removes the tape from her leg after the game. Or if you described for readers the beginning mo-

---

LEAVE 'EM WANTING MORE

The end of your story is the second most important part.
Check out the following examples of good endings.

The bell sounds loudly to signal the students' dismissal from class, but the students in in-school suspension don't pay much attention. They know that they still have another 245 minutes to spend here, sitting in silence.

> *—about what really happens in the in-school suspension room.*

In the last weeks of October, as this publication was being sent to the printer, Graham did not show up for class. While he said he enjoyed his day of leisure away from school, the administration here prepared his expulsion papers.

His second chance was over.

> *—about a boy who tried to repeat his senior*
> *year because he failed the first time.*

[Andrew] Shirley heads from the attendance office to his classroom. He walks at a normal pace, not too eager to go back. Head hanging low, he admits his defeat and says, "I guess I'd better think of a better excuse for tomorrow."

> *—about the school's new hall sweep policy and subsequent*
> *tougher enforcement of tardiness rules.*

Steve says he knows he has to work harder than other people, but he also knows that the handicap doesn't hold him back. He said, "I don't think of it as a disability or a handicap, more of just an obstacle to overcome."

> *—about identical twin boys, one of whom lost his leg*
> *in a lawnmowing accident when he was younger.*

ments of an English class, you could wrap the story up by describing the end of that very same class. However it works, try to coordinate your lead and your ending.

Remember Brian Lee Curtis dying of lung cancer from our discussion of leads? Here's how Sue Landry decided to end that piece:

> *Addiction is more powerful.*
> *As the graveside ritual ended, a handful of relatives backed away from the gathering, pulled out packs of cigarettes and lit up.*

See? The story is about the fact that people are dying of lung cancer younger and younger because they're starting to smoke younger and younger (Curtis was only 34 when he died). But the story raises the question of why don't people just quit? With that simple description of the scene following Curtis's funeral, the audience could see that dilemma first hand. That simple moment of people backing away from a funeral ceremony for a man whose smoking caused him to die of lung cancer and then pulling out their own packs of cigarettes to smoke speaks volumes in this story. Whenever I read this story aloud, my students always gasp at the irony. And that's what you want from your stories— some kind of reaction.

But what if you can't find a good scene to end with? **When in doubt, end with a good storytelling quote.** Sometimes it's difficult to end with a descriptive scene. It may be too trite or clichéd. But maybe in your interview process, someone gave you a storytelling quote (see Chapter 4) that really sums up what you wanted readers to think about. Why not end with that person's words? Why not let the audience's last words be the words of one of your sources?

LOOKING FOR EXAMPLES?

Check out these sources for great stories written in the narrative style.

Books:
Literary Journalism, Norman Sims and Mark Kramer, eds. (1995).
Somebody Told Me, Rick Bragg: a collection of the Pulitzer-Prize–winning writer's works.
South of Heaven, Thomas French: the Pulitzer-Prize–winning author spends a year at a high school in Largo, Florida.
Fire, Sebastian Junger: a collection of short stories investigating the most dangerous professions in the world.
Outside 25: the best writing from *Outside* magazine, including pieces from Jon Krakauer ("Into Thin Air") and Sebastian Junger ("The Perfect Storm").
A Hope in the Unseen, Ron Suskind: details the life of Cedric Jennings, a good student in a horrible school (expanded from Suskind's Pulitzer-Prize–winning article).
In Cold Blood, Truman Capote: one of the first works of "narrative nonfiction."
Into Thin Air, *Into the Wild*, *Under the Banner of Heaven*: more from Jon Krakauer.

Websites:
pulitzer.org—click on the dates at the top and look at winning examples of writing through the years.
sptimes.com—check out the extensive archive of stories like Roy Peter Clark's "Three Little Words" and Thomas French's "13: Life on the Edge of Everything."

Here's how Tom Hallman Jr. ended his story about the mentally retarded adults with kids of their own. Notice how the words of David Beem, another of the mentally retarded parents, leave the reader with both a sense of closure but also a sense that there's so much more about this issue that we as readers may not have even considered:

"We had [our children] here one day, and then they said we couldn't have them," [Beem] said. *"We don't know where they are. They don't write to us or nothing. We don't even get pictures. We think about them every day. It hurts us when we see kids."*

Beem thinks the state would allow them to adopt children if he and his wife had enough money.

So he plays the lottery.

"I won $300 and paid off bills," he said. "But if I won the big prize, I bet they'd let me have a child. I'm not a bad person."

In a word — wow.

Summary

Life lesson: The world is not black and white. There are no real definitive answers in the world. In most cases, answers only lead to more questions, and we strive to find those answers that never really come. But that doesn't mean we can't try.

And often, those answers that lead to more questions often start with good questions in the first place. That's where journalists come in. You provide a resource for your readers. You ask the questions that readers can't or won't or don't even think to ask. You provide the answers to some of those questions in the stories that you write and, in the process, lead readers to ask even more questions. You make your readers think, and you give them topics to think about, both topics that they want to know about and those that they need to think about.

And most importantly, you present that information in the context of an organized story.

The inverted pyramid structure does not work so well for high school journalists. There's not much you can say in an inverted pyramid story that your readers don't already know, nor is the inverted pyramid a compelling style of story if you actually want your audience to read what you've written.

So you've got to move beyond the inverted pyramid if you want to challenge your readers to think. You've got to think of your story like a fiction writer, in many ways, by providing a compelling lead, a clear transition to your point, a focused, relevant body and an equally compelling end.

Will the narrative style guarantee 100 percent readership? No. Nothing can do that. But it can guarantee better readership, and that's ultimately what you're striving for.

STUDY GUIDE

Terms and Concepts

Inverted pyramid — An organizational style that places the most important information in the beginning (lead) of the story and then places information in order of decreasing importance as the story progresses. In the story, the ending is the least important part of the story. A good style of writing for more timely, breaking news.

Narrative or literary journalism — An organizational style that follows a more "literary" format, meaning the story focuses on a face and that face's newsworthy conflicts. In this style, the ending of the story is the second most important part of the story after the lead. A good style of writing for more timeless stories.

Lead — The beginning of the story, usually the first paragraph or two. In the inverted pyramid, the lead generally contains the 5 W's and the H. In the narrative style, the lead establishes the "face" in the story and the conflict.

Try This

1. Look at the following story and see if you can tell what's wrong with it in terms of being appropriate for a high school publication. After that, discuss how you could tell this story better using what you've learned from this chapter.

   Once again, the Student Council is gearing up to collect money in its annual canned food drive. The money raised from this activity, which starts next Tuesday, generates thousands of dollars for needy families in the Carmel area.

   "Instead of collecting cans, we collect money, which the local food bank then uses to purchase food items that these families need," Student Body President Jane Manson said.

   This year marks the sixth year of the drive, and organizers said they hope to break a new record in money donated.

   "Last year we set the standard — nearly $8,000," Senate sponsor Fred Smalls said. "This year we're hoping for $10,000. It sounds like a lot, but we think it's doable."

   According to the latest state census results, Hamilton County has at least 8 percent of its citizens living at or below the poverty level. Even in affluent Carmel, the number stands at 6 percent.

   "We have needy families here in our own backyard," Manson said. "Even if we don't see it, they exist. The food drive just lets us help out our neighbors, those who are less fortunate."

   The canned food drive will last until Dec. 18.

2. Try to rewrite the story above using the suggestions you came up with from Question #1. Better yet, go out and write your own story using the techniques you've learned from this chapter.

CHAPTER 7

Proofreading *editing*

It's Not Just Proofreading Anymore

So, you've got a good story. Not great, but good. Solid. You have a point. You have good sources. You've included research. And observation.

And, of course, you've written something. A first draft. You have a beginning, a middle and an end. You've included gold coins throughout.

A good start.

Notice that I didn't say that you were done. Far from it, in fact. Now comes the hard part. The dreaded four-letter "E" word. The one that makes grown men cringe. The one that calls to mind forests of red-marked papers from years in school.

Edit.

I know, I know. You edit, you say. You go through your papers. You check for style. You make sure everything's spelled correctly. You make sure the research is accurate. You dot all the I's. You cross all the T's.

But that's only part of the process — an important part, but not the only part. But you're not alone. There are lots of other people just like you out there who think that editing consists of only one step. In journalism, we even have a name for that step — proofreading.

But proofreading isn't editing. It's definitely a part of the process, but not the only part.

Ask any professional writer, and he'll tell you about the editing process; you may get some varied responses, not many of them good. Stephen King shares an editorial bit of wisdom in his memoir *On Writing*. In it, King describes a jotted note he received at the bottom of a rejection letter. "Not bad, but puffy. You need to revise for length. Formula: 2nd Draft = 1st Draft — 10%. Good luck."

Good advice, and certainly a good place for us to start. As King says, "If you can't get out 10 percent of [your story] while retaining the basic story and flavor, you're not trying very hard." Remember, as we've already discussed, your readers are visual people. They don't have time to read. They don't want to read. So do whatever you can to make the time your readers do spend with your stories productive.

EDITING IN ACTION

THE ORIGINAL

Here's the story as it was originally submitted. It's a good start, but as you'll see, the reporter still has some work to do.

"The worst part of it is everybody knows…we had an assembly, the whole fifth grade was there. I guess it's my destiny, but it's ruining my life," said freshman Ryan Shaw.

"At least now I am in a new environment where I can keep it hush hush," he said. Although Shaw seems like an average boy with his perks there is truly more beyond that which meets the eyes.

"Everyday I take at least twelve pills…plus a Flinstone's Vitamin," said Shaw. This is how the average day of a person with hypertrophic cardiomypathy. Hypertrophic cardiomypathy is so rare that only 0.2 percent of the general population are believed to suffer from the genetic condition, which results in abnormal development of the heart, specifically a thickening of the heart muscles, usually in the interior areas of the lower ventricular chambers.

"I function almost like a normal kid, with a few setbacks such as no sports because of a chance of sudden death, which is rare even if you have this disease and you play sports. All my life I have wanted to play football…actually on a team. But because of my disease I can't," said Shaw. If Shaw wants even to go outside and mess around with his buds and participate in any physical activities, he must take pills before hand. There have been many difficulties for Shaw but some great things came out of this rare case.

"I have the most awesome battle wound," Shaw said as he quickly lifted his shirt to show the remains of a scar from surgery.

"I got tubes put in," said Shaw. Shaw believes that sports weren't meant for him. "I love sports with all my heart but this is Gods way…to show me to my destiny. I have always wanted to play football; maybe someday for the Denver Broncos, but in reality I know it will never happen. And even though my mom says not to…I do it anyway, almost everyday after school I head out to play football." Shaw says that his disease hasn't affected him a lot, and other than sports wise he runs a pretty normal life.

"Ever since I was little this disease has been affecting my life, sometimes bad and sometimes good. In the fifth grade everybody had to go down and learn about my disease and how easily I could get hurt while I was conspicuously sitting in the principals office in fear that I did something wrong. The teachers made a special effort to make sure nobody harmed me at recess…and I must say nobody touched me let alone talked to me for a month," said Shaw. Also, once in seventh grade

> Bring in an expert source here (a doctor perhaps) who can address the larger topic that you want readers to think *about* — perhaps to give readers a better understanding of other people, like Shaw, who have medical conditions so that they don't treat them differently than their "healthy" friends.

THE CORRECTIONS

Editing is more than just correcting for style and grammar. See how this story improves by looking at the content as well.

"The worst part of it is everybody knows,…we had an assembly; the whole fifth grade was there. I guess it's my destiny, but it's ruining my life," said freshman Ryan Shaw.

"At least now I am in a new environment where I can keep it hush-hush," he said. ~~Although Shaw seems like an average boy with~~
But Shaw's life is anything but ordinary.
~~his perks there is truly more beyond that of which meets the eyes.~~

"Everyday I take at least ~~twelve~~ pills…plus a Flinstone's Vitamin,"
12
said Shaw. ~~This is how the average~~ day of a person with hypertrophic
routine describes
ardiomypathy. ~~Hypertrophic cardiomypathy~~ is so rare that only 0.2
a genetic condition doctors believe
ercent of the general population ~~are believed to~~ suffers ~~from the~~
it.
~~enetic condition, which results~~ in abnormal development of the
The condition
eart, specifically a thickening of the heart muscles, usually in the nterior areas of the lower ventricular chambers.

"I function almost like a normal kid, with a few setbacks such as o sports because of a chance of sudden death, which is rare even if ou have this disease and you play sports. All my life I have wanted to lay football,…actually on a team. But because of my disease I can't,"
aid Shaw. ~~If~~ Shaw wants ~~even~~ to go outside and mess around with
Even
is ~~buds~~ and participate in any physical activities, he must take pills
friends
eforehand. ~~There have been many difficulties for Shaw~~, but some
Shaw said he's suffered through he said
great ~~things came out of this rare case.~~
experiences condition

"I have the most awesome battle wound," Shaw said as he quickly lifted his shirt to show the remains of a scar from surgery.

"I got tubes put in," ~~said Shaw.~~

Shaw ~~believes~~ that sports weren't meant for him. "I love sports with
said
all my heart, but this is God's way,…to show me to my destiny. I have always wanted to play football, maybe someday for the Denver Broncos; but in reality I know it will never happen. And even though my mom says not to,…I do it anyway. almost everyday after school I head out to play football."

Shaw ~~says~~ that his disease hasn't affected him ~~a lot~~, and other
said much
than sports ~~wise~~ he runs a pretty normal life.
his participation in said he

"Ever since I was little, this disease has been affecting my life, sometimes bad and sometimes good. In the fifth grade, everybody had to go down and learn about my disease and how easily I could get hurt while I was conspicuously sitting in the principal's office in fear that I did something wrong. The teachers made a special effort to make sure nobody harmed me at recess,…and I must say nobody touched me, alone talked to me for a month," said Shaw. Also, once in seventh grade he had to take a trip to the hospital, ending up on steroids.

"All throughout the year my cheeks were puffy and people kept asking me if I had my wisdom teeth pulled," Shaw said. It was the worst year in his life.

Shaw's grandfather had the disease and died when he was 82.

"I hope I make it that long…nobody thinks I can, but I will. If he did it, I can do it," said Shaw. The reason that people may be pessimistic about this rare condition is because this disease can develop undetected by doctors and cause unexpected death. Although Shaw knows he has this disease there is still a chance of unexpected death. There have been many setbacks for Shaw, but he considers it to be a blessing to be alive.

Shaw said, "When I get depressed about this I just think; man Ryan it could have been a lot worse…you got lucky, no matter what anybody says…you got lucky."

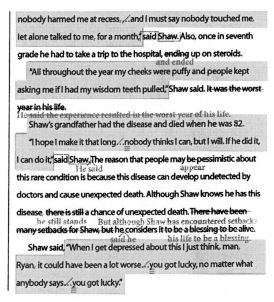

THE FINAL PRODUCT

If you edit properly, as you see here from the story on the previous pages, your end result will look more polished. Notice, as well, some of the reorganization of paragraphs to help the story flow more smoothly and make its point more clearly.

"The worst part of it is everybody knows. We had an assembly; the whole fifth grade was there. I guess it's my destiny, but it's ruining my life," freshman Ryan Shaw said.

"At least now I am in a new environment where I can keep it hush-hush," he said. But Shaw's life is anything but ordinary.

"Every day I take at least 12 pills plus a Flintstone's vitamin," Shaw said. This routine describes the average day of a person with hypertrophic cardiomypathy, a genetic condition so rare that doctors say only 0.2 percent of the general population suffer from it. The condition results in abnormal development of the heart, specifically a thickening of the heart muscles, usually in the interior areas of the lower ventricular chambers.

And Shaw isn't alone. According to John Carter, the leading pediatric surgeon at Central Hospital, while Shaw's condition is rare, many other students suffer from genetic conditions like Shaw's. "I think students would be surprised at the number of their peers who have some sort of major health concern," he said. "Sometimes these conditions manifest themselves physically, but much of the time they do not."

Carter added that most students with health problems don't want to be labeled. "I've found that most of these kids want to keep their conditions a secret — there's too much chance for misplaced ridicule — but, unfortunately, sometimes the word gets out," he said. "These kids are, for the most part, 'normal,' but they get ostracized by people who don't understand or care to understand. And that's where the real 'handicap' lies."

Shaw said that sometimes even school

officials add to the problem. "Ever since I was little this disease has been affecting my life, sometimes bad and sometimes good," he said. "In the fifth grade, everybody had to go down and learn about my disease and how easily I could get hurt while I was conspicuously sitting in the principal's office in fear that I did something wrong. The teachers made a special effort to make sure nobody harmed me at recess, and I must say nobody touched me, let alone talked to me, for a month." Also, once in seventh grade Shaw said he had to take a trip to the hospital and ended up on steroids.

"All throughout the year my cheeks were puffy and people kept asking me if I had my wisdom teeth pulled," Shaw said. He said that the experience resulted in the worst year of his life.

But despite his desire to fit in, Shaw said he does have limitations. "I function almost like a normal kid, with a few setbacks such as no sports because of a chance of sudden death, which is rare even if you have this disease and you play sports. All my life I have wanted to play football, actually on a team. But because of my disease I can't," Shaw said. Even if Shaw wants to go outside and mess around with his friends and participate in any physical activities, he must take pills beforehand.

Shaw said that sports weren't meant for him. "I love sports with all my heart but this is God's way, to show me to my des-

tiny. I have always wanted to play football, maybe someday for the Denver Broncos; but in reality I know it will never happen. And even though my mom says not to, I do it anyway. Almost every day after school I head out to play football."

But although Shaw said he's suffered through many difficulties, he also said some great experiences came out of this rare condition.

"I have the most awesome battle wound," Shaw said as he quickly lifted his shirt to show the remains of a scar from surgery. "I got tubes put in."

Shaw said that, with the exception of how he was treated in fifth grade, his disease hasn't affected him much; and other than his participation in sports, he said he runs a pretty normal life.

Although Shaw knows he has this disease, he still stands a chance of unexpected death. However, even with the condition, Shaw still has the potential to live a long life. Shaw's grandfather had hypertrophic cardiomypathy and died when he was 82.

"I hope I make it that long. Nobody thinks I can, but I will. If he did it, I can do it," Shaw said.

And even though Shaw has encountered setbacks, he said he considers his life a blessing. "When I get depressed about this I just think, man Ryan, it could have been a lot worse," he said. "You got lucky. No matter what anybody says, you got lucky."

But how? Now that's the trick. What follows in this chapter are step-by-step instructions on how to edit your text to make it tighter, more focused and, ultimately, more polished for your readers.

Step 1: Read It Aloud

When I was in high school, I participated on the speech team. My category was humorous interpretation, and for competition we would memorize a portion of a play which we would then present to an audience. In humorous interp, the idea was to get the audience to laugh. Trust me, it took a lot of work. I remember practicing quite a bit in preparation for speech tournaments.

But one of my first and most vivid memories of my speech experience was the auditorium (or cafeteria or lobby or wherever they put us from week to week) before any of the actual speech rounds began. The place, filled to the rafters with hundreds of speakers just like me, was a cacophony of sound. It reminded me of a high school gymnasium during a particularly raucous pep assembly. But on closer inspection, I noticed that many of the people in the room weren't actually speaking to anyone. In fact, the members of the assembly had managed to stake out small, individual four-to-five-foot areas all to themselves completely surrounding the location. As if this wasn't enough, what made the scene the most bizarre was the fact that these people were not even speaking to other people. In most cases, they were even facing the walls that surrounded the place, their arms flailing, their voices loud and clear, as if in heated discussion with the masonry.

It took me a while to figure the scene out. The students, you see, were practicing their pieces. They were honing their voices and sharpening their delivery. When I did understand the curious ritual, I soon found myself not just a detached observer but an active participant in the strange antics. All because I wanted to sound good. And sounding good, even if you're reading someone else's writing, takes practice.

Your own writing should be no different.

As a teacher of journalism, I try to read aloud good journalistic stories to my students almost every day. I want them to hear what good journalism sounds like. I want them to hear how award-winning journalists blend words and sentences and paragraphs into cohesive, memorable stories. And then I want them to transfer what they've learned to their own writing.

Good writing, after all, should sound good. It should have a tone and a pace. Good writing, like music, has an almost lyrical quality, the words and sentences ebbing and flowing seamlessly from beginning to end. Know this about your own writing and read it aloud to yourself or to a group of classmates. Not comfortable with one of those options? Then read it to the family dog. The wall. A picnic table. It doesn't really matter to whom you read the piece, only that you hear how the words sound.

On this first read-through, listen for a few different items. First, do you stumble over your own writing? Do you have trouble making sense of a sentence (maybe you have to stop, go back and re-read what you've written and even then you're not quite sure what you were going for)? Do you notice huge holes in your writing? Incomplete thoughts? Repeated words? Do you find yourself noticing the words on the page more than what those words are saying?

Chances are, your readers will notice all of that, too. On this first read-through, mark those passages and fix them. Then read the piece aloud again.

There's a variation of this method. Instead of you reading the piece, have someone else read your writing back to you. In this method you're looking for the same items, but sometimes having an outside reader — someone who's not familiar with your intentions for the piece — can be just what you need to catch any glaring mistakes. Or, for an even better variation, try both methods.

Step 2: Quotes

Grab a highlighter pen. Now mark everything in your story that appears in quotation marks. Seriously. Highlight all of the direct quotes. Now look back at what you've marked. Let's hope you have some quotes and you have enough of them spread evenly throughout the story. Readers like to hear the words of others, so a nice dose of quotes is necessary to help your stories come to life.

Check for Patterns

Before you start looking closely at the quotes, try to notice the structure. You may see and learn from a few items before you even start reading. For example, are all of your quotes relatively short? Then you may need to practice your interviewing skills. Maybe you're asking a lot of yes and no questions or maybe you're not skilled enough yet to get all of the important words down. Maybe you didn't ask the right questions in the first place. I'm not suggesting that all quotes should be lengthy, but a nice variety of length is more interesting.

JOURNALISM'S 10 DEADLY SINS

Here's a final checklist for you to use before you submit copy to your editors.

1. **Omit all exclamation points.**
   Reason: Exclamation points are subjective pieces of punctuation.

2. **Use the form (name) said, rather than said (name) (i.e. Smith said, not said Smith).**
   Reason: Subjects come in front of verbs, not after.

3. **Omit adverbs.**
   Reason: Adverbs are subjective words. If writers use strong nouns and strong verbs, they shouldn't need adverbs.

4. **Omit passive voice.**
   Reason: Passive voice makes the subject unclear. It is a timid way of writing, and it is often less concise. Remember to put the subject of the sentence in charge.

5. **Eliminate generalizations (words like most, all, none, some, everyone, no one, etc.).**
   Reason: These words are subjective unless writers have research to back up their claims.

6. **Avoid first and second person (I and you).**
   Reason: With few exceptions, journalists should use the third person. Fiction writers use first and second person; this is not fiction.

7. **Use past or present tense consistently.**
   Reason: Lack of consistency leads to confusion.

8. **Use the spell-check feature on your word processing software.**
   Reason: Correct spelling leads to credibility. Remember, however, that no computer can take the place of a good set of human eyes.

9. **Use the word "said."**
   Reason: Said is the most objective word for dialogue/quote attribution.

10. **Avoid these vague words:**

very	really	believe	nice	guy	some
most	feel	all	none	seem	thing(s)

Some of these writing quirks you may not even notice. When I first started writing journalistic stories, an editor approached me with one of my articles about the judo team. He held the piece in front of me and I noticed that he had marked all of the direct quotes in the story.

"Did you notice the pattern when you were writing this," he asked.

I took a moment to peruse the piece, and, after letting his marks sink in, the revelation dawned on me. In my story, literally every other paragraph was a direct quote. As a result, the article took on a sing-songy feel. Transition ... quote ... transition ... quote ... transition ... quote, and so on.

So take a look at your own quotes. See what you can, fix it and then move on.

Check for Content

Now it's time to look at the quotes themselves and what they say. Remember, you can't alter the content of the quotes. There's a reason why we highlighted the quotes, and not just to see any patterns that emerge as we just discussed. More importantly, the reason why these words fall inside quotation marks (and now underneath your highlighting) is because they are not your words. These are someone else's thoughts. These are someone else's opinions. Make sure you stay true to your sources and don't change the words within the quotation marks.

But you can still do a few odds and ends with quotes. First, look at each quote for content. Does each quote share an opinion or is it storytelling? Look back at your notes; are the quotes that you've used accurate and in the context of the questions that you asked? Do the quotes enhance the point of your story (what you want readers to think about)? Do you have enough sources (at the very least, a main

source and an expert source)? Are there any questions left that you'd like your sources to answer? Are your sources clearly labeled and do their titles show their relevance to the story?

If the answer to any one of these questions is "no," then you need to go back and fix the problem(s). In many cases, that means setting up and conducting a follow-up interview. But if you've completed your primary interview correctly (see Chapter 2), your sources should be prepared for any necessary follow-up.

Check for Style

OK. Let's assume that you've checked all of your quotes, you've made any necessary corrections and everything looks good. The answer to all of the questions is now "yes." You're ready to move away from your quotes.

Not quite.

Don't forget to check all of your direct quotes for proper style and spelling. As I mentioned earlier, you can't change the words in a quote (if a source uses bad grammar and you've read his words back verbatim and he said the quote was fine, then leave the bad grammar), but you can make sure the style meets your publication's guidelines.

And once you've completed that step, the quotes are done.

Step 3: Organization and Transitions

With the quotes marked off and corrected, take another look at your story. See what remains. Look now only at the words that are not highlighted — your words, you can say. There aren't as many as you thought, are there? A by-product of highlighting quotes and completing Step 2 is that the task of editing doesn't seem quite so daunting. By breaking up the text, you give yourself smaller "baby steps" to take along the way.

So with the words that are left, your next step in the editing process involves organization and its partner, transition. How your story flows from Point A to Point B and beyond is key to helping your readers navigate the words that you choose to share with them. Think of your story as a river, and your ideas are the water in that river. Your goal is to keep those words flowing from beginning to end. You don't want to do anything along the way to block the stream. How you organize your words is the key to that success.

Look back at your story, at the words that remain, and ask yourself another series of questions. Is your lead captivating? Is your point (what you want readers to think about) clear at the beginning of the story? Do you use transitions to guide readers from scene to scene and from source to source? At the end of the story (and at intervals in between for longer stories) do you come back to your main source and the "scene" you established in the lead? Do all of the parts of your story work together to enhance your point? Can you explain why all interviews, observations and research that you've included are relevant to your point?

Work to make sure all of these answers are "yes," and then move on.

Step 4: "To Be" or Not "To Be"

Let's take a moment to talk about the parts of speech. As journalists, we frequently discuss how important it is to remain objective (keeping our opinions out of our writing) as opposed to subjective (letting our opinions creep in). We'll dis-

---

GO AHEAD, BREAK THE "RULES"

You've heard the supposed "rules" of grammar. No doubt these have been ingrained in you since elementary school. Don't write sentence fragments. Don't use one sentence paragraphs. Don't start sentences with coordinating conjunctions. Sound familiar?

However, if you've read any books lately, you'll note that writers break these "rules" all the time. Of course, they don't just break them haphazardly. For the most part, these writers choose to disregard the guidelines with good reasoning in mind. Take a look at this example to see for yourself:

Sharks.
All around him were sharks. Dozens of them. Circling just below his feet. Getting closer and closer, inching toward his exposed flesh.
They were hungry.
And he was bleeding.

Let's see, that example uses four sentence fragments, three one-sentence paragraphs and one sentence that begins with a conjunction. But can you see how the writing style sets the tense tone of the story? In this case, the writer broke the rules for a reason. If you break the rules, make sure your reasoning is sound as well.

"BE" VERBS

Find 'em.
Get rid of 'em.

Forms of "be"

am

is

are

was

were

be

being

been

What to avoid

"be" + verb
(passive)

"be" + -ing
(weak)

"be"
(weak verb)

---

cuss this larger topic of objectivity v. subjectivity in Step 5, but we have to touch on it in this section. Because even certain parts of speech can be subjective.

For example, adverbs (mostly words that end in "–ly" with a few exceptions) are subjective because they tell how something happened or how much. (He ran slowly. He ate greedily.) Hence, subjective. Some adjectives are also subjective (a beautiful girl, a mangy dog, etc. Who are we to judge? Are we experts?). Consider the sentence, He had a strong grip. How do we know his grip was strong? Compared to whom? So take away adverbs and adjectives, and what does that leave us?

Simple — strong verbs and strong nouns. Two of the most important tools in your verbal arsenal are strong verbs and strong nouns. Starting from a noun standpoint, try using more details instead of

falling into the adjective trap. Instead of saying "the mangy dog," describe the dog as "a small, nondescript mixed breed with patches of hair missing above the left eye, revealing red, infected skin underneath." Name brands can also help to provide detail. Instead of saying "the man in the green cap drank a beer and smoked a cigarette," say "the man donned his John Deere cap high on his head, while a half-empty Coors Light sweated in front of him and a Marlboro dangled from his chapped lips."

That latter example in particular brings up a larger point, which is that it's difficult to discuss strong nouns and strong verbs separately. Just look at the verbs in that second sentence — "donned" and "sweated" and "dangled." Combined with the details, they provide a clearer picture.

Note, too, that I said strong verbs and strong nouns. With the verbs in particular, make sure those action words enhance the meaning of your story. Compare the sentence "He ran out of the room," to "He sprinted out of the room." Which one provides more detail? "He shut the door" versus "He slammed the door." Which one is more clear? Don't cop out of using more powerful language. It's easy to use weak verbs and vague nouns. Poor writers use them all the time. But if your goal is to actually get people to read what you've written, you'll spend some time editing those parts of speech in your story.

Speaking of weak verbs, let's take a moment to discuss the weakest verb of them all — "be." The word "be" is like a cancer in your stories. It says nothing. It enhances nothing. It just lies there, for the most part, and takes up valuable space in your stories. And, like cancer, the more you let it fester, the more problematic it becomes.

The biggest problem with the word "be" is that, in many cases, it transforms into something called passive voice. In the

English language, verbs come in two types, active and passive. In an active voice sentence, the subject comes before the verb:

The boy hit the ball.

In a passive voice sentence, the subject comes after the verb:

The ball was hit by the boy.

See what happened there? In the second sentence, the direct object (the ball) got put in charge. The subject (the boy) fell to the end of the sentence. To compensate, the verb (hit) had to change to make the sentence grammatically correct. And so a dreaded "be" word (in this case "was") appeared mid-sentence. And that form of the word "be" followed by another verb is the definition of passive voice.

So why is this bad? The sentence is still grammatically correct, right? True, but now the sentence is less clear and concise. The passive voice sentence is less concise because it now uses eight words to say the same thing that the active voice sentence said in five. And as far as clarity is concerned, remember way back to your elementary school education about parts of speech. What parts of speech do you absolutely need to make a complete sentence? A noun and a verb, right? Well, look at the second sentence and add a period after the verb.

The ball was hit.

It's a complete sentence. It has a noun and a verb. But now the subject (the boy) is unclear. Who hit the ball? Believe me, your readers will wonder the same thing, but, for the most part, they won't bother to find out the answer. Instead, chances are they'll stop reading.

So identifying passive voice is part of the solution. Fixing passive voice is the rest; and fixing passive voice is not always as easy as merely locating it.

From an editing standpoint, you first need to go through your story and mark the passive voice verbs. Realize that while you should avoid any use of the verb "be" (it's a weak verb), not every "be" verb indicates passive voice. Passive voice, you'll recall, is defined as a form of the verb "be" followed by another verb. So the sentence "John is tall" isn't passive voice. In this case, the form of the verb "be" functions as a linking verb for the adjective "tall."

Once you've identified the passive voice, now you can go back and fix it. To do that, ask yourself this question: "Who or what is doing the action?" The answer to that question should be your true subject. Once you've identified that subject, put it in charge of the sentence (in front of the action verb).

To illustrate, here's the sentence again:

The ball was hit by the boy.

There's that form of the verb "be" (was) followed by another verb (hit). So ask yourself the question, "Who or what is doing the hitting?" The answer? The boy. Put him in charge. Now your sentence should read correctly, "The boy hit the ball," and you've solved the problem.

With all of this discussion about verbs and verb use, there is still one notable exception—the word "said." "Said" is the most objective verb we have for quote attribution in the English language. I know some people will try to convince you that many more words exist to help spice up your writing. Words like "commented," "shouted," "moaned," "whined." I have even seen these people create whole lists of words to use instead of "said."

I offer two words of advice for you: Ignore them. Those people, while their intentions may be pure, know not what they do. I'll say it again, always use "said." I promise, you won't go wrong.

And another thing, use the word "said" after the name (or pronoun) of the person who said the quote. "I like cheese," Smith said. Not "I like cheese," said Smith. As with the passive voice, the latter example puts the verb in front of the noun. Can't remember that rule? Try this. Replace all of the proper names with their coordinating pronouns, like this: "I like cheese," he said. And "I like cheese," said he. Said he? Who's speaking here, Shakespeare? Said he? C'mon. Do the right thing and put that verb after the noun.

Step 5: Subjectivity

As we discussed in Step 4 and also in Chapter 1, journalists try to remain as objective as they can when writing stories. While we already know complete objectivity is a myth (see Chapter 1), journalists can still take steps to keep their writing as objective as possible. Adverbs and even some adjectives are off limits because they are, by nature, subjective words. Adverbs tell how or to what extent or degree something happens. Many adjectives do the same. As journalists, we can't make those judgment calls.

But other words can creep into your writing as well, words that, by their very nature, imply an opinion. Take a look at the chart in this chapter titled "Journalism's 10 Deadly Sins" to see some of these words to avoid. In some cases, words like "all" or "none" are too general. Case in point the following example:

All students look forward to spring break.

How do you know? Are you positive? Do you mean to say there's not one person who doesn't look forward to the vacation? Unless you have research to support your

---

AND ANOTHER THING, USE BETTER TRANSITIONS

You're not producing formal English essays, so don't write like you are.
Be wary of the words on the left,
and try using the more informal words on the right.

Avoid these words:	Try these instead:
Therefore	For example
Hence	But
Henceforth	In other words
Moreover	As a result
Thus	Besides
Conversely	Like
To sum up	Which
To conclude	Plus
In conclusion	Then
In short	So
In brief	
Admittedly	
Indeed	
Nevertheless	

use of these words, don't use them. Besides, as you learned in Chapter 1, it's much better to put an individual face on the story anyway.

So from an editing standpoint, look through your stories like lawn care professionals. Think of these words to avoid as weeds in your lawn, and they do nothing to your stories except to mar the overall beauty of the grass. Find them and root them out. Remove them from your writing forever.

Step 6: Style, Spelling and Grammar

And now you've finally made it to the part of editing that you once thought was the only part — proofreading. As you can see from the first five steps, there's a whole lot more to the process than you imagined. I know going through these steps takes a lot of work, but, believe me, there's a method to the madness.

First of all, if you've gone through the previous steps correctly and thoroughly, you will probably notice that you've eliminated a good percentage of the style, spelling and grammar mistakes along the way. It's sort of a by-product of following directions. For instance, there's no need to correct the spelling in a sentence if, in the editing process, you've decided to eliminate the sentence altogether.

But you should still give your story another once-over, just to be sure. You should have access to a style manual (either a local one that you've created through your own publications staff or, if you don't have one of those, a professional style manual — AP or CSPA, for example). Learn and follow the rules there. As I tell students, you don't have to memorize the rules (although some rules you will use so often that you'll

have no choice but to memorize them), but at least know that rules exist, and then know where to go to look up the answers.

And if the answers aren't in the style manual? Then go to the dictionary.

One final note — names are important. If it's one thing readers will notice, it's if you spell a person's name wrong in a story. Double-check the spellings of all names in your stories. Even if you think you know how to spell them, chances are you're wrong (Is it Catherine with a "K" or a "C?" "Kathryn?"). And why should you care about that? Because spelling people's names correctly leads to credibility. And, as we've discussed before, credibility in a publication is what it's all about. Without credibility, you have nothing in the world of journalism.

Summary

Editing a story involves much more than simply dotting the I's and crossing the T's. Meaningful editing means looking at the content as well and asking yourself if you've asked all of the appropriate questions and conducted all of the appropriate research. It also means becoming aware of your own opinions and biases and doing your best to eliminate them from your writing.

What good editing boils down to is thinking like your readers. What questions will they need to have answered? What sources will they want to hear from? How will they know how point A relates to point B and how source C is relevant to issue D?

Correcting style, spelling and grammar is part of the editing process, but it's not the only part. So leave yourself enough time in the editing process to give your writing a meaningful edit. Your readers will appreciate the effort.

STUDY GUIDE

Terms and Concepts

Proofreading — checking writing for punctuation, style and grammar. The final step in the editing process.

Editing — fixing a story for content as well as style.

Passive voice — a weak verb construction that places the subject after the verb and follows the form "be" + another verb.

Try to edit your own stories

1. Take a piece of writing you've completed, preferably one that incorporates all of the information gathering techniques we've discussed so far in this book.

2. Go through the editing process outlined in this chapter step by step. Be extremely cognizant of the steps as you go through them. By exaggerating each step, you will solidify your understanding of its role in the process.

3. Write a new draft of your story based on the corrections you have made.

For a twist, you can try having someone else edit your work. See what kinds of errors that person can find. Are they the same errors you found? If not, you may have discovered that you have a weakness in that area (say, with passive voice or with style). Find a way to compensate for this specific weakness in your own writing and add that strategy to your own list of editing steps each time you go through this process from now on.

CHAPTER 8

Dissection

How the Pieces of Writing Work Together

When I was in high school, we had to dissect things. Of course, I say "had to" like it was a chore. I actually enjoyed the process. I liked looking inside creatures to see how they worked, and I was continually amazed at how all of those individual parts could work together so seamlessly.

We dissected quite a few animals back then. If I remember correctly, we dissected a mutant earthworm (it was certainly larger than any backyard variety, I can tell you), a starfish and, of course, the obligatory frog. My older sister, who studied pre-med for a short time, even got to dissect a cat once (and it spent some time in our downstairs freezer right next to the Italian sausage links and the TV dinners), but I wasn't so lucky, although she did let me peek in on one of her sessions.

Today I'm not a biologist. My animal cutting days are far behind me. But I still get to use the concept of dissection in journalism.

If you've read this far, you've learned about all there is to know regarding the basics of good, people-driven journalistic writing. You know how to identify newsworthy stories. You know how to gather information. You know how to put that information together in a coherent form, and you know how to edit that information into a final, readable form.

You've looked at all of the individual parts that make up a whole story.

But before we move on, we'll take one final look at writing by going backwards. To facilitate this process, we'll use an excellent example of student work and "dissect" it into its individual parts. In this chapter, we'll start with the finished product along one side of the page, and along the other, we'll take a look at how all of the elements you've learned about so far work together to form that polished piece of writing.

So it's frog dissection without all of the formaldehyde smell or all of the gooey mess.

Happy dissecting.

The Story

STUDENT'S LEGAL RIGHTS QUESTIONED BY HIS "INAPPROPRIATE" HAIRSTYLE

By Sarah Hughes,
Carmel (IN) High School

Last year junior Alex Liederbach, tired of his long, shaggy haircut, decided to do something to stand out from the rest of the crowd. On April 19, he shaved both sides of his head, creating a Mohawk with Elmer's blue gel glue. The spikes averaged 10 to 12 inches long.

Liederbach's hairstyle attracted much attention during the school week of April 21. "Most of my friends thought it was cool," Liederbach said. "Most people wanted to know how I

The Dissection of the Story

A well-written headline can provide another means for readers to understand the point of this story. Readers know that this is a story not just about hair, but about legal rights.

The lead. The most important part of the story. Notice how this lead grabs readers' attention by using an observation (a "gold coin") to illustrate the situation. Note the strong, specific details:
Elmer's blue gel glue
spikes averaged 10 to 12 inches long
The lead also introduces readers to the main source in the story — the face of the article. It is through Liederbach's experiences that readers will understand the larger issue that the reporter wants them to think about.

The first of many storytelling quotes. Notice how Liederbach's own voice is clear as a result of good interviewing. What question did the interviewer ask to elicit this response?

Attribution: Always use name said (Liederbach said), not said name (said Liederbach). Also, look at consistent use of the word "said" throughout the story.

spiked it up and why I did it. I didn't get many negative reactions (from students). Most of my teachers just kind of laughed at it. My gym teacher, he was the one who sent me down to the dean in the first place, said I was distracting him. He was the only teacher who had any problems with it."

Protected by the First Amendment, every U.S. citizen is guaranteed his or her right to free expression. The 1969 U.S. Supreme Court ruling *Tinker v. Des Moines Independent Community School District* states, "It can hardly be argued that either students or teachers shed their constitutional right to freedom of speech or expression at the schoolhouse gate."

David Day, an attorney at the Church, Church, Hittle & Antrim law firm, has represented the Carmel Clay school district for more than 10 years. He said, "The courts have said that students don't lose rights because they're at school, but those rights have to be interpreted in light of the school setting."

As a result of his haircut, Lieder-bach was sent to student services. He

---

The transition to the point occurs here, in the middle of the quote. At this point in the story, we have a student with weird hair and, now, a teacher who wants him to change it. If we've read this far (and from the visual nature of the story there's a better chance that we have), we'll want to find out the result of this conflict.

This more formal transition elaborates on the main point of the story. What does the reporter want readers to think about? This is not just a story about a haircut but one about student's rights of free speech and expression. Notice how the rest of the story merely elaborates on this main focus.

Research. The reporter blends the court case into the text seamlessly. It's not like reading a lawyer's tort or a research paper; rather, the research is part of the story as a whole, tucked in between the gold coins of the observations and the solid, storytelling quotes.

The first of two "expert" sources. Day is credible because he's a lawyer, but he's more relevant because he is the lawyer for Lieder-bach's school district. When he discussed the "school setting," readers know he is referring to their own school.

Another gold coin. Between the lead and this point in the story, the reporter has provided information that helps enhance the said, "It wasn't really a big deal with the deans. (Administrative Assistant Robert) Grenda didn't have a problem with it at all, but because my gym teacher sent me down, he had to check more into it and confer with the other administrators about it. They called me back a couple of days later.

"They said I couldn't wear it up anymore because I could poke someone in the eye. It wasn't that big of a deal; I guess they just wanted to protect themselves and others because everyone's so crazy about suing each other. The next day I put cotton balls on my spikes because I didn't want to take it down yet. That way I couldn't accidentally poke anyone."

While Fred McGuire, Liederbach's sophomore physical education teacher, refused to comment, Grenda said, "I started getting calls from various teachers and I could see where it was a safety concern as much as anything, especially in physical education where there are people running in close proximity to other students."

In the early 1970s, one of Massa-

point of the story. But, as good reporters should always remember, she has not forgotten about the main face of this story. Liederbach's saga continued from the lead, and the reporter has picked up that tale here. Remember that the face of the story provides the framework through which readers can relate to the information. Students' free speech rights present a pretty weighty, complicated issue; Liederbach's experience with these rights helps readers to connect with the information they need to know.

The reporter has allowed the main source to continue speaking with excellent storytelling quotes. Again, what question (or questions) did the reporter ask to get such great responses? Notice how sources are allowed to express their opinions. Notice, too, how the reporter has kept a detached, objective stance in her own writing, allowing the sources to speak for themselves. Nowhere in the story does the reporter tell readers what to think, but she certainly gives them information to think about.

Two important points here: One, the reporter knew that readers would want to hear from the physical education teacher who sent Liederbach to the deans' office, so she made an attempt. Two, when the teacher refused to comment she knew enough to include that refusal in her story. That way, readers don't wonder why the teacher never had a chance to respond.

Since the teacher wouldn't respond, the reporter added another excellent expert source with Robert Grenda. Like the attorney earlier, Grenda is credible because he deals with discipline issues like Liederbach's as part of his job, but he is more relevant because he was the dean to whom Liederbach was sent.

chusetts' public schools threatened to suspend a male student for his shoulder-length hair. When his case reached the Massachusetts Supreme Court, it stated, "Within the commodious concept of liberty, embracing freedoms great and small, is the right to wear one's hair as he wishes." The court also tagged a condition along with the ruling, stating that the hairstyle must fit the basic requirement of not causing any distraction or violating any safety issues. This clause gave this school the right to ask Liederbach to cut his hair. Liederbach, who said he planned to get rid of his Mohawk, cut his hair after Houndstock on April 26. He said, "I was only going to keep it for a week anyways, and I had to get a job. It was pretty inconvenient because you can't fit in a car or anything."

Day said he believes it's not unreasonable for the schools to ask their students to dress or behave in such a way that does not disrupt the educational system. To prevent any similar problems, he said, "I would think that (students) need to read the student hand-

More research. Notice how this court case is relevant because it deals specifically with students' hair as it relates to free expression. Other cases dealing with students' First Amendment rights would be OK, but this Massachusetts case hits the issue squarely on the head (pun intended).

A written report can "state." For all other forms of attribution, use "said."

The phrase that begins with "This clause" is a subtle but effective way to make the transition back to Liederbach's situation and it points out the relevancy of the Massachusetts court case to the case at hand.

A good storytelling quote. It could make readers wonder whether the administration made too much of an issue of Liederbach's hair in the first place. Notice again how the reporter doesn't ask this question, but her placement of this particular quote from her main source causes readers to take pause.

A nice transition back to the attorney. His call to action for students to read the student handbook may be an opportunity for the reporter to present the information found there as some sort of alternative coverage. For more on that, see Section III of this book.

Don't change a source's words, but for clarity's sake, you may need to identify unclear words and phrases in parentheses.

book. That will tell you what you can and cannot do."

Despite his confrontation with the school's policy, Liederbach shares similar views as Day. He said, "I think the school has a right to have their own rules and everything. They have to keep the kids in line. I think our school is pretty good as far as rules and the dress code goes. They're not really that strict. I think it's pretty fair."

Once again, back to the main source. Everything is in relation to Liederbach's situation. The question here may have been something like "How do you think you were treated in this situation?" Readers would want to know, and the reporter knew enough to think like a reader and ask the question.

The grammatical agreement error here (school is an "it," not a "they") is correct as is because it falls inside the direct quote. Don't change a source's words, but make sure you verify exactly what the source said before you put his words in print.

Grenda said, "Seeing as it's a democracy, the biggest concern is infringing on other people's rights. If you offend other people with your statements, obviously that's not a good thing to do. If you cause disruption or distraction in class as a result of what you're saying, or a statement that you're wearing, then it's not a good issue.

Notice Grenda's use of the word "disruption." It occurs several times throughout the story (the Tinker case, the Massachusetts case and here) and it helps to give the entire story some semblance of unity and focus.

"I think we're fortunate that the majority of the people here do a good job of not offending others, and that's why we have a good climate. If you're here for education, you don't worry about the other issues. They'll take care of themselves."

Note the proper use of quotation marks when the quote continues into another paragraph.

When in doubt, end with a storytelling quote. Another technique is to come back to the gold coin that you established in your lead to provide closure. The ending of your story is the second most important part (next to the lead), and it should leave readers with some questions in their heads.

SECTION III

Alternative Coverage

Presenting Your
Information Visually

Your readers don't like to read. It's not that they don't know how, they just don't like to. It takes too much time, and time is of the essence in a high schooler's life. There's too much to do. Too much to see. Too much to experience. And if someone puts a bunch of text in front of average teenagers, guess what? They move on. They find something else more interesting, more worthy of their precious time.

Don't fight your readers. Work with them. Learn to take the factual informa-tion, the statistics, the numbers, the names, the dates, all of it, and present it visually.

This section is titled "Alternative Coverage" for a reason. This portion of the book isn't about mere sidebars or info-graphics; it's about so much more — an alternative, more visual way of covering your stories. It's about using these visual tidbits to enhance what you want readers to think about.

Read on and see for yourself.

CHAPTER 9

A Thousand Words

How to Reach Readers
Who Don't Want to Read

Have you ever watched Grandma try to navigate the Internet? If Grandma even owns a computer, chances are it's like watching a junior high boy work up the nerve to ask a girl to dance. Very slow. Very deliberate. Lots of hesitation. Now put your little brother or sister on the same computer. Like a fish in water, right? It's not that you or your younger siblings are any smarter than Grandma, you're just more adept at using technology.

So let's take that Grandma analogy even farther. Grandma probably gets her information in only a few predictable ways. She might subscribe to a newspaper. She has TV (but one that perhaps lacks cable or extended channels). Maybe she gets a magazine or two. She has a telephone (do rotary dials still exist?). And that's about it. As a result, she has time. Time to sift through the information. Time to read. Time to let the information make sense.

Now contrast the Grandma scenario to your own life. In some ways, you're a lot like Grandma. You get a newspaper delivered to your house. You have a telephone. You get magazines. You have TV.

But that's only the beginning.

On that phone, for instance, you probably have call waiting. And caller ID. Maybe you also have

your own cell phone. Chances are, it could have wireless access to e-mail and the Internet. I'll bet your TV has a lot of chan-

113

nels. 100? 150? More? How many of those are news channels? How many are devoted to pop culture (music and fashion and food)? How many to sports? Then add in computers. Maybe you have high-speed Internet. Maybe you chat online with your friends. Maybe you chat online using your high-speed Internet while you flip through channels on the high-definition TV in your bedroom while you talk to your boyfriend or girlfriend on your cell phone while you wait for another call to come through on your pager, and on your lap is the latest edition of some fashion magazine that you flip through casually with your free hand...

Gasp!

Knowing this about your readers, where does your school publication fall on the food chain?

The answer's kind of disheartening, isn't it? It's a problem, this lack of readership, and it's not one that will go away on its own.

So in order to solve the problem of readership (or lack thereof) we need to get back to Carl. You remember Carl the Caveman, right? You remember, of course, that he was the world's first storyteller. You remember that he used various tools to tell his stories — cave walls and paints and charcoal and the like. And you remember, too, why he chose to tell his stories in the way he did?

His readers, of course. The people for whom his stories were intended. And who were his readers? Other cavemen and women, certainly. But even more than that, they were people who couldn't read words (there were no written words in those days). They were people who lived in caves. They were people who put credence in keeping safe and hunting animals and staying warm.

So what did Carl write (or draw) about? He wrote about keeping safe and hunting animals and staying warm because that's what his readers needed and wanted to hear about. And he put those messages in caves where people would be more likely to read them. And he drew pictures to get his message across because people in his day couldn't read.

In Section I, we discussed how to tell written stories in such a way that would entice more people to read them. We discussed information readers need to know (broccoli) and how to present that information, in story form, in a way that makes readers want to read it (cheese). We discussed the difference between the inverted pyramid and the narrative style of writing and how the narrative style is more conducive for your readers. We discussed putting a face on stories and not necessarily telling readers what to think but definitely giving them something to think about. We talked about tools for information gathering — interviewing and observation and research — and how to blend the fruits of those tools into a story that hopefully makes readers take notice. We discussed how to find stories and how to narrow down the topics into individual slices of pepperoni in the larger pie of the subject.

So about writing, we discussed quite a bit. But now that we're this far and you're locked in for the long haul, I'll share this tidbit of information: Writing a story isn't always the correct answer and certainly it isn't the only answer.

Bigger Isn't Better

Time was that the more important a story was the more you'd write. Got a lot of sources? Add more words. Tons of research? More words. More prominent news? More words. Get the picture? I've worked with a lot of advisers over the years and I've seen a lot of publications, and that overriding trend still seems to dominate student press—the more important a story is, the longer the story is. Guess what? That trend is W-R-O-N-G. It's equivalent to turning writing into a math formula: Minor story = 300 words. Minor story that's a little more major = 600 words. Major story = 800 words. REALLY major story = 1,000 words and so on. But what kind of formula is that? The more important something is the bigger it should be? Abraham Lincoln wrote the Gettysburg Address on the back of an envelope. The Declaration of Independence is on one page. John Steinbeck's *Of Mice and Men* only contains six chapters. Heck, my last will and testament is only a few paragraphs long. Does the brevity of these documents make them any less important? On the contrary, these documents (my will notwithstanding) have stood the test of time perhaps because of their brevity. Their messages are clear and concise. If we measured importance by word count, then apparently the local phone book is the most important document that we own.

So I suppose this approach of writing longer stories was fine 20 years ago, when, like Grandma, readers had more time and

---

THE ROLE OF ALTERNATIVE COVERAGE

Actually, alternative coverage plays two roles—to enhance existing information and, in some cases, to replace that information. Here's how to set the two apart.

Enhance

In Sections I and II, you learned that good journalistic stories should feature a main face (someone who's affected by the news) and should answer the questions how and why.

As part of your information gathering, you may wind up with lots of relevant information (statistics, data, numbers, etc.) that are important but that would detract from the flow of your narrative.

Incorporating this information into alternative coverage that will accompany your main story is a great way to provide a visual layer for your visual readers. In this case, the alternative coverage works with your story to provide readers with the information they need.

Unless you're replacing the story entirely with alternative coverage, **try to incorporate alternative coverage into every story that you write.**

Replace

Sometimes stories are newsworthy but there's just no way to put a face on them (see the example on Page 117). Don't force a main source if none presents itself. Rather, just give the readers the information they need to know in visual form (alternative coverage) and get out.

In other words, if the only information your readers really need to know is that the state standardized test is next week, then just provide the relevant information (i.e., when the test is, where students need to go, etc.).

And sometimes, good use of alternative coverage can be even better than a typical story.

fewer distractions vying for their attention. But readers today, as you already know if you're this far along in the book, read differently than readers a generation or more ahead of them. They access their information differently. They process information differently. What that means for today's modern storytellers is that we had better provide information in a way that is conducive to the reading habits of our audience. We should provide information in a variety of different ways. Sometimes, of course, the written story is still the answer.

And sometimes it's not.

Mere words, therefore, do not equal importance. That's the old school of teaching. That's a main story? Write more. Not as important? Cut a few hundred words. But that way of teaching doesn't cut it anymore, not with today's readers.

No matter how good your article is, no matter how many gold coins you use, no matter how many storytelling quotes, the truth still remains that your readers don't really like to read. They don't have time. They don't have the desire (their teachers make them do too much reading as it is). The pessimistic bottom line is that no matter how much effort you put into writing a story, most people for whom the story is intended won't read it. Not because the story is bad, but because reading in most teens' lives is at the bottom of their to-do hierarchy.

But I'm an optimist, not a pessimist. I still think that readers will read if you give them a chance. Even more, I think they'll read if you give them a reason to.

This chapter is about what to do when just a story isn't enough. And how often is that? Just about always.

Trick Them into Reading

I say "trick" like it's a bad thing. I guess I mean something different. Whet your readers' appetites, maybe. Or intrigue them a little. Like watching a preview of a movie that shows you just enough to make you turn to your significant other and say, "I definitely want to see that when it comes out," a well done story should have the same effect. Only with journalism, readers don't need to wait until next May and attend a theater near them to get the story; it's right there in front of them just waiting to unfold.

At the beginning of Section I, we discussed dog manure and how high school publications (and even some professional ones) like to dress up what is essentially crap (badly written stories) with pretty designs and bows and ribbons. These publications say nothing but they look good doing it. They're like the air-headed blonde at prom — she looks hot, but sit her down to talk and it's almost as painful as passing a gallstone the hard way. Your readers are smart, and they'll look through the meaningless window dressing about as quickly as you can say "inverted pyramid." So the first time you try to put out your publication it's fine. But the next time? And the time after that? Forget it. You've lost those readers and you'll have a hard time getting them back.

And that's why we spent so long discussing good writing. It's the lifeblood of your publication. Without good stories, nothing else will matter. Learn to write good reader-driven stories, and learn to write them well. It's the content, after all, that matters. If the content is good, the design really doesn't matter. I can wrap up a diamond necklace in a brown paper bag and my wife will still kill herself trying to get inside. To keep going with analogies, journalism is like a house. You must start with a firm foundation — good, straight walls, solid concrete below, thick insulation, air-tight windows, a leak-free roof...

...and then it's time to decorate.

An Alternative to Storytelling

Section I of this book talked quite a bit about the how and why when telling a story — How does this story affect me? Why is this important? Why should I care? But the thing is, the who, what, when and where are still important. Those four W's tend to give readers the real "meat" of the story; they are the data that make a story relevant. They represent research and statistics and numbers, all of which play a role in journalism.

But in copy — in the story itself — they're just not that readable.

And sometimes, well, sometimes there's just no need for a story at all.

Here's an example:

"X" marks the spot for the end of the summer concert season at Deer Creek Music Center. On Sept. 30, X-Fest 20xx starts at 2 p.m.

This year's X-Fest features, on two separate stages, Stone Temple Pilots, Green Day, Fuel, P.O.D., Papa Roach and Disturbed. In addition to the music, organizers also offer an interactive concourse and extreme sports demonstrations. Also, special guest Rick Rockwell of "Who Wants to Marry a Multi-millionaire" fame acts as best man in a wedding that will take place on the main stage. Lawn seats are $30.

On Sept. 29 at 7 p.m., Deer Creek presents Jimmy Page and the Black Crowes. This performance is part of their "Live at the Greek" tour. Ticket prices are as follows: lower pavilion $75, upper pavilion $45, lawn seats $25.

Tuesday at 7 p.m. Christina Aguilera performs in her rescheduled, postponed concert originally scheduled for Aug. 6. Lawn seats are available for $25 and are "buy one, get one free."

Tickets for the above events are available online through the Deer Creek website at www.deercreek.com. One can also obtain tickets by phone at 555–5151 or at Karma Records at 146th Street and Meridian.

The story above is not horrible. Using our elements of news, it's timely (it would be published before the first concert listed, perhaps in early to mid–September), it's got proximity (the venue is nearby) and it's even got prominence (because of the headliners at the concerts). It contains information that readers want (and possibly need) to know.

But there's a problem.

Nobody will read it.

Now you could kill yourself trying to use the techniques we've learned from Sections I and II and attempt to write a people-driven story that will answer the how and the why. You could find someone at your school who's attended several of these concerts in the past or perhaps there's someone who works backstage at the venue and who has met several famous performers and who will have an opportunity to meet these performers. And if you've written this story for your publication and the above scenarios apply to you, then by all means write a narrative story for your readers.

But sometimes, these stories just don't exist. You could force a story (a kid in your school who wants to be a pop idol someday perhaps), but sometimes, as in this case, all you need to do is get the basic information out and then, just as quickly, get out.

I REPEAT, DON'T REPEAT YOURSELF, I REPEAT

Alternative coverage should expand your coverage, not make you cover the same thing twice. Here's an explanation and two types to avoid.

You should know by now that your readers are pressed for time. As a result, you should avoid repeating information in a piece of alternative coverage that you've already included in the story and vice versa. Remember that alternative coverage should enhance the story and expand its focus, not merely parrot what you've already said. Typically when a visual reader comes across repeated information, he will stop reading.

In particular, consider these two specific pieces of alternative coverage and why you should avoid them:

WHAT IT IS: THE PULLED QUOTE

Also called a liftout quote, this type of alternative coverage merely selects a story-telling quote from the story it accompanies and makes it REALLY BIG.

WHY IT'S BAD

The pulled quote just repeats information that already appears in the accompanying story. It lends nothing new to your article.

HOW TO FIX IT

Ask yourself, is there something else that I could put in this space besides a pulled quote? A fact box? A chart? A quiz?

Save pulled quotes as a last resort. In other words, don't plan around them. Only use them if you have no choice, like if, say, the story you planned to use winds up short and your deadline is in, like, five minutes.

WHAT IT LOOKS LIKE

"The pulled quote just repeats information that already appears in the accompanying story. It lends nothing new to your article."

Shall I say it a third time?

WHAT IT IS: THE MUGSHOT

This is usually a small head-and-shoulders photo of the victim, uh, I mean the source who's in your story.

WHY IT'S BAD

It gives readers very little information other than a face and a name. Also, typically, mugshots catch sources in "deer-in-the-headlights" poses, as if, in a moment, they'll also be fingerprinted and booked.

HOW TO FIX IT

Try using a candid photo and informative cutline or caption instead. You'd still show the source's face and name, but now he's be doing something newsworthy and relevant to your story, too.

WHAT IT LOOKS LIKE

Ima Mugshot
Consider these four words: "Turn to the right."

So how do you do it? Two words: alternative coverage.

Some designers use the terms informational graphics or infographics or even sidebars, but I have always preferred alternative coverage. They're all names for basically the same thing, **but alternative coverage really says what it is: an alternative way of telling a story rather than writing.** Remember that your readers are visual people. They like information presented to them in a visual format (which, with writing, is why we discussed the importance of incorporating observations into your stories). With design, alternative coverage provides even more avenues to share your information visually, especially those first four W's—who, what, when and where. Looking at the inverted pyramid-style story about the concerts, what in that story gives readers any more than those four W's? And since we've already determined that it's still necessary in the paper and that there's no other way to put a face on that story, then why present it in the way that you see? Why not try an alternative way, a more visual way, to cover that story?

Why not try this:

Tuesday
Who: Christina Aguilera (rescheduled from Aug. 6)
When: 7 p.m.
Cost: Lawn seats $25; buy one, get one free

Sept. 29
Who: Jimmy Page, Black Crowes "Live at the Greek" Tour
When: 7 p.m.
Cost: Lower pavilion $75, upper pavilion $45, lawn seats $25

Sept. 30
What: X-Fest 20xx (featuring Stone Temple Pilots, Green Day, Fuel, P.O.D., Papa Roach, Disturbed)
When: 2 p.m.

Cost: Lawn seats $30
Other attractions: Interactive concourse, extreme sports demonstrations, mass wedding featuring Rick Rockwell from "Who Wants to Marry a Multimillionaire" as the best man

For more information
www.deercreek.com
Tickets: Call 555–5151 or go to Karma records at 146th Street and Meridian

A couple of points to consider here. First, what information from the first story is not included in the second? Second, is the second story any longer than the first? Third, and perhaps more important, which of the two formats is more readable for your visual audience?

The first two questions are more rhetorical than actual. Both stories include the exact same information and both are roughly the same length. The reason I mention this is because those who are opposed to presenting stories visually often argue that the inverted pyramid can provide more information for readers and/or that presenting stories visually takes up more valuable space in their publications. Not so on both counts.

The third question, though, is the most important one: which is more readable? I hope you answered that the second story is; and if you fall into the demographic of the majority of your peers, chances are pretty overwhelming that that's what you said.

Enhance Your Narrative

Presenting information visually through alternative coverage can make the information you present to your readers more accessible. This holds true for information that your readers want to know and, perhaps more importantly, for the information that they need to know. With the concert story, **sometimes alternative coverage can be used instead of writing a story. But more often, you'll use alternative coverage to accompany and enhance a narrative story that you've written.**

Case in point, a student I taught once wrote a story about fire safety. Of course, as you know by now, "fire safety" is only a topic, so the larger angle — the thing she wanted readers to think about — was that students need to better understand fire safety in order to keep themselves and their families safe. The story that she wrote featured a student who had recently burned her house down. She didn't do it on purpose (that would have been another story entirely), rather, she had candles lit in her bedroom and she fell asleep. When she awoke, her room was engulfed in flames. She and her family were able to get out of the house, but the house itself was ruined, including all of the family's keepsakes and memories. Nothing was salvageable. The family had since built a new house, but it was still strangely devoid of any personality since nothing existed from their lives before the fire. The girl who caused the accident had still not forgiven herself for her mistake.

In the process of writing this story, the reporter visited the local fire station that put out the house fire and had an interview with the fire chief. He provided lots of great storytelling quotes in the body of the story, but he also provided the reporter with, literally, reams of literature about fire safety — statistics and brochures and instructions on what to do if your clothes catch on fire, etc. The information was certainly important enough to include for her readers, but there was just so much of it that she was certain (and rightly so) that if she included the information in the body of her story that it would ruin the flow of her otherwise quite readable narrative story and readers would be turned off by it and would not read what she had written.

But the information was still valid and important, and the reporter wanted to make sure that readers could access it. What to do?

Alternative coverage.

The published story included three different pieces of alternative coverage that accompanied the main narrative:

1. A graph that showed current local fire statistics (the fire fighters answered nearly 3,000 calls during the most recent year, 343 of which were fire-related)

2. A step-by-step instructional chart that told readers what to do to survive a fire in their home.

3. A multiple-choice quiz titled "Are you fire safe?" that contained 15 questions about typical fire-related information (i.e., It is necessary to change smoke detector batteries: A. every other month. B. when the seasons change. C. once a year. D. every other year. The answer, by the way, is C.).

The students on staff conducted a reader poll after that issue came out where they gathered a cross section of 25 student readers, gave them some pizza and had them comment on how and what they read in the publication. Nearly 75 percent of the students read the information in the graph and the step-by-step chart, and more than 90 percent of them did the quiz. Of those, a vast majority read the accompanying story, too. Contrast those findings to another story we published in the same issue about a student who found out that her mother had breast cancer which contained no alternative coverage other than some photos; less than 20 percent read that story and the majority of the readers didn't even read more than the headline and accompanying summary deck.

Which all goes back to the original premise established in this book: Your readers are visual people, and if something doesn't grab their attention right away, they won't waste their valuable time finding it.

Meet the Reads of Your Needers

Consider the professional publications that you or your friends read on a regular basis. Think about the magazines you subscribe to. And now think about the publications your parents subscribe to, or your grandparents. Are they the same? Sometimes they are, but I think eventually you'll find a pretty definite dividing line between your tastes in periodicals and your parents.' I mean, how many of your grandmothers are reading *Seventeen* and *Cosmo Girl*? And how many of you or your friends are perusing *Business News Weekly*? When you consider the publications that you like, there's something about those publications that you're drawn to. And we're looking beyond content here, by the way. I mean, no offense to the publishers of *Teen Beat*, but how earth shattering is an exposé on lip gloss? Or an in-depth study on skirt styles for fall? Of course the content is important to you — in many cases it's information that you want to know anyway — but beyond that, you might take a look at how that information is presented.

I think you'll find a definite difference, the biggest of which is the amount of visual storytelling that occurs in your publications versus those others geared toward a more adult crowd. And why not? We already discussed at the beginning of this book how you and your parents read differently. It's not that you're dumber or less sophisticated; you're just different. And you're different because your lives are different. Your experiences as a child have been different. The way you've learned to access information is different. The amount of information at your disposal is different.

So not worse. Just different.

Which means your own publications — the ones you produce — need to be different, too, to match the way your readers read. There's a phrase we use in the world of journalism — **Meet the *needs* of your *readers*** — that reflects the necessity of providing the information that your readers both want and need to know in your publications. But take that phrase and switch a few letters and you're left with this — **Meet the *reads* of your *needers*.** This sentence is just as important because it refers to the way your readers access information. Certainly providing information that your readers need to know is important, but if your readers aren't reading that information because of the way it's presented, then why bother? You need to balance both. The first part of this book addressed how to make your writing more visual. This section will attempt to address the rest of the elements on the page. Writing visual stories is part of the equation.

Alternative coverage is another vital part.

Marketing to Readers 101

We've established that you, if you're true to your demographics, purchase periodicals that look a certain way because they are geared toward you and your reading habits. As well those publications should be. After all, magazines are in a big, competitive business. Don't believe me? Take a look at your local bookstore's magazine collection the next time you visit. There are literally hundreds of magazines vying for your attention, many of them that fall into the same categories. Now the big misunderstanding is that magazines are made for you — that the magazine places within it information that you will read because you are the most important part of that magazine's business. Some people believe that the money you pay for your subscription or for your over-the-counter purchase helps to pay for that magazine.

Not so. In fact, your subscription money, in most cases, means very little to those publishers. What matters is the money generated from advertising dollars. Magazines don't sell you entertainment; rather, magazines sell audiences to advertisers. And the more of an audience that magazine has, the more it can charge for advertising.

Consider another medium for a moment — television. One of the biggest television events of the year happens to be the Super Bowl. And if you follow the news at all, you'll know that the stations that carry the Super Bowl tend to charge an exorbitant amount for commercial air time each year (in 2005 for Super Bowl XXXIX, the going rate was $2.4 million for a 30-second commercial spot). And why? Because millions of people watch the Super Bowl. More so, in most years, than any other television event. For advertisers, that means that millions of people can potentially see their messages, as opposed to smaller audiences the rest of the year. This means, ultimately, that the media that carry those messages can charge more money. And money, in the world of business, is what it's all about.

So what does this discussion have to do with you and your reading habits? Actually, quite a bit. Take a look again at those magazines that you read. You can bet that the publishers of those periodicals spend a lot of money to research their demographic markets. After all, they're trying to sell you to potential advertisers, and the more of you they can entice to pick up their magazines, the more money they can charge and, subsequently, make.

Chances are, though, that you don't have a lot of money. You don't need it. The research has already been done. You know the publications that are geared toward your audience because you probably subscribe to them already, so all you need to do is to look more carefully at how those publications design their information. My guess is that you'll start to see a lot of similar trends — more photos, more alternative coverage, fewer stories. But don't take my word for it; check it out for yourself. And when you're done looking, take the ideas you've gained from the experience and see how the concepts might apply to your own publications. Did you see a timeline of summer concerts? Could you use that idea to visually depict your own school's marching band schedule? Did you see a photo montage of hot make-up products for the fall? Could you use that same idea to show a prom "survival kit"?

Summary

Your audience definitely reads in a pretty specific way. For the most part, your readers like information presented to them visually. The evidence is in the publications that they already regularly read — the periodicals that they actually go out of their way to purchase.

You can learn a lot from those professional publications that are geared toward people in your demographic, not so much in the content of those publications but in how those publication present information. And what you'll find is that these publications rely heavily on alternative coverage — an alternative to writing a story, in other words—to present information.

Always remember that you have two important responsibilities as a journalist. First, you must meet the needs of your readers; you must provide them with information that they need to know. But second, you must meet the reads of your needers. You have to understand how your readers read so that you can provide that information that they need to know in such a way that makes them want to read it.

We discussed broccoli in Chapter 1. Later, we talked about how to put cheese on the stories you write (with observations, for example). These remaining chapters will show you how to create even more cheese using design techniques, which will make the stories you do write even more palatable.

STUDY GUIDE

Terms and Concepts

Alternative coverage—A different, more visual way of telling a story. Either enhances or replaces the traditional written story.

Pulled quote—Also called a lift-out quote, a type of alternative coverage that merely selects a passage from the story it accompanies and makes it really big. Should be avoided.

Mugshot—A small head-and-shoulders photo of a source in a story with the source's name underneath. Should be avoided.

Practicing with Alternative Coverage

The story below is representative of a typical beat report for a journalism student. Using this story, brainstorm possible ideas for alternative coverage that could either enhance the existing story or replace it. Remember to think about data and statistics as well as more global concepts that would intrigue a wider audience.

Public Library to Screen Film 'Finding Neverland'

By Ben Linder, Carmel (IN) H.S.

Almost no child goes through his or her life without seeing or hearing the story of Peter Pan, a fantasy tale about remaining young and refusing to grow up. Many people do not realize the interesting story of the genius behind the scenes of the infamous tale, though.

On April 15, the public library will show "Finding Neverland," the recent film telling the story of J.M. Barrie, the man who wrote Peter Pan, and where he drew inspiration for the story.

Released last year, "Finding Neverland" contains an all-star cast, including Hollywood stars such as Johnny Depp, Kate Winslet and Dustin Hoffman. The film shows Barrie's relationship to three young boys who would rekindle his creativity and inspire Peter Pan.

Sophomore Kasey Lloyd saw and enjoyed the film. According to her, the film touched her and made her think. "[The movie] started out really bad, and I was angry that I went, then it got better and it made me sad. It made me cry," Lloyd said.

Kay Williams, senior library assistant at the public library, said that one of her most important jobs is deciding which movies to screen. In the past, the library has shown "The Motorcycle Diaries" and "The Bourne Supremacy." According to her, "Finding Neverland" was not a hard choice. "I saw it, and I thought it was really well done," Williams said.

The film will be shown on April 15 in the Program Room of the public library.

The library welcomes anyone to attend the event, and free popcorn will be provided. Those interested should stop by the Audiovisual Desk at the library to pick up a free ticket.

Williams said she believes those in attendance will enjoy the film, and she encourages everyone to come. "It's just a good, old-fashioned, feel-good kind of movie," Williams said.

CHAPTER 10

Alternative Coverage 101

A Practical Guide to Visual Presentation

Some call them informational graphics, or infographics for short. Some say sidebars. Still others call it visual coverage. Call it what you will, it's all the same. And for your visual readers, alternative coverage is one of the most important elements that you can provide—an alternative to the way you would normally tell the story. And what's that "normal" way? Writing it into the story, of course.

Chapter 9 discussed how readers today access information differently than readers a generation or more ahead of them. They process information differently. What that means for today's modern storytellers is that we had better provide information in a way that is conducive to the reading habits of our audience or else we'll lose that audience. We should provide information in a variety of different ways. Sometimes, of course, the written story is still the answer.

And sometimes it's not.

This chapter is about what to do when a story just isn't enough, or when a story isn't even appropriate in the first place. Knowing what you now know about your readers means that every story you write for your publication should either be alternative coverage or be enhanced by al-

ternative coverage. This chapter is a practical guide to the multitude of ways to present information visually.

The examples contained within these pages are just that—examples. They are not meant to be copied as is. Rather, take these ideas and try to make them work for your own publication. Better yet, once you've seen what's here, go out and find your own examples—create an "idea file"—and keep them in a convenient place that you can refer to when you're stuck.

In addition, the following examples by no means constitute an exhaustive list. Each is merely an example of the hundreds of ways that you can present information visually. These examples should get you thinking about alternative ways to tell stories. The rest, of course, will be up to you.

Alternative Coverage: The Basics

Alternative coverage takes so many forms that it would be impossible to show them all here. Rather, use the information found within as a springboard to further discovery. Once you've learned about some of these different types, go to other publications—magazines, newspapers, brochures—and see what other examples you can find for yourself. Then, borrow and enhance these ideas to create alternative coverage of your own. Keep in mind that your visual information should enhance your point.

EXAMPLE

TYPE   Bio box

DESCRIPTION   A list of relevant, statistical information about one or more of the sources in your story.

A BELCHING LEGEND
Senior Tim Hauptman's burping credentials are impressive

Showing winning form, senior Tim Hauptman (above) belches the alphabet during a recent competition.

Hauptman's belching resume:
1985 – Lil' Tykes Burping Bonanza (first place)
1987 – The Toddler Burp-O-Rama (first place)
1992 – The Burp Cup (honorable mention)
1995 – Ted's Taco Hut Burp Extravaganza (second place)

TYPE   Checklist

DESCRIPTION   A list of information that readers can use to help them prepare for an event. Checklists are good because, if done properly, they can make the alternative coverage something that readers can actually use and interact with, rather than just look at passively.

BEFORE YOU GO TO THE BELCHING CONTEST
Want to be prepared? Don't forget these items on the way to this Saturday's Burp Bash.

☐ Three two-liter bottles of soda (at least. Burping champion Tim Hauptman recommends that the soda be warm).
☐ Four green peppers, sliced. (In a pinch, according to Hauptman, he's resorted to eating dandelions, but they don't provide the same punch).
☐ Three super-stuffed bean burritos (later you can attend the Flatulence Festival).
☐ A blanket (Seating is on the lawn).
☐ Nose plugs (Did we mention the smell?)

TYPE   Comparison chart

DESCRIPTION   Especially useful to contrast two or more products or services. Readers can visually relate to your concept by seeing like elements set against one another.

THE BENEFITS OF BELCHING
A healthy burp does wonders for your physical well being. Compare the lungs of a burper v. a non-burper.

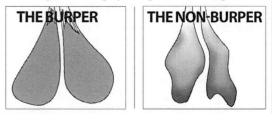

THE BURPER   THE NON-BURPER

EXAMPLE

TYPE Fact box

DESCRIPTION Interesting statistical data that enhances your story. As with many of these other types of alternative coverage, fact boxes may contain numbers or figures that, while important, might not be visual enough if included in the written story and, therefore, might detract from the flow of the story itself.

BURPING BASICS

Everything you need to know about competitive belching

- Competitive belching is one of the earliest sports. Evidence of burping for sport dates back to the Roman Empire.
- It's possible to hear a championship burp from space.
- The Bronze Burper is a traveling trophy that is awarded to the burping points champion each year.
- The youngest winner of the Bronze Burper was 9-month-old Elias Marshall. Marshall was later stripped of his prize when judges discovered that his mother had mixed illegal gas-producing tablets into his formula bottle.

TYPE Glossary

DESCRIPTION Words and definitions that will help readers to better understand the accompanying story.

BURPING A TO Z

- **The croaker** – A long, jagged burp that sounds like the maiming of a large bullfrog. Because of its sustainability and volume, the croaker is the basis of many other belches.
- **Blurp** – A bad burp, either because of volume, length or both.
- **Burpette** – A female burp competitor.
- **Burp surprise** – When a burp results in accidental vomiting.
- **Burp stink** – The result of an unusually odiferous belch.

TYPE How-to box

DESCRIPTION Step-by-step instructions for readers to help them complete a certain task that is relevant to the story.

BURPING 101

Wanna know how the pros do it? Here's how.

Step 1: Get a large two-liter of warm soda.

Step 2: Breathe deeply.

Step 3: Chug the soda from Step 1.

Step 4: Wait. You can't rush a good burp.

Step 5: Let 'er rip.

EXAMPLE

TYPE Map

DESCRIPTION   Maps are interactive and instructive, particularly if you're identifying a place not well known by your readers.

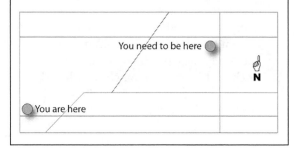

GETTING TO BURPSTOCK
Use this map...or just follow the aroma.

You need to be here

You are here

N

TYPE Photo essay

DESCRIPTION   A collection of storytelling pictures and cutlines that visually enhances or replaces the story.

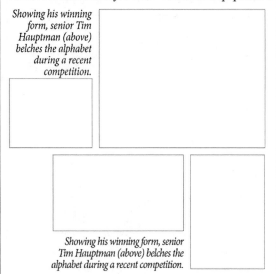

A PICTURE IS WORTH 1,000 BELCHES
Check out these scenes from last weekend's Burpapalooza.

Showing his winning form, senior Tim Hauptman (above) belches the alphabet during a recent competition.

Showing his winning form, senior Tim Hauptman (above) belches the alphabet during a recent competition.

TYPE Pie chart/graph/bar chart

DESCRIPTION   Ways to compare items visually. Pie charts show how individual elements make up a whole. Graphs show trends over time. Bar charts compare two or more items.

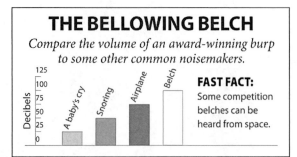

THE BELLOWING BELCH
Compare the volume of an award-winning burp to some other common noisemakers.

Decibels
125
100
75
50
25
0

A baby's cry
Snoring
Airplane
Belch

FAST FACT:
Some competition belches can be heard from space.

EXAMPLE

TYPE   Q&A

DESCRIPTION   Great for quick human interest or expert source interviews.

ONE-ON-ONE WITH A BURPING LEGEND

National belching champion Jared Campbell shares his gaseous secrets with the world.

Q: Why did you get involved in competitive belching?

A: Ever since I was a kid I've been good at making noises with my body, and since there's no armpit fart noise league I went with the burping.

Q: What's the secret to a successful burp?

A: A lot of people will tell you that it's the type of soda you drink or the food you eat. But I think you just have to be a really disgusting person. I mean, I've been burping since I was a kid because I didn't care what people thought. Neither did my parents. I guess I chalk that up to years of unhindered practice.

TYPE   Quiz

DESCRIPTION   Visual readers like interaction. Quizzes provide a wonderful combination of interaction with learning opportunities.

TEST YOUR BURPING BRAINPOWER

Think you know belching? Take this quiz to find out.

1. When was the first ever belching competition?
A. 1904   C. 1924
B. 1914   D. 1934

2. Jared Campbell has the record for the most national wins. How many medals has he earned?
A. 3   C. 5
B. 4   D. 6

3. How many burps does the National Burping Foundation officially recognize?
A. 2   C. 4
B. 3   D. 5

Answers: 1) A. Competitive belching was introduced at the 1904 Chicago World's Fair. 2) C. His most recent win was in May 2005. 3) B. They are as follows: the squeaker, the wet warhorse and the boomer.

TYPE   Quote collection

DESCRIPTION   A collection of storytelling quotes from relevant sources that can provide added insight to your story. Make sure that the information in a quote collection is different from the information in the story. Don't repeat information; rather, use the quotes to enhance the rest of the story.

SOUND OFF

Local burping competitors share their thoughts.

"I've always said that a good burp takes three things – time, patience and a really sensitive stomach."
• **Senior Paul Goodlove**

"Burping competitively is lots of fun, but I hate contests in enclosed spaces. The smell makes my eyes water."
• **Junior Diedre Cranberry**

"People always make fun of me 'cause I'm little. Let me tell you, though, I may be small, but I burp huge."
• **Freshman Carter Chipman**

EXAMPLE

TYPE   Ratings

DESCRIPTION   Evaluating something on a comparative scale. Great for reviews of books, movies, music, plays, restaurants, etc.

WHERE'S THE BURP?

Our guest reviewer, burping champion Alex Tubman, ranks local restaurants for their ability to produce mammoth belches.

Ken's Taco Hut Rating: 2
Comment: I expected more from Ken. I mean, heck, they've got a menu item called the "Gutbuster." But all it did was make me sick.

Mr. Christie's Indian Cuisine   Rating 4
Comment: The burps just kept on coming. The only downfall was the price.

School cafeteria   Rating: 5
Comment: Granted I ate on "Mystery Monday," so I can't vouch for the other days of the week, but I'll tell you, I've never had that much gas in my life.

Ratings guide:
1 = Burp? What burp?   4 = Outstanding
2 = Below average   5 = Look at me, ma! I'm
3 = Solid burp for the buck   peeling paint off the walls!

TYPE   Step-by-step box

DESCRIPTION   Similar to the "How-To" box, this type of alternative coverage illustrates a process or complicated series.

THE ANATOMY OF THE BURP

Belches don't just happen. Local gastrointestinal doctor Paul Phoenix describes how it works.

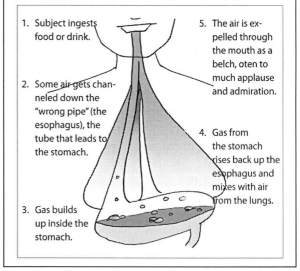

1. Subject ingests food or drink.

2. Some air gets channeled down the "wrong pipe" (the esophagus), the tube that leads to the stomach.

3. Gas builds up inside the stomach.

4. Gas from the stomach rises back up the esophagus and mixes with air from the lungs.

5. The air is expelled through the mouth as a belch, oten to much applause and admiration.

EXAMPLE

TYPE   Timeline

DESCRIPTION As the name implies, this type of alternative coverage shows major events over a block of time. You can divide by any time denomination — seconds, minutes, years, eons — it all depends on what story you're trying to tell.

A DAY IN THE LIFE OF A BURPER

Here's the routine of champion belcher Marilyn Johnson.

6 a.m. Wake up. Eat three brown sugar and cinnamon Pop Tarts. Drink two cans of diet soda ("I'm trying to burp, not get fat," Johnson said.).

7:30 Arrive at school. Warm-up belching with other belchers in her burping group. These are short, controlled belching bursts.

9 The first big burp of the day. Johnson waits until the bell rings to use her burp to dismiss her second period class ("The teacher even looks forward to my burp," Johnson said.).

Noon Lunch. One bean burrito, two more cans of warm diet soda and carrots.

3 p.m. After-school burping practice. This usually depends on the day. According to Johnson, Tuesdays and Thursdays are designed for burp endurance. The rest of the week is for volume.

10 Several more cool-down burps before bed ("If I don't get at least 100 in, I can't sleep," she said.).

STUDY GUIDE

Terms and Concepts

Bar chart — Compares two or more items.

Bio box — A list of relevant, statistical information about one or more of the sources in your story.

Checklist — A list of information that readers can use to help them prepare for an event.

Comparison chart — A piece of alternative coverage that compares or contrasts two or more similar products or services.

Fact box — A list of interesting statistical data that enhances your story.

Glossary — A list of words and definitions that help readers to better understand the accompanying story.

Graph — Shows trends over time.

How-to box — Step-by-step instructions for readers to help them accomplish a certain task.

Map — Shows where an event is located and, possibly, how to get there.

Photo essay — A collection of storytelling pictures and cutlines that visually enhance or replace the story.

Pie chart — Shows how individual elements make up a whole.

Q&A — Simple listing of questions posed to a source and the source's responses.

Quiz — An interactive piece of alternative coverage that presents information relevant to a story in test form.

Quote collection — A collection of storytelling quotes from relevant sources that provide added insight to your story.

Ratings — An evaluation of something on a comparative scale.

Step-by-step box — Illustrates a process or complicated series.

Timeline — Shows major events over a period of time.

Start an Idea File

1. Get a blank spiral notebook or, better yet, an empty three-ring binder and some divider sheets.

2. Divide the notebook into several sections, titled as follows:
   A. Writing
   B. Alternative coverage
   C. Photography
   D. Design
   Note: You can make as many more of these dividers as you see fit.

3. Start gathering information to fill in the alternative coverage section. Find a wide variety of elements in each of the categories. Make sure you stretch your barriers; look in publications that you wouldn't normally read. Find elements that catch your eye. The more you have, the better.

4. This notebook will serve two purposes:
   A. It will solidify your understanding of the terms and concepts you've learned in this book.
   B. It will give you a place to go when you're stumped for ideas. Keep in mind that you should never use someone else's work for your own purposes (that would be illegal); the idea file's purpose is to give you a starting point, a place to go for inspiration. You might see something in the file, for example, and say, "I like this idea. I think I can borrow some of the concepts from this piece and enhance them to meet the more specific needs of my readers."

Packaging

Putting the Pieces Together

You're almost there. You've got all the tools—the stories, the alternative coverage, everything. Now it's time to put it all together into cohesive, coherent pages. This section will show the nuts and bolts—the basics—of page layout and design. It will show you how to "package" information together into something that your readers are more likely to read.

But as with the other parts of this book, this section on packaging and design is only a start. The variations of these concepts are infinite. What you'll find here are guidelines to point you in the right direction. When you're done, it will be up to you to take those guidelines and run with them.

CHAPTER 11

Design 101

Page Creation

In the world of design, the key phrase is "points of entry." If you want to get readers to actually access the stories that you've written, you've got to get them to stop and then linger on those stories for a few moments because the longer they stay, the more chance there is that they'll read. And while they're lingering, you've got to entice them to want to read.

You've got to suck them in like a good movie preview and get them to want to find out more. You've got to determine what those readers need to know and present that information in a way that makes them want to read it. At every turn, you've got to give them something new and not repeat what you've said earlier.

As we discussed in Chapter 9, you've got to "meet the reads of your needers."

We've talked about visual readers so much at this point that you're probably saying the words over and over again in your sleep. If so, then good, you've just about got it. If not, then I'll talk about them one more time for emphasis because we can never forget about our readers. Without them, then your publications serve no purpose. Let's assume, then, that you've written some solid stories. You've got a bunch of great angles— stories for your readers to think about. After all, good stories are the lifeblood of your publication. So if stories are the lifeblood, then good design is the rest of the body. It's what readers see first; and the more interesting the design is, the more chance you have to get your visual readers to stop and take notice.

Points of entry are the key.

Readers are pretty predictable. At least they are after extensive study. There are several professional groups out there that charge a lot of money to study readers. They study older readers and younger readers. Women readers and men readers. Non-English speaking readers and multilingual readers. In other words, just about every demographic you can think of, somebody's studied that group's reading habits. As a result, we know, for the most part, how people like you — teenagers, kids in high school — actually access information. We know what you like and don't like. We know what makes you stop and take

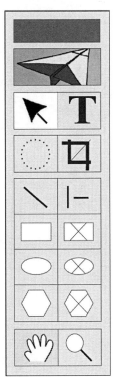

THE DESIGN

Below is the design template we'll be using for much of this chapter. It uses the student rights story from Chapter 8 as its centralized focus. The other stories on the page are not real and are positioned for illustrative purposes only. Is this a "perfect" design? Read the chapter and then decide for yourself.

TECHNOLOGY RULES

Nobody seems to know what's acceptable and what's not. Do you?
Page 3

All the news that's printed to fit

DAILY SNOOZE

RUMMAGE sales

Where your crap is someone else's treasure
Page 8

December 4, 20XX

School year to end early due to lack of interest

Low attendance leaves administrators no choice but to cancel learning until further notice

BY IMA FRAIDNOT
Global High School

Lorem ipsum dolor sit amet, consectetuer adipiscing elit, sed diam nonummy nibh euismod tincidunt ut laoreet dolore magna aliquam erat volutpat. Ut wisi enim ad minim veniam, quis nostrud exerci tation ullamcorper suscipit lobortis nisl ut aliquip ex ea commodo consequat. Duis autem vel eum iriure dolor in hendrerit in vulputate velit esse molestie consequat, vel illum dolore eu feugiat nulla facilisis at vero eros et accumsan et iusto odio dignissim qui blandit praesent luptatum zzril delenit augue duis dolore te feugait nulla facilisi. Lorem ipsum dolor sit amet, consectetuer adipiscing elit, sed diam nonummy nibh euismod tincidunt ut laoreet dolore magna aliquam erat volutpat. Ut wisi enim ad minim veniam, quis nostrud exerci tation ullamcorper suscipit lobortis nisl ut aliquip ex ea commodo consequat.

Duis autem vel eum iriure dolor in hendrerit in vulputate velit esse molestie consequat, vel illum dolore eu feugiat nulla facilisis at vero eros et accumsan et iusto odio dignissim qui blandit praesent luptatum zzril delenit augue duis dolore te feugait nulla facilisi. Nam liber tempor cum soluta nobis eleifend option congue nihil imperdiet doming id quod mazim placerat facer possim assum.

NOT THE FIRST TIME

Lorem ipsum dolor sit amet, consectetuer adipiscing elit, sed diam nonummy nibh euismod tincidunt ut laoreet dolore magna erat volutpat. Ut wisi enim ad minim veniam, quis nostrud exerci tation ullamcorper suscipit lobortis nisl ut aliquip ex ea commodo consequat. Duis autem vel eum iriure dolor in hendrerit in vulputate velit esse molestie consequat, vel illum dolore eu feugiat nulla facilisis at vero eros et accumsan et iusto odio dignissim qui blandit praesent luptatum zzril delenit augue duis dolore te feugait nulla facilisi. Lorem ipsum dolor sit amet, consectetuer adipiscing elit, sed diam nonummy nibh euismod tincidunt ut laoreet dolore magna aliquam erat volutpat.

Ut wisi enim ad minim veniam, quis nostrud exerci tation

SEE QUITTERS ON PAGE 3

Splitting *legal* Hairs

BY SARAH HUGHES
Carmel (IN) High School

Student's 'disruptive' hair addresses free speech rights

Last year junior Alex Liederbach, tired of his long, shaggy haircut, decided to do something to stand out from the rest of the crowd. On April 19, he shaved both sides of his head, creating a Mohawk with Elmer's blue gel glue. The spike averaged 10 to 12 inches long.

Liederbach's hairstyle attracted much attention during the school week of April 21. "Most of my friends thought it was cool," Liederbach said. "Most people wanted to know how I spiked it up and why I did it. I didn't get many negative reactions (from students). Most of my teachers just kind of laughed at it. My gym teacher, he was the one who sent me down to the dean in the first place, said I was distract-ing him. He was the only teacher who had any problems with it."

Protected by the First Amendment, every U.S. citizen is guaranteed his or her right to free expression. The 1969 U.S. Supreme Court ruling *Tinker v. Des Moines Independent Community School District* states. "It can hardly be argued that either students or teachers shed their constitutional right to freedom of speech or expression at the schoolhouse gate."

David Day, an attorney at the Church, Church, Hittle & Antrim law firm, has represented the Carmel Clay school district for more than 10 years. He said, "The courts have said that students don't lose rights

SEE HAIR ON PAGE 3

Hair Raising: According to junior Alex Liederbach, physical education teacher, Liederbach's spikes, which averaged 10 to 12 inches in length were a "disruption" in class. The U.S. Supreme Court defined students' free speech and expression rights in the landmark 1969 case *Tinker v. Des Moines*, stating that students are allowed to express themselves as long as that speech is not disruptive to the learning environment.

STUDENT RIGHTS 101

Court cases have peppered history regarding what First Amendment rights students do (or do not) have (U.S. Supreme Court cases in bold)

Year	Case	Decision
1969	*Tinker v. Des Moines Independent Community School District*	Students may express themselves as long as speech isn't "disruptive" to learning environment
1989	*Hazelwood School District v. Kuhlmeier*	Schools can censor the content of "school-sponsored" student publications
1995	*Kincaid v. Gibson*	A college in Kentucky violated a student yearbook editor's rights when it censored her publication.
2002	*Mahan-Iey v. Aldrich*	A school district in Michigan violated a public high school student's First Amendment rights when it suspended him for his speech on an off-campus private Web site.
2003	*Dimedi v. Wooster (OH) City School District Board of Education*	The courts upheld a school board's decision to censor the student newspaper because the information within was potentially defamatory in nature.

*Student Press Law Center/***Source**

Lunch ladies urge students to pack own meals

School employees can't keep up with demand for tater tots, chipped beef, slaw

BY URI NORMOUS
Global High School

Lorem ipsum dolor sit amet, consectetuer adipiscing elit, sed diam nonummy nibh euismod tincidunt ut laoreet dolore magna aliquam erat volutpat. Ut wisi enim ad minim veniam, quis nostrud exerci tation ullamcorper suscipit lobortis nisl ut aliquip ex ea commodo consequat. Duis autem vel eum iriure dolor in hendrerit in vulputate velit esse molestie consequat, vel illum dolore eu feugiat nulla facilisis at vero eros et accumsan et iusto odio dignissim qui blandit praesent luptatum zzril delenit augue duis dolore te feugait nulla

facilisi. Lorem ipsum dolor sit amet, consectetuer adipiscing elit, sed diam nonummy nibh euismod tincidunt ut laoreet dolore magna aliquam erat volutpat. Ut wisi enim ad minim veniam, quis nostrud exerci tation ullamcorper suscipit lobortis nisl ut aliquip ex ea commodo consequat.

Duis autem vel eum iriure dolor in hendrerit in vulputate velit esse molestie consequat, vel illum dolore eu feugiat nulla facilisis at vero eros et accumsan et iusto odio dignissim qui blandit praesent luptatum zzril delenit augue duis dolore te feugait nulla facilisi. Nam liber tempor cum soluta nobis eleifend option congue nihil imperdiet doming id quod mazim placerat facer

We can't take much more, Cap'n: Buried in a sea of breakfast cereal, cafeteria workers Alobie Normal and Darlene Clementine raise white flags to indicate their location. "These kids," Normal said. "They want too much. I am but only one person."

SUPPLY AND DEMAND

The daily usage at the most popular dishes from the cafeteria

Cole slaw	4,200 pounds
Tater tots	75,000 tots
Chipped beef	1,400 pounds

"We can't take much more of this. We're drowning in the fruit of our success. Literally."
- cafeteria manager Ellena Dover

notice and what makes you want to just turn the page.

And guess what the research shows about you and your peers' reading habits? You guessed it — you're visual people. As a result, the publications that you read — including your school publications — should be visual, too.

But you can't just expect haphazardly to throw a bunch of items — photos, alternative coverage, stories — on the page and expect readers to access them. They're visual people, but their not mind-readers. Not only do you have to make the stories visual, you also have to organize the bits of information in a coherent form that makes accessing that information easier. Design doesn't just happen. You've got to plan good design with the needs of your readers (and the reads of your needers) in mind.

This is where points of entry and, ultimately, page design come into play. **Every page that you design should have several points of entry — places where your readers actually enter your story and access information.** Anything can be a potential point of entry — a photo, a headline, a piece of alternative coverage, a lead — and in many ways we can predict with some success which point readers will go to first and second and so on, remembering, of course, that the ultimate goal is to get those readers to actually read the story itself, which is often, unfortunately, the final point of entry. And, to be honest, many readers will never read those stories you've written, no matter how hard you've agonized over them.

But the information in that story is still important, and, even if your readers don't actually read the story, they should still, as they say, "be able to discuss the stories intelligently at the dinner table" even if all they've read are the many other visual pieces of information on the page besides the stories. Think of these points of entry as layers, and as you peel off each layer, you need to reveal new and different (although relevant) information.

Chapter 10 discussed alternative coverage and all of its forms. This chapter will show you how to organize that alternative coverage — along with photos, stories, headlines, etc. — into coherent, visual, readable pages.

DESIGN TERMINOLOGY

Seen as a whole, all of the elements — the article, the photos, the alternative coverage — work together to tell the story for readers. But what are all of those things? The diagram below shows you the vocabulary you'll need to talk about design like a pro.

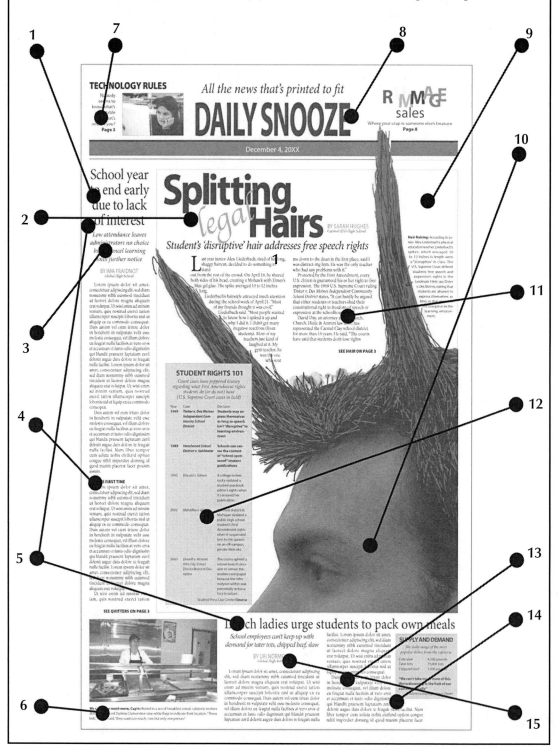

1. **Headline**—Incorporates both a subject and a verb. Present tense. Summarizes the content of the story it covers. Summary decks (see below) are optional to use with headlines.

2. **Title**—Generally missing either a subject or a verb, titles try to grab readers' attention with catchy plays-on-words but often don't tell much about the story underneath. Designers *must* use a summary deck (see below) with a title.

3. **Summary deck**—Used underneath a title or headline, it provides additional information for readers.

4. **Subhead**—Sort of like a title within a story, a subhead breaks up large chunks of gray text.

5. **Hierarchy**—To signify importance of stories, put larger headlines higher on your page. They should get smaller as readers descend the page.

6. **Cutline**—Also called a caption, good cutlines are the most widely read copy in any publication and should contain at least two sentences (see Page 146, "Writing Cutlines That Cut It").

7. **Teasers**—Sort of like "windows" to the content inside your paper.

8. **Nameplate**—Also called a flag, it's the logo of your publication.

9. **White space**—Simply, space on a page with nothing in it. Good white space should "escape" off the page. "Trapped" white space has no escape.

10. **CVI**—Center of Visual Impact. The largest element on your page. A good rule is that the CVI should be 2.5 times bigger than other elements on the page.

11. **Ragged text**—Like this block of text where one side of the text is left uneven. Creates a more casual look, which makes it a good technique for feature pages.

12. **Alternative coverage**—A visual way of telling stories. See Chapters 9 and 10 for more information.

13. **Justified text**—Like this block of text where each line stretches from one side of a column to the next creating smooth lines. Creates a more formal "look" to a story, which makes it great for news pages.

14. **Text wrap**—When text flows around other elements on a page.

15. **Byline**—The name of the person who wrote the story.

OTHER DESIGN TERMS

Folio—A line at the top of an inside page that tells readers vital information like the issue date, page number and section.

Photo credit—A byline for a picture.

Refer—A box inside a story indicating that other relevant stories can be found inside the publication.

Jumpline—Used when a story is too long to fit on one page. The first part is at the end of the first page indicating where the story "jumps" to. The second part is at the beginning of the second page indicating where the story "jumped" from.

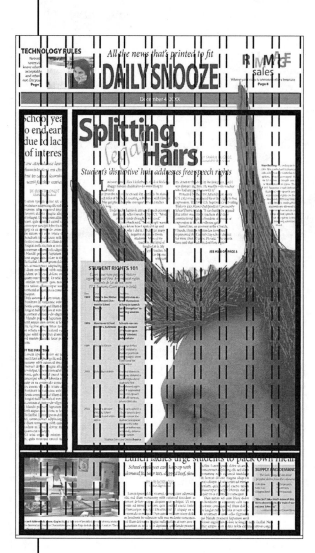

PLACEMENT

Good design doesn't just happen. There's an underlying framework to it all. Here's how it works.

THE GRID SYSTEM

Most of today's print publications are divided into equally spaced, vertical columns. In some cases, designers even go so far as to divide their pages horizontally as well (hence, a grid system).

The dotted lines at the left, illustrate how this page has utilized an 11-column format. This larger number allows for more design options. Notice, for example, how the body text in the "School year to end early" story fills two columns while the body text in the "Cafeteria workers" story fills up three columns. In that latter story as well, you can see how the designer was able to use the columns to create a text wrap (see previous page) to marry the alternative coverage with the rest of the story.

You can really use as many columns or grids as you want on a page. Just know that more grids, while they do create more options, can create more confusion for the novice designer.

RECTANGULAR PACKAGING

The dark solid lines included on this page try to get you to notice how all of the elements for each story on this page — the photos, alternative coverage, display text, stories, etc.—create rectangles. This design technique is called packaging.

Using that term — packaging — think of each story you write as a present. You have a rectangular box in which to fit everything. And then those individual boxes that contain all the parts of each story — the packages— need to fit together with other packages to make an entire page.

This technique wasn't always the standard in journalism. See the graphic on the next page to understand the evolution to modular design.

DESIGN THROUGH TIME

*Newspapers have gone through several design evolutions
since the beginning. Here's a brief rundown.*

Gray Suit Times

TRADITIONAL "GRAY SUIT"

Think *Wall Street Journal*. Lots of columns, lots of text. Not very
readable for more visual audiences.

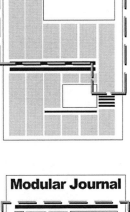

MODERN/"L-SHAPED"

Fewer columns. More photos. Stories simply extended into the
next story, creating interesting "dog-legs."

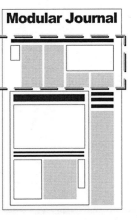

MODULAR/RECTANGLES

Everything fits into a geometrical package. Most of today's
papers fall into this category.

The Way We Read

The point of good design is to get readers to stop and then linger on your page. The longer readers stay on a page, the more likely that they will actually read your stories. See the explanation of this pattern on the next page.

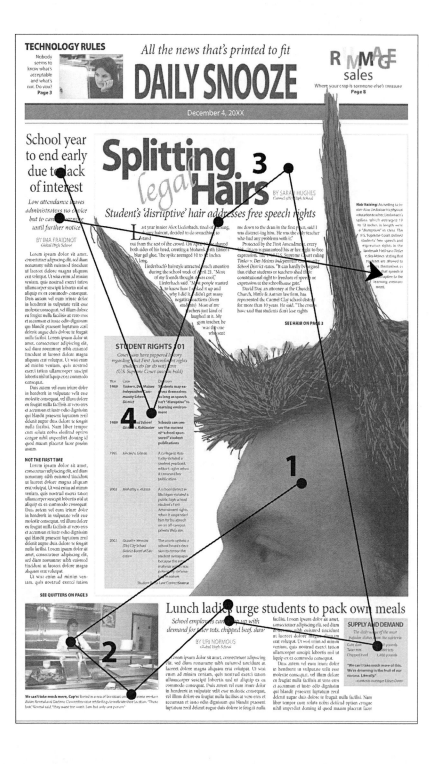

1. **THE DOMINANT IMAGE**
   It starts here. Make sure your dominant (or CVI) is big enough to stop readers as they flip through the pages.

2. **PHOTOS AND CUTLINES**
   Good photos are worth 1,000 words, but enhancing them with a few more (in a well written cutline) can do wonders to enhance the point of your story.

3. **HEADLINES, TITLES AND SUMMARY DECKS**
   Say something here that's worthwhile. Continue to detail the focus of your story to intrigue readers to want to read it.

4. **ALTERNATIVE COVERAGE**
   Take that relevant data and make it visual, and then package it in the context of the rest of the design to enhance (and not repeat) the content of the story.

THE Z PATTERN

A more traditional style of design

Purists prefer this design pattern. But notice that, like the larger design, the Z pattern ensures that readers cross as many stories as possible. The more stories readers cross, the more likely it is for them to read.

Details, Details, Details

Just like with writing, design has its share of minutiae to work with. Below is the briefest of descriptions of some of the major details that you'll deal with. And like with writing, it's this attention to detail that turns something good into something great.

AN ISSUE OF SPACE

Don't cram every square inch of your page with information. Too much info can actually turn off your visual readers. Here's what you need to know.

White space

Literally, space with nothing in it. Use white space to draw readers' eyes to what you want them to see. Like this:

Made you look.

Try not to "trap" white space. It should always have an "escape" off of the page (see "Design Pitfalls" on the next page).

Picas (pronounced **pie'** *cahs*)

The general unit of measurement in journalism. Six picas = 1 inch. In general, keep one pica of space around all elements on your page.

| pica | pica | pica | pica | pica | pica |
one inch

Also, 12 points = 1 pica. So when you use 12-point type, you use type that is 1 pica tall from ascender to descender (see "Types of Type" below). Like this: 12-point type pica

---

TYPES OF TYPE

You can literally spend years studying typography.
Here's what you need to know in about a minute.

Serif—Fonts that have little "feet" attached to them.

Sans serif—Like the title of this graphic, text that has no "feet."

Serifs

Ascender

Boom, baby

X-height

Baseline   **Descender**

Rules of thumb:

A "family" of fonts includes all of its different variations—bold, italics, etc.

Don't use more than two different font families (generally one serif and one sans serif) when you design. This leads to consistency of your publication.

DESIGN PITFALLS
Avoid these potential problems with design.

Widow—A lone bit of text hanging below a paragraph.

Orphan—A lone bit of text hanging at the top of a column.

Trapped white space—White space that escapes off the page = good. White space that doesn't = bad.

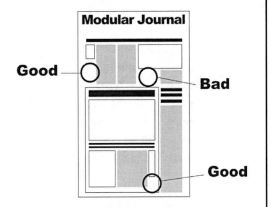

Tombstone—The result when two headlines from two different stories butt up against each other.

Tombstone

es cheese Students revo

Photography's Role in the Design Process

Let's face it, photos are the first thing visual readers look at when they see a page.

Subsequently, cutlines (or captions)—the text that accompanies photos—are the most widely read copy in any publication. Here's how to get them right.

THE SEVEN C'S OF PHOTOJOURNALISM
Keep these guidelines in mind when planning for and shooting photos to enhance your stories.

Composition—How the photo is put together. See the graphic on page 147 ("Photo Composition Guidelines") for more explanation.

Candid—The opposite of "posed." Take pictures of people doing whatever they do that makes them newsworthy.

Clarity—Two definitions: A) Physical clarity of the photo. Is the photo free of scratches and "grain?" B) Clarity of message. Is the photo a good storytelling picture?

Contrast—Like clarity, two definitions: A) Physical contrast of blacks and whites (or color). B) Contrast in message. Readers are drawn to differences—in age, gender, etc.

Cropping—Most pictures aren't perfect right off the camera. A photographer must do some trimming to allow the photo to fit the design and to draw attention to the central image.

Color—Self-explanatory, but remember that some photos look better in black and white.

Cutline—Some call them captions. It's the text that accompanies a photo. See the graphic on the next page for more information.

WRITING CUTLINES THAT CUT IT

More than a few great photos have been ruined by bad cutlines.
Here's how to write them correctly.

Cutlines should:

1. Be at least two sentences long.
2. Have the first sentence written in present tense, describing what's going on in the photo.
3. Have the second sentence (and any subsequent sentences) written in past tense, giving readers additional information that will enhance the point of the accompanying story.
4. Not start with a name, unless the person in the photo is a prominent figure (like the president of the United States or Spongebob Squarepants).

Cutlines should not:

1. Overuse the "-ing" phrase at the beginning of the first sentence (i.e. "Diving for the ball," or "Eating until her intestines explode").
2. State the obvious.
3. Restate information already included in the story or in other pieces of alternative coverage.

Bad Example

Journalism teacher Jim Streisel makes a point in class. Streisel often makes points in class.

Good Example

A few hours before the final deadline of the December issue, *HiLite* newspaper adviser Jim Streisel gives staff members a few suggestions for the design of front-page story. Streisel said that teaching newspaper provides fantastic real-world experiences for his students, experiences they may not get in other more traditional classrooms. "These kids are making an actual product," he said. "They have a real audience, real readers, and that gives them more of a sense of ownership and responsibility in the quality of the product. You just can't teach that in every classroom." *Photo by John Shi, Carmel (IN) H.S.*

E.D.F.A.T.

Remember this acronym when planning for and shooting photos.

Establishing—Take a few shots that set the scene. Show lots of people in one frame.

Detail—Zoom in for close-ups that show emotion and reaction. Show only one or two people per frame.

Framing—Be aware of your surroundings and how they help to draw attention to your center of interest.

Angle—Try to see the world in a way that readers aren't used to seeing it. Take a shot from up high or down low. Try different approaches than just straight forward ones.

Time—Spend enough time at an event to get the whole story. Don't expect to shoot a basketball game in the first few minutes of the first quarter.

The 411 on Photo Composition

Good photos don't just happen. Photojournalists spend a lot of time preparing for good storytelling shots. See how these guidelines of composition—the way a photo is set up—lead to solid pictures.

PHOTO COMPOSITION GUIDELINES

Why do professional photos often look better than the ones you took on your vacation?
These guidelines for the "C" of composition ("The Seven C's of Photojournalism" on Page 145) might help.

Simplicity—Keep backgrounds uncluttered.

Framing—Be aware of how elements in your viewfinder add depth to your photo.

Lines—See how elements connect through real and implied lines. Lines should lead to what you want viewers to see.

Rule of thirds—Keep the action of the photo at one of the intersections of lines in the diagram.

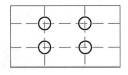

Balance—Two types: Asymmetrical, which is more dynamic, and symmetrical, which is more static.

Mergers—There are three types to avoid.

Complete—objects seem to grow out of people's heads.

Border—people's hands and feet get cut off at the edges of the photo.

Near—Colors blend together too closely.

Good Photo Dissected

Look at this photo by John Shi (Carmel [IN] H.S.) and then look at how it meets the guidelines of good photo composition.

Simplicity
The background is uncluttered. In fact, the photographer has purposely blurred the background so that it does not detract from the subject.

Asymmetrical balance
The subject of the photo is on the left, yet the photo is balanced because the laughing girl's eyes draw viewers back. Also, the subject has some space to look into.

Framing
The slightly out-of-focus students do a wonderful job of framing the subject of this photo, giving it the illusion of depth.

Lines
Notice the "lines" that lead from both the main subject's and the girl's eyes.

Rule of thirds
What we're supposed to focus on – the subject's face – is located near the top left third of the picture. The laughing girl is toward the bottom right (see the grid).

Mergers
There are a couple of border mergers (the top of the main subject's head, the girl's chin), but they seem to still work here.

WHAT A CATCH: As Carmel downs the ball inside Warren Central's 15-yard line, seniors (from left) Andy Glaser, Nick Willy, David Hanger and Kevin Loughery cheer on their team during the state championship game. The team went on to score a few plays later to tie the game at 7–7 against the three-time defending state champions. Carmel lost 35–14. *Photo / Todd Mewhinney, Carmel (IN) H.S.*

Give Photo Evaluation a Try

Evaluate the photo above in terms of the seven C's of photojournalism and the six elements of photo composition. Remember, of course, that these are guidelines, and photos may not meet all of the criteria.

The Seven C's

1. Is this photo *candid* or posed?
2. Is the photo physically *clear*? Is the message of the photo clear?
3. Is there enough physical *contrast* in tone in this photo? Is there a contrasting message?
4. Has this photo been *cropped* well? Could it have been cropped another way? How so?
5. Is this photo better in black and white, or would it have been better in *color*? Why?

6. Does the *cutline* follow the guidelines? Is it informative? As a reader, what else do you need to know?
7. *Composition* (see below).

Photo Composition

1. Is the background *simple* and uncluttered? How did the photographer manage to keep it that way?
2. Does the photo utilize *framing*? How so?
3. Are there any *lines* (either real or implied)? What direction do they lead, if any?
4. Does this photo use the *rule of thirds*? Where?
5. What kind of *balance* does this photo use? Is it balanced? How do you know?
6. Are there any *mergers* in this photo? If so, what kind(s)?

The Dummy

Even the best designers do some sketches before they sit down at the computer. Quick thumbnail sketches and more formal dummy sheets (shown here) can help designers plan and work out glitches quickly to make the final design process more painless.

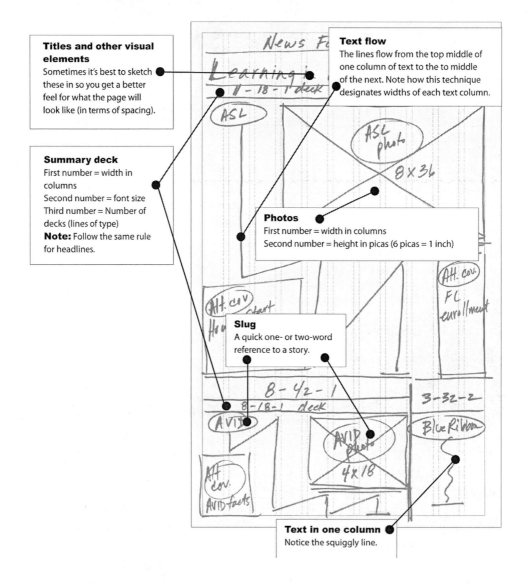

Titles and other visual elements
Sometimes it's best to sketch these in so you get a better feel for what the page will look like (in terms of spacing).

Text flow
The lines flow from the top middle of one column of text to the to middle of the next. Note how this technique designates widths of each text column.

Summary deck
First number = width in columns
Second number = font size
Third number = Number of decks (lines of type)
Note: Follow the same rule for headlines.

Photos
First number = width in columns
Second number = height in picas (6 picas = 1 inch)

Slug
A quick one- or two-word reference to a story.

Text in one column
Notice the squiggly line.

THE FINISHED PRODUCT FROM THE DUMMY AT LEFT

PAGE 2 • THURSDAY, SEPTEMBER 30, 2004 • NEWS

HiLite

Learning in Silence

School introduces American Sign Language course, enrollment exceeds that of many other world language classes

By Stephanie Nowell
snowell@hilite.org

Sophomore Emma Hensong's seventh period class differs from a typical world language class. This class remains silent.

American Sign Language (ASL) is in its first year at this school.

"ASL is a lot of fun. It's really different, but I love learning a whole new way to communicate with others," Hensong said.

Assistant Principal Tim Smith said teachers thought about offering ASL two years ago.

ASL went to the school board twice. "The first time around, there were still some questions on who was going to be involved with it and how it was going to be taught," Smith said.

However, the board approved it for this school year. "A lot of first-year programs take a year or two to get going and get developed, but obviously we had no problems filling (ASL) and had to turn kids away," Smith said.

Students choose to take ASL for several different reasons. "I took sign language because I already knew some sign language, and I wanted to know more. It also sounded like a really fun way to get my foreign language credits," Hensong said.

ASL teacher Bryan Bush said many students take the class because they want to converse with deaf friends and family members, and some even want to enter the field of speech pathology.

There are also students who take ASL because traditional world languages seem difficult. "There are the students who didn't do as well in Spanish or French, and they took the class because they thought, 'Well, maybe this will be easier for me,'" Bush said.

According to Hensong, ASL is not too difficult. "You can get a good grade as long as you work hard and try your best," she said.

Although Hensong knew some sign language upon the start of the class, students represent all skill levels. Some students have had no previous experience with sign language, while others have already been exposed to ASL.

A main difference between ASL and other languages stands that the classroom is generally a lot quieter. "We're using our bodies instead of our voices to communicate. It's a three-dimensional language," Bush said.

"A lot of learning sign language is getting the students to tap into their own body language," Bush said.

Bush plans to try and add ASL II for next year. He has surveyed the students to determine interest.

Putting their signing skills into practice, sophomore Jennifer McNamara (left) and sophomore Emma Hensong act out a real-world situation of asking each other if they are deaf. This year marks the school's first time offering American Sign Language (ASL), and 168 students fill its six classes. Students who pursue sign language can later become interpreters, as several colleges offer sign language interpretation as a possible minor.

Courtesy Amy Bishop / photo

Hensong said she would take ASL II because this is her only world language. Students need two years of the same language to graduate. "If (ASL II) wasn't offered, then I would have to take two years of another language my junior and senior year. It would mean a lot of students would have to take a second language, and this course wouldn't really count towards foreign language credits to graduate," Hensong said.

To quiz his students, Bush signs a word, and the students write the English equivalent. Later in the year, he will have dialogues with them where the student will sign.

Bush uses various games to teach his students. One is called "Who's the leader?" The students stand in a circle with one person in the middle. One person is a leader and performs various actions. The rest of the group follows, and the center person tries to determine who leads.

This game helps to develop peripheral vision, which is very important in sign language. In ASL, eye contact means eye-to-eye not eye-to-sign, so in order to maintain eye contact and converse, peripheral vision must be very strong. The person in the center must see as much of the circle as possible at the same time.

"I like playing different games in the class because it is a different way of learning, and it makes the class more fun," Hensong said.

According to Bush, there are many benefits to taking ASL. "I think it helps them raise their own self-awareness and to limit their inhibitions about how they express themselves non-verbally. It enables them to better read body language from other people, even if it's not formal ASL."

Bush also said, "After this class, I hope every student will re-evaluate the term disability." He said he wants students to look at individuals with limited skills as fully capable humans beings as long as certain resources are in place to help them.

Hensong said, "ASL helps me realize what's going on around me. I notice body language and eye contact a lot more now than even just a month ago."

A few things taught in the class include introductions, giving directions and describing the weekend. Students also discuss cochlear implants and attend events at the Indiana School for the Deaf.

"I'm really looking forward to going to sporting events at the Indiana School for the Deaf. ASL is exposing me to a whole new culture I would've otherwise been blind to," Hensong said.

During class, Bush said that he tries to rely on signing as much as possible and speaking sparingly. He said, "My goal is to speak less and less as the students acquire more vocabulary and grammar structure. Whenever I can rely on signing or gestures, I try to rely on that because I think it's a more effective way to get the students to focus in on body language."

"I would really encourage students to sign up for ASL if they have an open class period next year," Hensong said. "Even if you never use ASL outside of the classroom, the new skills you take away will be used for the rest of your life."

How to Start a Class

1. The person wanting to start the class comes up with an outline describing who can be in the class, the curriculum and who it benefits.

2. The principal and an assistant principal then approve the outline and send it to the curriculum advisory committee.

3. If the committee okays the proposal, it then goes to the school board.

4. The board then has to approve the class for it to begin.

Source: Principal Tim Smith / source

2004-05 Foreign Language Enrollment	
French I:	65
Spanish I:	436
Latin I:	75
German I:	47
Japanese I:	45
ASL:	168

Because more than 200 students signed up to take ASL, over 32 students were cut to fit the class size.

Source: ASL Teacher Bryan Bush / source

AVID maximizes students' potentials

School offers new elective with hopes to teach students skills necessary for success

By Marc Fishman
mfishman@hilite.org

Freshman Sean Gleason said he feels more motivated about his schoolwork than ever before. He pays closer attention to the notes he takes and is generally a better student.

These are the first results, so far, of Achievement Via Individual Determination (AVID), a new elective course offered at CHS that Gleason and other freshmen currently take.

The decision to bring AVID into CHS started when the 10 to 12 member committee, a team formed to look at curriculum needs for sophomores through seniors when the Freshman building opens next year, looked at certain curriculum needs. Nancy Campbell, AVID teacher and co-coordinator, said that the committee wanted to reach the students who were falling through the cracks with their schoolwork. After observations and evaluations of the program, the committee found AVID to be the best class for those specific students.

Counselor Corinne Johnson acts as the other AVID co-coordinator. She said that the class should help students maximize their potential to get better grades. "(AVID) is for students in the middle. They have the ability to be successful, but have not been," Johnson said.

In the actual class, students learn different study skills. They learn methods of taking notes, such as the Cornell system that requires students to write questions about their notes so that they thoroughly understand them. They also learn methods to keep their schoolwork organized in binders.

Tutorial sessions stand as another benefit of AVID. Campbell says tutorial sessions usually consist of five to six students who have similar questions in a specific subject. An adult then helps them solve their problems as a group.

For Gleason, AVID is already working. "The reason that my grades were down before was because I could never find my papers," Gleason said.

Diagnostic teacher Linda Gleason said that the class helps her son. She said that AVID teaches Sean to keep his schoolwork all together and take his notes seriously.

Although AVID helps people become better students, it is not strictly focused on academics. According to Campbell, the class benefits students socially also. "The skills they learn in this class are hopefully something that they will want to take on in their personal life," Campbell said. "It's not just for academics."

AVID started in California, but it is steadily making its way to schools all over the country. Carmel Clay is the fourth school district in Indiana to add AVID to their curriculum. Other school districts include Washington Township and Lawrence Township.

As the teacher, Campbell said that the students have mostly reacted in a positive way to the course. "I feel kids realize (these skills) are a need," Campbell said. "It's a different way of doing things, so there can be a bit of resistance. But (the students) have been enthused."

Sean said, "Before, I just wasn't motivated to come to school. Having Mrs. Campbell breathing down my neck with my notes has actually been pretty good."

Learn About AVID

The AVID curriculum focuses on writing, inquiry, collaboration and reading.

In addition to regular training for the class, teachers and administrators attend AVID's summer institutes to learn AVID teaching techniques.

Over 2000 middle and high schools across 30 states and 16 countries use AVID.

Since 1990, more than 30,000 AVID students have graduated from high school and gone on to college.

www.avidonline.org / source

Looking through his binder, freshman Sean Gleason finds himself more organized through taking AVID. Organization, along with note-taking, marks a skill that the class focuses on.

Samuel Poole / photo

CHS named national Blue Ribbon school

By Stephanie Nowell
snowell@hilite.org

At the close of afternoon announcements, hundreds of students marched through the halls cheering and clapping during their fourth period class.

This school received the national "No Child Left Behind - Blue Ribbon Schools" award. The award honors schools that either improve drastically or contain students who perform at superior levels, according to the National Department of Education web site.

This school is one of only two Indiana public high schools receiving this award. The other school is Zionsville Community High School. A total of 14 schools in Indiana earned this award.

Principal John Williams said, "This award is a national recognition of the work that our staff and students do everyday. What this award does is to validate what we do, and that is to make CHS a great place to be. I also think that it should make us very grateful for what we have. Carmel is a unique place, we have resources that other schools only dream of. It is nice to know that we are taking advantage of our opportunities."

In response to this award, students paraded through the halls in celebration. One such march was sophomore Jennifer McNamara's English teacher Kristi LeVeque released McNamara's class for a break. They then joined other classes in walking through the school, picking up more students as they progressed.

The walk ended in the varsity gym. Williams talked to the students, and, after allowing them all one final cheer, he gave them seven minutes to return to their classes.

Williams said, "I was torn between being proud and excited about what I felt was a genuine reaction to students who are proud of their school and being concerned that we had kids out of class, some without permission. I wanted to acknowledge their pride and enthusiasm. At the same time, I wanted them back in class where they were supposed to be."

McNamara agreed with the idea of the celebratory walk. She said, "I'm just happy to be in Carmel. It's a big honor to know that all our hard work paid off. It's great to be in a school where you can get out of class and march around the school because of an award we got. We have a terrific drama department, marching band, sports teams and overall student body."

Don't Be a Dummy, Make One

Go ahead and photocopy the blank dummy sheet below to practice your dum-mying skills. Or, better yet, make a blank dummy sheet that fits the needs of your own publication.

STUDY GUIDE

Terms and Concepts

Angle—When referring to a photo, it's the perspective that the photographer used to take the shot (high, low, etc.).

Balance—Photo composition and design term. Two types: asymmetrical, where large images on one side balance smaller images on the other, and symmetrical, where images on both sides are of equal size.

Byline—The name of a person who wrote a story.

Candid—Photos of people doing whatever makes them newsworthy. The opposite of posed.

Clarity—Refers to a photo's physical clarity (free of grain, in focus) and clarity of message.

Composition—How a photo or page is put together.

Contrast—Refers to a photo's physical contrast (whites and blacks) and the contrast in content (age, size, etc.).

Cropping—Trimming of a photo to fit design needs and to draw attention to the subject.

Cutline—Also called a caption, a description that accompanies a photograph.

CVI—Center of visual impact. It is the largest element on a page.

Detail shot—A close-up photo.

Dummy sheet—A rough sketch of the elements on a page that designers use before they move to the computer.

Establishing shot—A photo from a distance that sets the scene.

Folio—A line at the top of an inside page that tells readers vital information like issue date, page number and section.

Framing—Photo composition term. How elements in a photo surround the subject.

Headline—A short summary at the top of a story. Incorporates both a subject and a verb.

Hierarchy—Placing larger headlines higher on a page. Signifies importance of those stories.

Jumpline—Used when a story is too long to fit on one page. Tells readers where the story goes and, on the second page, tells where the story jumps from.

Justified text—Lines of type that are even on both sides.

Lines—Photo composition term. Elements create real and implied lines that draw readers to the subject of the picture.

Mergers—Photo composition term. Where elements in a photo blend together (near), with other objects (complete) or with the edge (border).

Modular design—A design system where everything fits into rectangles.

Nameplate—The logo of your publication. Also called the flag.

Orphan—A lone bit of text that appears at the top of a column.

Photo credit—A byline for a picture.

Points of entry—Places on a page where your readers actually enter your story and access information.

Ragged text—Lines of type that are uneven on one or both sides.

Refer—A box inside a story indicating other relevant stories that appear somewhere else in the publication.

Rule of thirds—Photo composition term. Keeping the action of the photo at one of the intersections of imaginary lines if you were to divide the photo both horizontally and vertically into three equal sections.

Sans serif—Fonts that have no feet (or serifs) attached to them.

Serif—Fonts that have feet (or serifs) attached to them.

Simplicity—Photo composition term. Keeping backgrounds uncluttered.

Subhead—Breaks up large chunks of gray text. Sort of a title in the middle of a story.

Summary deck—A smaller headline underneath either a headline or title. Gives readers additional information about the story.

Teaser—Information (usually above the fold of the paper) that entices readers to open the paper by giving a window to the content inside.

Text wrap—When text flows around other elements on a page.

Title—At the top of a story, it's generally missing either a subject or verb. May use a play on words to grab readers' attention.

Trapped white space—White space that does not escape off the page.

White space—Space on a page with nothing in it.

Widow—A lone bit of text hanging below a paragraph.

Continue Your Idea File

1. Use the notebook you started in Chapter 10.

2. Start gathering information to fill in the section labeled Design. Find as many good examples as you can. Make sure you stretch your barriers; look in publications that you wouldn't normally read. Find elements that catch your eye. The more you have, the better.

3. Challenge yourself on a few of the examples to see if you can identify the following:

   A. The names of the elements on each page.

   B. The column structure of the page(s).

Chapter 12

The Total Package

Combining Stories and Visuals

All this talk about writing stories, compiling alternative coverage and designing packages doesn't mean much if you can't see it in action. Up to this point, everything is merely theory.

Like reading excellent examples of narrative stories, this chapter will attempt to help you make sense of the concepts by seeing them in action on actual newspaper pages. Keep in mind that these examples are merely that — examples. They aren't perfect. In fact, some would argue that no design is ever perfect; it just meets deadline. Therefore, the pages you'll see in this chapter are critiqued in two categories "what works" and "what could be better." The concepts listed within those categories are meant to give more global direction in terms of design itself, and not just to critique the specifics on each page. For example, if you see a comment that discusses the page's use of a photo essay to tell a story, note how you might apply that same concept to a story or page that you are designing.

The pages in this chapter are also organized by category, showing some of the more common types of pages that you might see in a publication, from news pages to feature pages to opinion pages and other categories in between. But you may have different categories in your own publication. Or you may have a different format — a tabloid or a magazine, for example. No matter. Some design concepts are universal, so you'll be able to take the suggestions herein and apply them directly, while others are more specific to the type of publication you're working with. If this is your case, by all means go out and find professional examples of the type of publication you're dealing with. Publications, after all, come in all different shapes, sizes and colors. Find the ones that best meet your needs and, as you should use the pages that follow, use those pages to give you even more ideas about how to organize information for your readers.

In the end, though, practice makes perfect. Once you feel comfortable with these design and packaging concepts, go out and do some designs on your own. And like the pages you see here, critique them in terms of what works and what could be better.

Good luck.

Front Page

What Works

1. The lengthy caption/cutline is a nice touch. The most widely read types of copy in any publication are cutlines. Use this to your advantage to provide even more information.

2. The dominant image (or "CVI," for Center of Visual Impact) sits slightly above the natural fold of the paper. CVIs don't need to be completely above the fold, but at least part of them should show to entice readers to open the publication. Also, CVIs should enhance the story. This photo illustration shows the metaphoric "tug of war" between men's and women's sports.

3. The timeline helps to provide a more relevant, global angle to this story.

What Could Be Better

3. The timeline has dark text on a dark background and, therefore, makes it hard to read.

4. The "teaser" photos are too square. Square photos are static, while vertical and horizontal photos tend to appear more dynamic.

5. The top teaser photo faces off the page. Not all photos have a direction, but some do. See how the band photo leads readers into the story that it accompanies.

Front Page

What Works

1. The "Magnifying" graphic certainly enhances the point of the story.

2. The alternative coverage about spyware enhances the main story by providing relevant information that will help readers to better understand the content of the story.

3. The teaser photos here are more vertical and horizontal. See how those shapes lead to better visual interest.

What Could Be Better

4. The mugshot doesn't provide much information other than a face and a name. Ask yourself, could this space be better utilized by something else?

5. The photo for this story doesn't really enhance the point very well. The lengthy cutline is good (since cutlines are the most widely read copy in any publication), but the photo should be of people, not of a banner. Always remember that, to be news, a story must affect people. Make sure your photos show those people and how they're affected.

News

What Works

1. The dominant photo isn't bad. It shows two students actually doing what it is that makes them newsworthy — in this case, sign language.

2. The graphic here is relevant to the story it enhances. The point of the story is that ASL is fast becoming a popular class; the numbers here support that claim visually.

3. The designer has avoided a possible tombstone of headlines here using several techniques:

   A. Using a sans serif headline on the left and a serif one on the right.

   B. Allowing for slightly more white space at the end of the AVID headline.

   C. Using a one-deck headline and summary deck on the left and a two-deck headline with no summary deck on the right.

   D. Varying the sizes of the headlines to show hierarchy.

   E. Using a thin "rule line" to separate the articles.

What Could Be Better

4. The photo of the kid at the desk is square (static) and boring (also static). Can you think of other ways to take this photo that might be more storytelling and dynamic? Try different angles rather than just straightforward ones.

Learning in Silence

School introduces American Sign Language course, enrollment exceeds those of many other world language classes

By Stephanie Nowell
snowell@hilite.org

Sophomore Emma Hessong's seventh period class differs from a typical world language class. This class remains silent.

American Sign Language (ASL) is in its first year at this school.

"ASL is a lot of fun. It's really different, but I love learning a whole new way to communicate with others," Hessong said.

Assistant Principal Tim Smith said teachers thought about offering ASL two years ago.

ASL went to the school board twice. "The first time around, there were still some questions on who was going to be involved with it and how it was going to be taught," Smith said.

However, the board approved it for this school year. "A lot of first-year programs take a year or two to get going and get developed, but obviously we had no problems filling (ASL) and had to turn kids away," Smith said.

Students choose to take ASL for several different reasons. "I took sign language because I already knew some sign language, and I wanted to know more. It also sounded like a really fun way to get my foreign language credits," Hessong said.

ASL teacher Bryan Bush said many students take the class because they want to converse with deaf friends and family members, and some even want to enter the field of speech pathology.

There are also students who take ASL because traditional world languages seem difficult. "There are the students who didn't do as well in Spanish or French, and they took the class because they thought, 'Well, maybe this will be easier for me,'" Bush said.

According to Hessong, ASL is not too difficult. "You can get a good grade as long as you work hard and try your best," she said.

Although Hessong knew some sign language upon the start of the class, students represent all skill levels. Some students have had no previous experience with sign language, while others have already been exposed to ASL.

A main difference between ASL and other languages stands that the classroom is generally a lot quieter. "We're using our bodies instead of our voices to communicate. It's a three-dimensional language," Bush said.

"A lot of learning sign language is getting the students to tap into their own body language," Bush said.

Bush plans to try and add ASL II for next year. He has surveyed the students to determine interest.

Putting their signing skills into practice, sophomore Jennifer Eckhamm (left) and sophomore Emma Hessong try out a real-world situation of asking each other if they are deaf. This year marks the school's first time offering American Sign Language (ASL), and 168 students fill its six classes. Students who pursue sign language can later become interpreters, as several colleges offer sign language interpretation as a possible major.

Hessong said she would take ASL II because this is her only world language. Students need two years of the same language to graduate. "If (ASL II) wasn't offered, then I would have to take two years of another language my junior and senior year. It would mean a lot of students would have to take a second language, and this course wouldn't really count towards foreign language credits to graduate," Hessong said.

To quiz his students, Bush signs a word, and the students write the English equivalent. Later in the year, he will have dialogues with them where the student will sign.

Bush uses various games to teach his students. One is called "Who's the leader?" The students stand in a circle with one person in the middle. One person is a leader and performs various actions. The rest of the group follows, and the center person tries to determine who leads.

This game helps to develop peripheral vision, which is very important in sign language. In ASL, eye contact means eye-to-eye not eye-to-sign, so in order to maintain eye contact and converse, peripheral vision must be very strong. The person in the center must see as much of the circle as possible at the same time.

"I like playing different games in the class because it is a different way of learning, and it makes the class more fun," Hessong said.

According to Bush, there are many benefits to taking ASL. "I think it helps them raise their own self-awareness and to limit their inhibitions about how they express themselves non-verbally. It enables them to become a language from other people, even if it's not formal language," Bush also said. "After this class, I hope every student will re-evaluate the term disability." He said he wants students to look at individuals with limited skills as capable humans beings as long as certain resources are in place to help them.

Hessong said, "ASL helps me realize what's going on around me. I notice body language and notice it more now than even just a month ago."

A few things taught in the class include giving directions and describing the weekend. Students also discuss cochlear implants and attend events at the Indiana School for the Deaf.

"I'm really looking forward to going to sporting events at the Indiana School for the Deaf. ASL is exposing me to a whole new culture I would've otherwise been blind to," Hessong said.

During class, Bush said that he tries to rely on signing as much as possible and speaking sparingly. He said, "My goal is to speak less and less as the students acquire more vocabulary and grammar structure. Whenever I can rely on miming or gestures, I try to rely on that because I think it's a more effective way to get the students to focus on body language."

"I would really encourage students to sign up for ASL if they have an open class their first year," Hessong said. "Even if you never use it outside of the classroom, the new skills you take can be useful for the rest of your life."

How to Start a Class

1. The person wanting to start the class comes up with an outline describing who can be in the class, the curriculum and who it benefits.

2. The principal and an assistant principal then approve of the outline and send it to the curriculum advisory committee.

3. If the committee okays the proposal, it then goes to the school board.

4. The board then has to approve the class for it to begin.

Assistant Principal Tim Smith / source

2004-05 Foreign Language Enrollment

Language	Enrollment
French I:	65
Spanish I:	436
Latin I:	75
German I:	47
Japanese I:	45
ASL:	168

Because more than 200 students signed up to take ASL, over 32 students were cut to fit the class size.

Counselor Chris Wheeler
ASL teacher Bryan Bush / source

AVID maximizes students' potentials

School offers new elective with hopes to teach students skills necessary for success

By Marc Fishman
mfishman@hilite.org

Freshman Sean Gleason said he feels more motivated about his schoolwork than ever before. He pays closer attention to the notes he takes and is generally a better student.

These are the first results, so far, of Achievement Via Individual Determination (AVID), a new elective course offered at CHS that Gleason and other freshmen currently take.

The decision to bring AVID into CHS started when the 10 to 12 member committee formed to look at curricula for sophomores through seniors. In the freshman building last year, looked at certain specific needs. Nancy Campbell, AVID teacher and co-coordinator, said the committee wanted to help students who were "caught in the cracks with their schoolwork." After observations and evaluations of AVID's program, the committee found AVID to be the best class for those specific students.

Counselor Corinne Johnson acts as the other AVID co-coordinator. She said that the class should help students maximize their potential to get better grades. "AVID is for students in the middle. They have the ability to be successful, but have not been," Johnson said.

In the actual class, students learn different study skills. They learn methods of taking notes, such as the Cornell system that requires students to write questions about their notes so that they thoroughly understand them. They also learn methods to keep their schoolwork organized in binders.

Tutorial sessions stand as another benefit of AVID. Campbell says tutoring sessions usually consist of five to six students who have similar questions in a specific subject. An adult then helps them solve their problems as a group.

For Gleason, AVID is already working. "The reason that my grades were down before was because I could never find my papers," Gleason said.

Diagnostic teacher Linda Gleason said that the class helps her son. She said that AVID teaches Sean to keep his schoolwork all together and take his notes seriously.

Although AVID helps people become better students, it is not strictly focused on academics. According to Campbell, the class benefits students socially also. "The skills they learn in this class are hopefully something that they will want to take on in their personal life," Campbell said. "It's not just for academics."

AVID started in California, but it is steadily making its way to schools all over the country. Carmel Clay is the fourth school district in Indiana to add AVID to their curriculum. Other school districts include Washington Township and Lawrence Township.

As the teacher, Campbell said that the students have mostly reacted in a positive way to the course. "I feel kids realize (these skills) are a need," Campbell said. "It's a different way of doing things, so there can be a bit of resistance. But (the students) have been enthused."

Sean said, "Before, I just wasn't motivated to come to school. Having Mrs. Campbell breathing down my neck with my notes has actually been pretty good."

Looking through his binder, freshman Sean Gleason finds himself more organized through taking AVID. Organization, along with note-taking, marks a skill that the class focuses on.
Samuel Fowler / photo

Learn About AVID

The AVID curriculum focuses on writing, inquiry, collaboration and reading.

In addition to regular training for the class, teachers and administrators attend AVID's summer institutes to learn AVID teaching techniques.

Over 2000 middle and high schools across 30 states and 16 countries use AVID.

Since 1990, more than 30,000 AVID students have graduated from high school and gone on to college.

www.avidonline.org / source

CHS named national Blue Ribbon school

By Stephanie Nowell
snowell@hilite.org

At the close of afternoon announcements, hundreds of students marched through the halls cheering and clapping during their fourth period class.

This school received the national "No Child Left Behind - Blue Ribbon Schools" award. The award honors schools that either improve drastically or contain students who perform at superior levels, according to the National Department of Education web site.

This school is one of only two Indiana public high schools receiving this award. The other school in Zionsville Community High School. A total of 14 schools in Indiana earned this award.

Principal John Williams said, "This award is a national recognition of the work that our staff and students do everyday. What this award does is to validate what we do, and that is to make CHS a great place to be. I also think that it should make us very grateful for what we have. Carmel is a unique place; we have resources that other schools only dream of. It is nice to know that we are taking advantage of our opportunities."

In response to the award, students paraded through the halls in celebration. One such student was sophomore Jennifer McNamara. English teacher Kristi LeVeque released McNamara's class for a break. They then joined other classes in walking through the school, picking up more students as they progressed.

The walk ended in the varsity gym. Williams talked to the students, and, after allowing them all one final cheer, he gave them seven minutes to return to their classes.

Williams said, "I was torn between being proud and excited about what I felt was a genuine reaction to students who are proud of their school and being concerned that we had kids out of class, some without permission. I wanted to acknowledge their pride and enthusiasm. At the same time, I wanted them back in class where they were supposed to be."

McNamara agreed with the idea of the celebratory walk. She said, "I'm just happy to be in Carmel. It's a big honor to know that all our hard work paid off. It's great to be in a school where you can get out of class and march around the school because of an award we get. We have a terrific drama department, marching band, sports teams and overall student body."

News

What Works

1. Using this concept of "scatter coverage" is a great way to share a lot of factual information in a visual way. Note all of the different types of alternative coverage that this page employs. This technique wouldn't work for every page that you design, but it works well here.

2. This "buyer's guide" is a practical piece of alternative coverage that students can actually use — they can take it with them when they head down to the festivities to give them a map.

3. A photo essay is a nice way to tell recently old news. Because it has already occurred, we don't want provide readers with a written story, but the photos and cutlines can serve the same purpose while also providing a new look at something that has already passed, particularly if that event ties in with something ongoing, as it does here.

What Could Be Better

4. The timeline, at points, becomes a little difficult to follow, possibly because it covers two separate lines. However, the pieces of additional information that stem off of the timeline are a neat way to provide fun tidbits.

The Homecoming Guide: A Timeline of Events

1

Today: *Hawaiian Day*

Tomorrow: *Blue and Gold Day*

Distribution
HiLite — 30 Minutes — 10 to 10:30 a.m.

PENNY WAR ENDS
After opening for Tuesday and Wednesday, the Penny War will finish. Last year the sophomores won.

CONSTRUCTION FOR CHARITY
Each class will construct a playhouse. They will be auctioned off during the Homecoming game. The money goes to each class' charity.
4 to 6 p.m.

PEP RALLY *Pep Rally*
10 to 10:30 a.m.

PRINCIPAL SPEAKS
John Williams will address the crowd on issues of involvement and spirit.

DANCING
Charisma, the cheerleaders, and the Step team will perform their routines.

CHAMPIONS
The Legs King and Kiss Queen, elected by online voting, will be announced.

CLASS RIVALRY
According to student body president Roy Metts, the senior idea of Homecoming is a competition between the classes. This culminates with the class chants and another secret event.

BEFORE THE RACES

A Talk with DJ Jef Hill

NIGHT FESTIVITIES *Saturday:*

TAILGATING *Tailgating* 4 to 7 p.m.
While only about **400** people arrive regularly, senior Blue Metts expects nearly **700** before the game against Terre Haute North.

A Man and His Grill

HALFTIME
Homecoming queen will be announced. A smaller version of the daytime parade will ride through the stadium and the marching band will perform.

HOMECOMING DANCE
Dance

Past Queens
2001: Elizabeth Gaustad, Purdue University
2002: Lindsey McDaniel, University of Florida
2002: Ashley Doose
2004: Annie Graham, University of Illinois

2

A Buyer's Guide to the Homecoming Booths

Organization	Product	Cost
Spanish Club	Takiras (Spanish Cookies)	N/A
French Club	Soft Drinks, Water	$.50, $1
Chinese Culture Club	Fortune food, Pocky the Panda	$.50, $.25
Key Club	Henna Tattoos	$.25
Gay Straight Alliance	T-shirts	$5
House	Karaoke, Cookies	N/A
Latin Club	Gatorade, Snack food	N/A
SAGE	Buttons, Baked Goods	$1
Freedom's Answer	Voter registration	N/A
German Club	Straw pops	$.25

A Listener's Guide to the Homecoming Bands

Stage One

Band 1: Sean Connery Live
Genre: Early '80s Disco
Songs:
* "Schweinful Android"
* "Sabotage"
* "Helena"

Band 2: Trauma Project
Genre: Heavy Metal
Songs:
* "Find Things Out"
* "Untainted"
* "March to War"
* "Suffocate"

Stage Two

Band 1: The Outcome
Genre: Alternative Rock
Songs:
* "Tormented"
* "That was That"
* "Enough is Enough"
* "Slow Stream"

Band 2: The Awesomes
Genre: Punk Rock & Roll
Songs:
* "I Hate Hardcore"
* "Kamikaze Kindergarten"
* "Deal Grandma"
* "Nerck Song"

3

5k Charity Run/Walk
A Photo Essay by Nicole Beckage

Football Field
Home

Race Results
1. Seniors
2. Juniors
3. Sophomores
4. Freshmen

4

TRIKE RACES
$9 - student teams and faculty teams will fight for this year's crown.

HISTORY OF THE 3-WHEELERS

The Beginning:
The event started about 20 years ago in order to broaden Homecoming. It began with 64 teams.

The Origin of the Trikes:
Participants built or provided their own trikes until Senate bought a set from an Anderson bike shop. Each bike costs around $1,000 to replace.

A conversation with junior Philip Davis
Q: What team are you captain of?
A: A member of the Doomed Outside of the Lost Arc.
Q: Why the curious name?
A: It combined all of the movie titles of the Indiana Jones trilogy.
Q: What does your trike look like?
A: I'm doing an Indiana Jones, with the hat, whip, and a leather jacket if I can find one. We would have you pictured standing at St. James St.

TRIKE'S PAST GLORIES

Past winners	Best costumes
1993 Brian Adams's team	The Pixies
1994 Adam Powell's	Pink Panthers
1995 Playboy Bunnies	Team Bacon
1996 No Base	Team Music Boys
1997	
1998	
1999	
2000	
2001 The Final Revenge	
2002 The Final Revenge	
2003 Team Bacon	

Sports

What Works

1. As on the previous page, see how the photo essay can tell a story visually. Notice, too, how the lengthy cutlines provide relevant details for readers. Since cutlines are the most widely read copy in any publication, there's a good chance that readers will read these.

2. See how the text design enhances the point of the story. It uses the same colors from the photos and uses a playful text treatment that goes along with the tone of the pictures.

3. The pictures themselves show good photography techniques in that they stop the action pretty well, they are candid and they have simple, uncluttered backgrounds.

What Could Be Better

4. The story at the bottom has a better chance of not being read because it is so gray. Is there a way to tie in an additional photo or piece of alternative coverage (besides the bar graph) that would give readers a reason to move their eyes down there?

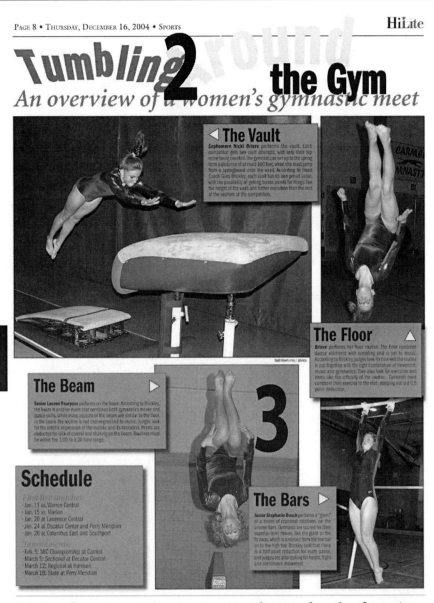

PAGE 8 • THURSDAY, DECEMBER 16, 2004 • SPORTS   **HiLite**

Tumbling 2 around the Gym

An overview of a women's gymnastic meet

◄ The Vault

Sophomore Nicki Briere performs the vault. Each competitor gets two vault attempts, with only their top score being counted. The gymnast can run up to the spring from a distance of at most 100 feet, when she must jump from a springboard onto the vault. According to Head Coach Gerry Brickley, each vault has its own preset value, with the possibility of getting bonus points for things like the height of the vault and better execution than the rest of the vaulters at the competition.

The Floor ▲

Briere performs her floor routine. The floor combines dance elements with tumbling and is set to music. According to Brickley, judges look for how well the routine is put together with the right combination of movement, music and gymnastics. They also look for execution and items like the difficulty of the routine. Gymnasts must complete their exercise to the mat; stepping out is a 0.5 point deduction.

The Beam ►

Senior Lauren Nearpass performs on the beam. According to Brickley, the beam is another event that combines both gymnastic moves and dance skills. While many aspects of the beam are similar to the floor, in the beam the routine is not choreographed to music. Judges look for the artistic impression of the routine and its execution. Points are deducted for lack of control and shaking on the beam. Routines must be within the 1:10 to 1:20 time range.

The Bars ►

Junior Stephanie Rouch performs a "giant," or a series of repeated rotations, on the uneven bars. Gymnasts are scored for their superior-level moves, like the giant or the fly pack, which is a release from the low bar on to the high bar. Brickley said that there is a half-point reduction for every pause, and judges are also looking for height, flight and continuous movement.

Schedule

First five matches
- Jan. 11 vs. Warren Central
- Jan. 15 vs. Marion
- Jan. 20 at Lawrence Central
- Jan. 24 at Decatur Central and Perry Meridian
- Jan. 26 at Columbus East and Southport

Tournaments
- Feb. 5: MIC Championship at Carmel
- March 5: Sectional at Decatur Central
- March 12: Regional at Harrison
- March 19: State at Perry Meridian

Women's gymnastics team cuts players for the first time

Greyhounds hope that smaller numbers will help players develop, allow for improvement on last year's Regional appearance

By Trish Smyth
tsmith@hilite.org

After fifteen years as a no-cut sport, the women's gymnastics team lowered the number of gymnasts this year, decreasing in size from the 22 girls on last year's roster to 16 on this year's.

"There's a lot less people, and the coaches get to work more with the individuals," sophomore Nicki Briere said. "Last year we had 22, and that made it hard with one coach per 11 lads. One coach per eight lads is a lot easier to work with."

Head Coach Gerry Brickley cited the large number of gymnasts last year as the main reason for removing the no-cut policy. "We've always tried to keep it a no-cut program, and that's worked for the last 15 years, but we just keep getting more and more girls that are interested, and it just started getting too big."

Junior Stephanie Rouch said that she expected the removal of the no-cut policy to have a positive impact on the team. "I think it'll make us stronger because it'll be easier to work harder since there'll be more space."

"The big thing is, you have a limited amount of space, (a limited) amount of equipment, and if you have too many girls, you have a lot of girls sitting around not able to work," Brickley said. "(You have) a limited number of coaches to work with twenty-two girls... an of practice just doesn't the team is more manageable

Senior says that the gym less individual attention than had 22 girls. "Last year girls, and it had a about it. We all got along, were only two coaches, couldn't get around to all of the all of the time. So it's 16 girls this year. It's easier for (Brickley) and (Assistant Coach Cindy Mayrose) to get around to us and to give more individual attention."

Thirty-one girls attended the September call-out meeting and 20 decided to try out for the team. The coaches watched the girls for three days to looked for basic skills. "We also looked at attitude, work ethic, who was sitting around and who was

up working. For the most part, that was not a problem. Everyone seemed to have a pretty good approach to things. It mostly came down to the skill level," Brickley said.

"It's harder (to get on the team) if you only specialize in one event, you have to be really good in that event, but they're not looking for basic skills in each of the (events)," Rouch said. Gymnastics includes four events: the vault, the balance beam, the parallel bars and the floor exercise.

Even though four freshmen were cut from the team, Brickley said that the no-cut policy did not affect team morale. "We had great team morale those last two teams. As big as they were, they all worked well together; they all got along. A big team shouldn't make that easy; you would expect with that many girls it wouldn't have worked as well.

"It's kind of sad, because usually everyone gets on it," Rouch said, "but most people were pretty happy about (the change), because it was a lot harder with so many girls there to get things done. (The girls who were cut) were freshmen, so we weren't attached

to them yet."

According to Brickley, the athletics department allowed coaches to decide whether or not to pursue a no-cut policy. "They'll pretty much let the Head Coach run the program the way they want to run it. They understand why (I made my decisions). The no-cut policy was my policy, they just approved that. It was no problem switching over."

Meanwhile, limiting the team to gymnasts with basic gymnastic skills raised the quality in the level of the gymnasts. "We came close last year, qualified out of the Sectional as a team, and then qualified one girl to State. We pretty much kept the core people from last year, and we've got some new talent coming in that I think will also help us out," Brickley said.

Brickley encouraged the freshmen who did not make the team to try out again next year. "I told them, keep working, staying in the gym, working on the skills. We hope to see ten next year, because we've got five seniors and there will at least be five openings on the team next year. We hope they keep trying."

Cuts for selected Carmel sports teams

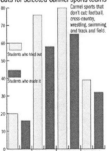

Carmel sports that don't cut: football, cross-country, wrestling, swimming and track and field.

Students who tried out

Students who made it

Gymnastics   Boys Soccer   Girls Soccer   Girls B ball

Sports

What Works

1. This designer has made careful consideration to put two very different sports on the same page. Why? Because if you place only, say, women's basketball information on a whole page, what if readers aren't interested in women's basketball? Putting additional stories on a page gives readers more reason to linger, and the longer they linger, the more chance there will be that they'll access the information you have provided.

2. The graphic at the bottom is another interesting variation on how to tell a story visually.

What Could Be Better

3. This headline could have used a summary deck to accompany it. Notice how it's difficult to tell what readers are supposed to think about here (because of the lack of that point of entry).

4. This page is a poor example of hierarchy. The larger headlines and titles should be at the top of the page and get smaller as readers descend. This page has been reversed.

5. There's too much white space here. Some white space is good, and, thankfully, this white space is not "trapped." But when you see this much blankness, you have to ask yourself, "Is there something else that I could have included her that would have given readers even more information?" What would you do?

Page 6 • Thursday, December 2, 2004 • Sports　　　　　HiLite

Carmel basketball teams focus on teamwork, staying healthy

Last year the men's and women's basketball teams both started with injuries to key players, senior Josh McRoberts and junior Melanie Thornton. But this year, both teams are fortunate to have healthy starting lineups.

Thornton, who was out for the first eight games of last season, is healthy and ready to start the season. The women's team has just one injury. However, the younger players have stepped up. Thornton said one of her main roles on the team is to be a leader and to encourage her teammates to reach their goals.

The women also have adapted well to new head coach Scott Bowen. Bowen previously was an assistant coach for Carmel men's basketball. "They have made me feel extremely welcome. Change is difficult, but they have been open and eager to learn," Bowen said. According to Bowen, the players have been focusing on the team aspect. Forward and junior Jessica Ionescu said, "We need to come together as an offensive team and utilize all of our threats."

Thornton mentioned that a main goal is to win the Sectional. "We have the skill to do it, we just need to stay healthy and play as a team," Thornton said.

According to men's Head Coach Mark Galloway, the men's team will play through McRoberts for success. "[McRoberts] is a great passer and is very unselfish. We need to get [McRoberts] the ball every time down the floor because he will draw a double team. Then we need perimeter players to step up and hit shots," Galloway said.

Though McRoberts is a star player on the team, he said he doesn't think about it getting him out of focus because of confidence in people around him. "Sharing the ball is easy because I trust my teammates. I know I have good guys around me," McRoberts said.

The men's team lost several seniors and has added younger players to the starting lineup. "This year's team is more disciplined and overall fundamentally sound," Galloway said. He also mentioned that they are playing well as a team, but they are not as deep this

year and need players to step up. Forward and junior Tyler Kinges will be out for a few weeks with an ankle injury, and players will need to fill his role temporarily. Galloway said they need to know and understand their roles on the team.

Both the men's and women's teams have started their seasons well. The men's team is ranked fifth in the state and defeated Brownsburg and Hamilton Southeastern to start the season with a 2-0 record. McRoberts played well with 29 points, 12 rebounds and five blocks against Brownsburg. He scored another double-double against Hamilton Southeastern with 18 points and 16 rebounds. Guard and senior Ben Myers added 16 points and forward and junior Eric Schneider added 14 points in the victory over Hamilton Southeastern.

The women's team lost its first game against Valparaiso in the Lafayette Jeff Tip-Off Classic, but has won its last four games to improve to a 4-1 record. Carmel upset Hamilton Southeastern, which was ranked second in the state. Guard and junior Stacia Shepherd scored 14 points, and Thornton added 10 points in the 55-53 victory.

Both the men's and women's teams have had significant contribution from freshmen. Forward and freshman Danielle Havel scored 15 points in the victory over Hamilton Southeastern. On the men's team, guard and freshman Daniel Moore showed his quickness with five steals in the team's victory over Hamilton Southeastern.

The men's team plays at Noblesville tomorrow night at 7:30. According to Galloway, Noblesville is good at cutting, screening and shooting. "We will have to defend well and we can't afford to make mistakes. Noblesville doesn't make many mistakes," Galloway said.

The women play at Warren Central tonight at 7:30. Bowen said the keys to winning this game will be "containing their athleticism, being aggressive and rebounding."

Bowen said the team look like they will be successful. He said, "Hopefully people will come support our Lady Hounds as much as the men's team this year."

Todd Montgomery / photos
Clockwise from top: Driving by the Hamilton Southeastern defender, freshman Danielle Havel dribbles towards the basket. Havel scored 16 points against the Royals last Saturday night. Top right: Senior Ben Myers rises to the basket. Myers helped the team with 16 points, including two three-pointers. Bottom right: Going for the layup, junior Melanie Thornton helps lift Carmel to victory over Hamilton Southeastern. Thornton had 10 points against the Royals.

Greyhound swimmers strut their strokes

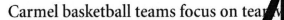

Junior Alyssa Rosinko — Butterfly

•**About the stroke:** "I think fly is the hardest stroke to accomplish. It is definitely the most tiring stroke."
•**CHS record holder:** Emily Ayers '96, 0:55.45
•**State record holder:** Katie Robinson, South Dearborn '02, 0:54.64
•**National record holder:** Misty Hyman, Shadow Mountain (AZ), 0:...
•**Ranking at State last year:** First with time of 0:58.43.
•**Personal best time:** 0:57.84

Senior Sebastian Cousins — Freestyle

•**About the stroke:** "Freestyle is the fastest stroke. It is the easiest to learn but the hardest to perfect."
•**CHS record holder:** Mike Reynolds '95, 4:30.01
•**State record holder:** Brian Hartley, North Central '01, 4:16.73
•**National record holder:** Jeff Postoff, Upland High School (CA), 4:16.39
•**Ranking in State last year:** First in the 500-freestyle, time of 4:36.02

Todd Montgomery / photos
Carmel Greyhound swimmers Sebastian Cousins, Emily DiBenigno, Alyssa Rosinko and Megan Sparks perform the freestyle, breaststroke, backstroke and butterfly respectively.

Freshman Emily DiBenigno — Breaststroke

•**About the stroke:** "It is important to be narrow when you're swimming breaststroke. Finishing your kick hard and timing are also important."
•**CHS record holder:** Katie Simmons '00, 1:02.91
•**State record holder:** Laura Swander, Center Grove '99, 1:01.98
•**National record holder:** Jessica Hardy, Woodrow Wilson (CA), 1:00.41
•**Ranking at State last year:** N/A

Sophomore Megan Sparks — Backstroke

•**About the stroke:** "You have to concentrate on hip rolls and keeping your shoulders out of the water."
•**CHS record holder:** Lindsey Carlberg '98, 0:56.43
•**State record holder:** Jenni Anderson, Chesterton '01, 0:55.24
•**National record holder:** Misty Hyman, Shadow Mountain (AZ), 0:53.68
•**Ranking at State last year:** Third with personal best time of 0:57.70

Taylor Baughman and John Flora / infographics

Feature/Calendar

What Works

1. This is an interesting variation on the traditional calendar page that you see just about everywhere. Notice how it uses a visual "theme" to tie all of the elements together.

2. The addition of additional "things to do" at the bottom of the page is a nice way to branch readers away from just the typical school-related activities.

What Could Be Better

3. Some of the text on the photos is difficult to read. Always be aware of how "content dictates design," not the other way around. If your design is distracting from what you really want readers to see (in this case, the information inside the boxes), then make modifications to accommodate those problems (i.e., lighten the photo).

The *HiLite* Guide to Winter Break

From athletics to entertainment, this guide provides various activities taking place from today through Jan. 3.

New Releases
- Tomorrow
  - "The Aviator"
  - "A Series of Unfortunate Events"
- Wednesday
  - "The Flight of the Phoenix"
  - "Meet the Fockers"
- Dec. 25
  - "The Darkness"
  - "Fat Albert"

Freshman Danielle Hawl goes up for a shot against Cathedral. Both the men's and women's basketball teams will play over winter break. For more information and schedules look at page 6.

Sports
- Friday - Pacers versus Toronto Raptors at 7 p.m.
- Sunday - Colts versus Baltimore Ravens at 8:30 p.m.
- Wednesday - Pacers versus Philadelphia 76ers at 7 p.m.
- Dec. 25 - Pacers versus Detroit Pistons at 12:30 p.m.
- Dec. 26 - Colts versus San Diego Chargers at 1 p.m.
- Dec. 27 - Pacers versus New Orleans Hornets at 7 p.m.
- Dec. 28 - IU versus Ball State at 8 p.m. at Conseco Fieldhouse

All games are at Conseco Fieldhouse or RCA Dome.

Entertainment
- **"A Christmas Carol"**
  - at IRT from now to next Thursday
  - price: $19 to $49, contact: 635-5252
- **First Bank Yuletide Celebration**
  - at Hilbert Circle Theater now to Wednesday
  - price: $28 to $58, contact: 639-4300
- **"A Beef and Boards Christmas"**
  - now to Dec. 31
  - price: $27 to $49, contact: 87...
- **"Santa vs. The Snowman 3D"**
  - at IMAX theater from now to Dec. 30
  - price: varies, contact: 2333-4629
- **"The Elves and the Shoemakers"**
  - at the Children's Museum until Jan. 3
  - price: $9.50, contact: 334-3322

Holiday Festivities
- **Kroger Christmas at the Zoo**
  - Now to Dec. 30 from 5 to 9 p.m.
  - price: $8, contact: 630-2001
- **Gingerbread Village at Conner Prairie**
  - now to Dec. 30
  - price: $5.50, contact: 776-6000
- **Jolly Days Winter Wonderland**
  - now to Jan. 5, 10 a.m. to 5 p.m.
  - price: $11.50, contact: 334-3322
- **Santa on the Circle**
  - Saturday from 12 to 3 p.m.
  - price: Free, at Monument Circle
- **Holiday in the Heartland**
  - Indiana Historical Society
  - price: Free, contact: 232-1882
- **Holiday Public Skating**
  - Indiana Skating Academy
  - price: $3.75, contact: 237-5555

Carly Anderson / photo

Reynolds Light Display
December 16 to 31

What: Reynolds 12th Annual Outdoor Christmas Light Display
Where: Reynolds Farm Equipment
Ind. 37 and 126th St.
Fishers, IN 46038
When: Today to Dec. 30
Contact: 849-0810

A display of lights on all day and night. Santa visits from 6 to 9 p.m. on this Saturday.

Local Sledding Hills
1. **Cool Creek Park**
   2000 E. 151st Street
   Carmel, IN 46033
2. **Brookshire Golf Course**
   12120 Brookshire Parkway
   Carmel, IN 46033
3. **West Park**
   116th Street and Towne Road
   Carmel, IN 46032
4. **Forest Park**
   701 Cicero Road
   Noblesville, IN 46060

Evan Brown / photo

Feature/Entertainment

What Works

1. Using these "kicker heads" is a nice way to organize information on your page and bring it all together, particularly when all of the information revolves around a single theme, as this page does.

2. See how large initial capital letters can become their own points of entry. Use them sparingly, though. Maybe once (or twice) per page. Too many "drop caps" and you run the risk of confusing readers and, worse, occasionally spelling some subliminal words that you didn't mean to.

What Could Be Better

3. There's no dominant image here (CVI). It's difficult for readers to decide where to go first.

4. Notice, again, how this page doesn't use hierarchy properly. This headline is larger and bolder than the one above it.

5. This photo faces the wrong way. The girls' eyes lead readers off of the page.

PAGE B4 • THURSDAY, DECEMBER 2, 2004 • ENTERTAINMENT   HiLite

THIS ISSUE'S TOPIC: HOLIDAY SHOWS

Holiday Entertainment

With the Holiday Season in full swing, many options are available to the Carmel area

As the Holiday season creeps up on everyone in the city of Carmel, students and citizens are provided with many new entertainment opportunities. With the opening of [the] Spectacular alone, new entertainment choices and options have been introduced for students to enjoy. Two sisters perform for the first time together in the annual "Holiday Spectacular" performed by all choirs here. Other students perform in the Holiday classic, "The Nutcracker," also provides a memorable evening for those who attend.

COOKING CORNER: SUGAR COOKIES

A Touch of Sugar

Supplies:
- 1/3 cup Shortening
- 1/3 cup Margarine
- 2 cups Flour
- 1 tb Milk
- 3/4 cup Sugar
- 1 Egg
- 1 ts Baking Powder
- 1 ts Vanilla Extract

Steps:
1. Preheat oven to 350 degrees
2. Grease a 12 inch baking pan
3. In a small bowl, mix flour, baking powder and salt at a medium speed.
4. In a large bowl, mix sugar, butter and shortening until creamy.
5. Next, beat in egg and vanilla extract.
6. At a low speed, mix in milk and flour.
7. Bake in oven for 18 to 20 minutes until the edges are slightly brown.
8. Let cookies cool on a wire rack.
9. Place on a plate and serve to friends and family!
10. Enjoy the cookies along with the Holiday season.

BEHIND THE CURTAIN

Holidays are Spectacular as sisters perform together

By Neil Abrendt
nabrendt@hilite.org

"Yes, I'm tired after it's over. And yes, it takes away from my schoolwork, but it's totally worth it in the end," Campbell said. "It's worth all the work and you get to spend time with a lot of great people and learn a lot about performing and just entertaining your audience."

Familiar favorites, like "Jingle Bells" and "Silent Night" have made their way onto the roster for the performance, which runs December 9 to 12. Audience members might hear some new tunes this winter, however. Unless, of course, they've already heard "Joyful, Joyful" from the movie "Sister Act II." But it isn't likely that they have. The choir will also perform "Bell Carol of the Kings," a compilation of "We Three Kings" and "Carol of the Bells."

"Sometimes we'll do a familiar song but our directors will choose an arrangement that's just a little bit different," Campbell said. "And I think that's neat for the audience to come hear something that they know, but it's not the everyday stuff that they hear on their CDs at home."

One of the biggest presents for her this festive season is the chance to finally share the performing experience with a person she knows fairly well, her younger sister, Emily. "It's really exciting to be performing with my sister because we've never performed together before," Campbell said. "We've been performing for years, but always separately, so it'll be really neat to be on stage together singing at the same time."

Campbell has high hopes for the concert and said viewers will be stunned. "It's one of those things where the audience walks out saying 'Oh my gosh I'm so glad I went.' I saw all of my friends and I can't wait to come back next year.'"

Freshman Emily Campbell and senior Elizabeth Campbell rehearse for the upcoming performances of "Holiday Spectacular." The show takes place on Dec. 9 and 10 at 7:30 p.m. and Dec. 11 and 12 at 2 p.m. Tickets are on sale at the bookstore or at the door for $6 for those and $7 for balcony. Nicole Backup / photo

Talent Runs in the Family

Freshman Emily Campbell follows in older sister's footsteps through school choir and other school involvements

By Bing Chen
bchen@hilite.org

As temperatures drop and clothes become thicker, the winter season wouldn't be complete without the school's annual "Holiday Spectacular." Every year in early December, the "Holiday Spectacular" meshes the talents of all the performing arts and drama departments.

Freshman Emily Campbell has attended the show every year in the past even before she reached high school. Her sister, senior Elizabeth Campbell, sang with the school choir, and this influenced Campbell to also participate in performing arts. "The freshman choir and I really like it because she's a really great singer. She influenced me a lot," Campbell said. Although the freshmen don't participate as involved as the older choirs work helps her understand the work and dedication needed for the "Holiday Spectacular." "[For choir], I would say work really hard and respect your teachers because it is a lot of work," she said. "The freshman choir works hard in class because that's the only time we have except for two or three major rehearsals."

Campbell stresses the importance of participation for incoming and current freshmen. Getting involved with activities provides a way to meet new people and enjoy school. "Choir is a lot of fun, and it's a great way to spend part of the day," Campbell looks forward to the opening of the "Holiday Spectacular."

PHOTO CORNER: HOLIDAY SPECTACULAR

Nicole Backup / photos

Today	Tomorrow	Saturday	Monday	Tuesday	Wednesday	Dec. 9	Dec. 10	Dec. 11	Dec. 12
Rehearsal 6 to 9 p.m.	All day choir rehearsal / Ambassador performance at St. Luke's	Rehearsal 6 to 10 p.m. / Rehearsal 6 to 10 p.m.	Rehearsal 6 to 10 p.m.	Opening night 7:30 p.m. performance / Photo night		2 p.m. performance / 7:30 p.m. performance		2 p.m. performance	

CHS Dancers take part in Holiday Original, "The Nutcracker"

By Eda Zhang
ezhang@hilite.org

At first senior Ashley Jones didn't want to do it. But after several years of persistence, and the addition of pointe shoes, ballet took the place of tap dancing in Jones' heart and became her favorite form of dance.

Jones began dancing ballet at 10 years old with the encouragement of her mother, who danced all her life and used to dance professionally at one point. This year Jones looks forward to performing in what's become a tradition: the Central Indiana Dance Ensemble's (CIDE) fifth annual "Nutcracker" production.

"About four years ago I went away to a summer dance camp in Alabama with the American Ballet Theatre, and so many girls were talking about the "Nutcracker." I went home and asked my mom why we didn't do one. So after that my mom tried as hard as she could to form a company that lets teenagers and younger dancers perform more, especially the "Nutcracker." So, in a way, me and my friends started the tradition of dancing a "Nutcracker" each year, with so much help from my mom (who is the director) and the rest of the management," Jones, who performs as the sugar plum fairy, said.

CIDE, a non-profit, regional, pre-professional ballet company, will perform the "Nutcracker" in the Westfield High School auditorium. But, according to Jones, performing in Westfield mostly makes no difference for the many CHS students involved. "We never ran into the kids at Westfield, and everyone there is so nice," she said. "They have a great performance facility, and it's not too far away from Carmel. We actually rehearse in Carmel at Performer's Edge and just perform at Westfield. We all love to show people what we do and that we do it well. So performing in Westfield has never presented a problem, just as long as we are dancing. Most of the girls go to school together, which helps us with scheduling around homecoming..."

Practicing pointe, senior Ashley Jones rehearses for her upcoming roll as a sugar plum fairy in the CIDE production of the "Nutcracker." Performances are tomorrow at 7:30, Saturday at 2 and 7:30, as well as Sunday at 2. Nicole Backup / photos

Feature/Student Section

What Works

1. The use of the dominant visual works well to anchor this page. This type of visual is called a photo illustration, since it has been manipulated by the designer to illustrate his story.

2. These candid photos around the page mix well with the photo illustration and allow readers to see these bands in action.

3. The visual technique used here — having the different musicians respond to the same question — is a nice break from the typical student band story.

What Could Be Better

4. It might be nice to incorporate a more informative headline (or title) and summary deck or even a short couple of paragraphs to really bring out the timeliness of this information; the bands will perform together soon. Here's where they'll perform and why.

Feature/Human Interest

What Works

1. Notice the planning on this page. This designer has tried to approach this story using a holistic approach — she's considered the focus of the interview and how she can enhance that focus with visual elements. The dressmaker's dummy is the dominant image around which all of the other elements revolve.

2. The playful use of typography here blends well with the tone of the article.

3. The Q&A format, while it wouldn't work for every story you write, works well when part of a larger publication that contains more narrative stories.

4. Notice how the cutlines enhance the angle of the story. A reader could read these cutlines and never actually read the interview and still know enough about the story to speak intelligently about it at the dinner table.

What Could Be Better

5. Try to design another story onto this page in addition to the seamstress story. What if readers aren't interested in this girl and her avocation? Perhaps a sidebar story about other students who pursue their passions (similar but not the same as the seamstress) would help to broaden the scope of the story and give readers more reason to understand why the information is important and how it affects them. Give them a reason to linger on the page.

'Rocker Chic' junior Teddi Bickers creates her own
one-of-a kind clothing

Seamstress 2 Style
with

By Teresa Easwaran
teaswaran@hilite.org

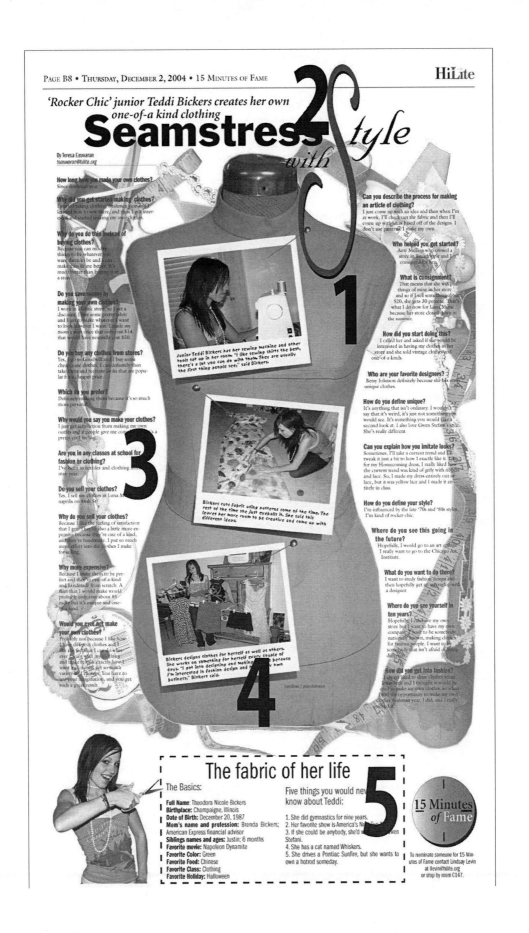

How long have you made your own clothes?
Since freshman year.

Why did you get started making clothes?
I started taking clothing freshman year and I learned how to sew there, and then I got interested and started making my own clothes.

Why do you do this instead of buying clothes?
Because I can make things to be whatever you want them to be and I can make them fit me better. It's much better than buying it at a store.

Do you save money by making your own clothes?
I work in a fabric store, so I get a discount. I buy some pretty fabric and I get to make whatever I want. I make my own cute clothes that only cost $14 that would have normally cost $50.

Do you buy any clothes from stores?
Yes, I go to Goodwill and I buy some cheap cute clothes. I can definitely then take them and recreate looks that are popular for a cheaper price.

Which do you prefer?
Definitely making them because it's so much more personal.

Why would you say you make your clothes?
I just get satisfaction from making my own outfits and if people give me compliments, a pretty cool feeling.

Are you in any classes at school for fashion or clothing?
I've been in textiles and clothing all year.

Do you sell your clothes?
Yes, I sell my clothes at Luna Music in napolis on 86th St.

Why do you sell your clothes?
Because I like the feeling of satisfaction that I get. They're also a little more expensive because they're one of a kind, and they're handmade. I put so much more effort into the clothes I make for selling.

Why more expensive?
Because I make them to be perfect and they're one-of-a-kind and handmade from scratch. A shirt that I would make would probably only cost about $5 more but it's unique and one-of-a-kind.

Would you ever not make your own clothes?
Probably not because I like how I have different clothes and I like that feeling I could whatever I want with my clothing and I put in such detail. I have a variety and I change. You have to use your imagination, and you get such a great result.

Junior Teddi Bickers has her sewing machine and other tools set up in her room. "I like sewing thirts the best, there's a lot you can do with them. They are usually the first thing people see," said Bickers.

Bickers cuts fabric using patterns some of the times. The rest of the time she just eyeballs it. She said this leaves her more room to be creative and come up with different ideas.

Bickers designs clothes for herself as well as others. She works on something for herself every couple of days. "I got into designing and making clothes because I'm interested in fashion design and having my own business," Bickers said.

Can you describe the process for making an article of clothing?
I just come up with an idea and then when I'm at work, I'll check out the fabric and then I'll come up with ideas based off of the designs. I don't use patterns. I make my own.

Who helped you get started?
Amy Mullins who owned a store in Broad Style and I consigned clothes.

What is consignment?
That means that she will put things of mine in her store and so if I sell something about $20, she gets 30 percent. That's what I do now for Luna Music because her store closed down in the summer.

How did you start doing this?
I called her and asked if she would be interested in having my clothes in her store and she sold vintage clothes and one-of-a-kinds.

Who are your favorite designers?
Betsy Johnson definitely because she has really unique clothes.

How do you define unique?
It's anything that isn't ordinary. I wouldn't say that it's weird, it's just not something you would see. It's something you would take a second look at. I also love Gwen Stefani's style. She's really different.

Can you explain how you imitate looks?
Sometimes, I'll take a current trend and I'll tweak it just a bit to how I exactly like it. Like for my Homecoming dress, I really liked how the current trend was kind of girly with ribbon and lace. So, I made my dress entirely out of lace, but it was yellow lace and I made it entirely in class.

How do you define your style?
I'm influenced by the late '70s and '80s styles. I'm kind of rocker-chic.

Where do you see this going in the future?
Hopefully, I would go to an art college. I really want to go to the Chicago Art Institute.

What do you want to do there?
I want to study fashion design and then hopefully get an internship with a designer.

Where do you see yourself in ten years?
Hopefully, I'd have my own store but I want to have my own company. I want to be somebody nationally known, making clothes for famous people. I want to be somebody that isn't afraid of being different.

How did you get into fashion?
I've always liked to draw clothes what I wore and I thought it would be cool to make my own clothes, so when I had the opportunity to make my own clothes freshman year, I did, and I really loved it.

The fabric of her life

The Basics:

Full Name: Theodora Nicole Bickers
Birthplace: Champaigne, Illinois
Date of Birth: December 20, 1987
Mom's name and profession: Brenda Bickers; American Express financial advisor
Siblings names and ages: Justin; 6 months
Favorite movie: Napoleon Dynamite
Favorite Color: Green
Favorite Food: Chinese
Favorite Class: Clothing
Favorite Holiday: Halloween

Five things you would never know about Teddi:

1. She did gymnastics for nine years.
2. Her favorite show is America's Next Top Model.
3. If she could be anybody, she'd want to be Gwen Stefani.
4. She has a cat named Whiskers.
5. She drives a Pontiac Sunfire, but she wants to own a hotrod someday.

15 Minutes of Fame

To nominate someone for 15 Minutes of Fame contact Lindsay Levin at llevin@hilite.org or stop by room C147.

Opinion

What Works

1. The editorial cartoon is used well here. Remember that an editorial cartoon is not just a tool to illustrate a larger story; it should be considered as a visual column all its own. The only difference between an editorial cartoon and a written column is that the cartoonist chooses to share his viewpoint with drawings rather than words.

2. It's often difficult to make opinion pages more visual. This page uses graphics well to keep the page from being too gray.

3. Column logos should show your paper's personality (I hope you have one) while remaining professional. The logo can set the tone for the information to be found within the column itself.

4. Notice how no ads appear on this page. This should always be the case with an editorial page.

What Could Be Better

5. This may seem minor, but this left side page is supposed to be an editorial page, and the "Op/ed" page should appear on the right page ("Op/ed" stands for "opposite the editorial" page). That being said, the actual editorial page should include the staff editorial (see next page). The op/ed page should include other viewpoints. Readers should come to rely on where they can find certain information, including the staff editorial (which many journalists say may be the most important article you write in each issue).

HiLite

5

Realizing life away from here

Currently Playi[illegible]
"Round Here"
by Counting Crows

3

This summer I went to [illegible]ego with my family for [illegible] weeks. It was a great vaca[illegible] because I got to experience beauti[illegible]ful scenery, dreadful highways, them[illegible] parks, beaches and a differ[illegible] all in one area. I saw histor[illegible] San Diego, the Zoo and W[illegible] Park, Disneyland and Universal Studios Hollywood as well as several other attractions. And my family and I relaxed in the sun quite often.

The trip provided quite a change from daily life here, which was cool for a while, but I definitely wanted to go back home as soon as possible. I missed my friends and the comforts of home. But I liked California, too, and it helped me appreciate wildlife and the rest of the world.

Having lived here for six years, I'd pretty much settled for Carmel life. I know that, despite what we might think, Carmel is not the center of the universe. Going to the west coast helped me see that better. Carmel may be the center of the state that America loves to drive through (that's the non-Hoosier translation of "Crossroads of America"), but the city has no meaning or place in the rest of the country.

Carmel is a city a bit out of balance and full of plenty of interesting, though like-minded, people. We seem to have a great school, yes, as we are a Blue Ribbon School, we "were great" and now we "are family." The school atmosphere may be good, but we aren't the best in the nation at everything. We are quite gifted but not quite perfect.

We put stock in items that don't necessarily matter in the grand scheme. We strive to have more and "the best" without regard to the world beyond. One should get through life without needing coffee to survive. (It tastes gross anyway, except in frappucinos.) Life isn't about having North Face fleeces, acting hard or popping your collar. Life isn't about the money you have (or your parents have). Carmel's mayor, in this materialistic tradition, has attempted to grab all the land he can. Home Place? Let's call it Carmel, even though the residents are against it. Clay Township? Carmel. Westfield, a separate town who doesn't want to be annexed? Let's make it part of Carmel. With his grab-all mentality, Mayor Jim Brainard seems to embody and endorse the materialistic spirit of this city. That's just great.

It really doesn't matter what city we consider ourselves in; there are so many bigger things in life. Sometimes, these come to Carmel directly. We see the importance of good choices when area students die horrifically in car accidents. Two years ago, when a club committed to fighting global AIDS got U2's Bono on a video calling us "car-MEL" high school, students started to think about trying to stop the spread of this disease.

A political season excited our school, but most students took their parents' positions after all the examinations and thoughts. A friend of mine said, "I'm for Bush, but I'm pro-gay rights and pro-choice." It made more sense when I saw that his parents' van had a Bush-Cheney '04 sticker.

Carmel is a positive community with quality schools, and many choose to live here all their lives. There is nothing wrong with that, as long as we understand that there is a world and problems outside this blessed community. Taking a little time away from here, possibly at college, may be all it takes to remember there are people different from us. Many suffer from poverty, lack of jobs, dangerous towns and streets and other problems we don't usually face here.

I get to go to London this winter break, and I can't wait. I'll be there with all of my friends, yeah, but I also hope I can experience the culture, problems, politics, opinions and people from another country. I've been to England before, and at that point my family met a charming couple who owned a small bed-and-breakfast in a coastal town called Eastbourne. They were spirited, animated and living an amazing life in a scenic town which was flanked by white cliffs. It was great to understand them, and see another way of life in another area.

I just hope that the rest of Carmel can understand the splendor and the trouble that happen outside our town. It's amazing. ***Matt Welch is the front page editor for the HiLite. Contact him at mwelch@hilite.org.***

1

Graphic Perspective

Saying good-bye to an American hero

Currently Playing:
"A Country Boy Can Survive"
by Hank Williams Jr.

He considered himself a typical country boy, walking along life's path while whistling to Hank Williams, Jr.'s song "A Country Boy Can Survive." He was tall and thin and had very much the look of a country boy, his mother, Melanie Smith, said. "He always had this ornery smile with a gleam in his eyes. It's that look. His eyes were always so bright, even as a baby, he just had that smile that always had the little orneriness stuck in there."

It was no surprise, to his friends or family then, when Thompson signed a year early for the U. S. Marines Corps during his junior year at Eastbrook High School. His mother, who remembers that five of Thompson's birthday cakes when he was little had military themes, said Thompson, his brothers and friends were always obsessed with playing with guns, airplanes, fighting the bad guys and adventure. "They just always wanted to be the good guys," she said.

Thompson just wished one of his older brothers, Phillip, who just finished his four years of active duty, didn't steal the thunder by joining the Marines before him.

Thompson was also tempted to wait a year for Casey Stanley, Thompson's cousin and best friend, who's a year younger, so they could sign up together on the buddy system, but decided to enlist early and join as soon as he graduated high school. Stanley, after he finished high school, joined Thompson at Camp Pendleton as a Lance Corporal of an amphibious assault vehicle crew.

During Thompson's first tour in Iraq, his mother would receive some form of communication from him, typically an e-mail, daily. That tradition followed into his second tour, but during the last couple of months, Smith and other loved ones knew the push into Fallujah would be a difficult one, for he barely had any time to write or call anyone.

Nonetheless, according to Smith, Thompson thought (the services) had a very important job to do there. He had seen a lot of the results of Saddam Hussein's rule, and it hurt him terribly. He felt they were there, and the people really appreciated them being there, because that would bring them their freedom.

His mother received a phone call from Thompson on Friday, Nov. 12, just three days before his death. He asked about his family, Stanley's medial condition (he sustained injuries to his back), and the upcoming holiday season. She told him he'd receive a large package soon of Christmas gifts, which included the much-desired homemade beef jerky to share.

He then, she said, asked what she wanted for Christmas. Smith said, "'I want to be there in Iraq with you.' He laughed and said, 'Well that's not going to happen. I'm here so you are there, and my family is home. So they can sleep at night and be safe.' I don't think that's atypical of any military person serving there. They all feel like their job is keep it there so it doesn't come home like 9/11.

"He said he was there so that people could have the freedom to do what they wanted to do, say the things they wanted to say and be who they wanted to be. Freedom isn't free, and we have to pay the price for it," Smith said.

Thompson has become a hero to his family and Stanley, not for just paying the price for freedom with his life, but for being the country boy they loved. Stanley said Thompson's ultimate sacrifice will make him become a better Marine because it makes him appreciate what he's doing for this country even more.

Smith knows Thompson wouldn't want to be remembered as exceptional, he was like everyone he served with. She can see him saying, "It's just the way it is. We're all like this."

When asked how Smith thought Thompson would like to be remembered, and the advice he'd give to teenagers, she said, "I think much of his "gung ho" philosophy is what Lance would tell teenagers. Set your goals high, and go for it, just go for it whatever it is. He really thought that school was very important. He would tell everyone to work hard. That's our job in life to get your goal, meet your dreams," she said.

She continued to say, "Be all you could be," until Stanley jokingly reminded her that it was an Army phrase, and Thompson would have never used an Army slogan. She laughed, said, "Strike that," and rephrased it to say, "Be proud of what you are and what you believe in." ***Sarah Hughes is the editor in chief for the HiLite. Contact her at shughes@hilite.org. Thompson's family has set up a scholarship for seniors at Eastbrook High School.***

Donations can be sent to:

Cpl. Lance M. Thompson Memorial Scholarship Fund
Marion School Employees Federal Credit Union
[illegible] E. Main Street
Gas City, IN
[illegible]

Name: Corporal Lance M. Thompson
Personal Motto: "Gung Ho"
Favorite Song: "A Country Boy Can Survive" by Han[illegible]
Age: 21
Branch of Service: Second Battalion
5th Marines
Weapons Company
Stationed at Camp Pendleton, CA
Specialty: Field Communications, communicated co[illegible]es of air strikes and enemy positions when atta[illegible]
Length of Tour: Second seventh-month tour in Ira[illegible]
High School: Eastbrook High School Class of 2001
Relation to CHS: Mother, Melanie Smith is a special services teacher here
Died: Nov. 15, 2004

2

Chameleon says: It's not a soup kitchen

Currently Playing:
The Afternoon: Forever Afternoon (Tuesday?)
by Moody Blues

The Noblesville Food Bank is one of those visionary projects where the owner's idealism and benevolence cannot hide reality: the establishment lacks something fundamental. Boxes that spill over with food form mazes around the disheveled rooms and litters of cats roam the outside grounds. Mold decays boxes of bread and jugs of milk, and random bags of food have burst open. This attracts swarms of strange, large bugs.

For my community service, I stacked food crates, maneuvered food crates, emptied less full food crates into more full food crates, for efficiency, then unloaded additional food from the delivery truck to repeat the process. Throughout my three hours as a serf for the food bank, I had no contact with the people my actions benefited. My interactions were limited to my fellow detainees and, of course, the crates.

Community service paints the pleasurable visual of connection and solidarity between the people forgotten by society and those more fortuitous who decide to help them. Current dogma states that the volunteers will either 1) appreciate their life more after exposure to the less fortunate and/or 2) swell with pride over the magnanimity of their deeds. Administrators everywhere, in schools, jails and rehabilitation centers, instituted community service as a corrections policy; the deviants will learn the joy of charity, they thought, renounce their destructive habits and find meaning and life in mutual aid.

Far from enriching or enlightening, the work reminded me of my past experience as a Kroger bagger, a job filled with senseless, repetitive shuffling and ordering food for faceless customers. Industrial, assembly-line labor, whether labeled community service or not, is assembly-line labor; an environment that does not inspire change, nor does it feel like punishment; the work merely crushes and constricts the spirit, vaguely similar to enslavement, encouraging passionate rebellion once free.

And my fellow workers agreed. None of them thought they had suffered or gained insight or understanding. Instead, I listened as people traded secrets about how to achieve the best legal high.

Lies, fantasies, delusions! O! we said, people have no idea. Clueless, bumbling, bureaucrats, we said. Forced service, we said, is idiotic and causes more resentment and anger at those rules we already loathe.

When I first learned of my future service, I expected real interaction with the people marginalized by society. Instead, although the owners swore they distributed all the stored food, I felt detached from any charitable purpose. ***Nathan Claus is a news editor for the HiLite. Contact him at nclaus@hilite.org***

The debate on sex education v. abstinence only plan

Currently Playing:
"Let's Talk About Sex" by Salt-N-Pepa

Synopsis: According to advocatesforyouth.org, Congress has allocated over $500 million since the fall of 1996 to fund abstinence until marriage programs. President Bush has stated publicly that schools that do not teach only abstinence will not receive federal funding.

Andy Glaser (AG): Abstinence-only education programs are the most effective because they present the facts and dangers of early sexual activity. This is the best course of action for educators because it is the healthiest decision for a teenager to make.

Ben Linder (BL): I agree with you in the sense that abstinence exists as the only foolproof approach to avoiding STDs and teen pregnancy. Those are the facts of the matter. However, an abstinence-only educational plan will not reverse the decisions of society's teens about whether or not to have sex, and it is, therefore, important to teach alternate forms of safety (i.e. condoms).

AG: Nice vague reference to society. Although promoting condom use may be safer than unprotected sex, I believe that teaching about condoms undermines the goal of teaching abstinence in the first place. Saying "abstain, but if you don't, here's a condom," is like telling students not to smoke, but giving them nicotine patches in case they do chose to smoke.

BL: Here's a realistic analogy for you: obviously, this school advocates sobriety for all its students. It in no way endorses any teenager drinking alcohol. However, this school always promotes the "Prom Promise" campaign in which students agree not to drink *and drive*. The school undoubtedly realizes that it's naive to think no stud[illegible] will drink on prom night, so they tell the students th[illegible]est way to conduct themselves in such circumstanc[illegible] the responsibility of our educators to do the same [illegible] comes to sexual activity.

4

AG: While it is true that not all teenagers w[illegible] it is the responsibility of the educators to tell te[illegible] dangers of sexual activity. Interpersonal rela[illegible] teac[illegible] Lila Torp uses a sex simulation where stud[illegible] dangers of sexual activity. She presents the [illegible]stinence is the only certain way to stay safe. While no[illegible] students will listen, it is important that they are educa[illegible] so that they understand the consequences of their acti[illegible] When the statistics are considered, abstinence is obviously the safer choice since one in four sexually active teens has an STD.

BL: Nobody disputes the fact that abstinence is the safest sexual choice to make, but Torp also had this to say about sexual education: "If you present the facts, abstinence advocates itself." This obviously points out that shielding a student from all of the facts will only create a dangerous curiosity, which is precisely why it's important to present all of the facts (including abstinence *and* safe sex alternatives) and let the students make their own decisions.

AG: No one is shielding students from the facts, they're teaching the facts. But most teens don't take into account the emotional and psychological injury that can result from making the wrong decisions. According to Robert Rector, author of *Teens at Risk*, most females regret their first sexual experience. This isn't a question of teenagers' choices; they will make their own decisions. Even so, it is important that they know what they are getting themselves into.

BL: Exactly. So if you admit that students will make their own decisions, then what about those students who hear all of your abstinence-only programs and still decide they want to have sex? Is society (yet another vague reference) to leave them out to dry and to fend for themselves when they have an unwanted child or a life-threatening STD because our health teachers couldn't include the use [illegible] contraception or condoms in their lesson plans? I hap[illegible] to think that's ridiculous, and those students, while less responsible, still deserve to know alternatives.

AG: It's a choice everyone has to make. It is not the *sole* responsibility of the school. Parents should educate their children and students should educate themselves. What one person thinks is the right choice may not be; the point is that had that person made different choices, he or she wouldn't have needed the alternative education. And that's something everyone has to consider.

Andy Glaser and Ben Linder are reporters for the HiLite. Contact them at aglaser@hilite.org and blinder@hilite.org.

Opinion

What Works

1. Here we see a properly placed staff editorial. Notice how the body font is different from the normal treatment for body copy. While not necessary, this treatment helps to separate and enhance the staff editorial, making it stand out on the page.

2. In this case, the editorial cartoon actually accompanies the staff editorial. However, notice how it doesn't merely illustrate the text. Although it is related to the editorial, it could just as easily stand alone.

3. Both the staff editorial and the editorial cartoon relate to an objective news story that appears earlier in the publication. Because of the infrequency of publications in high school journalism, it's not a bad idea to have elements relate.

What Could Be Better

4. All of the columns of body copy in the stories on the left side of this page are the same width. This can be a little monotonous. Try mixing it up a little between stories.

New games, shows should have less violence

Graphic Perspective

Mustafa Hameed 12/10/04
HAPPY HOLIDAYS, BOYS...

2

Mustafa Hameed / art

Our Perspective

We go to the movie theaters, and we see it. We watch television, and we see it. We go home, and we see it. Everywhere we go, media violence is at every corner we turn, and it is affecting students by making them more immune to violence. First of all, shows on TV are portraying more and more violence as time goes by. An example of this is the World Wrestling Entertainment's show, "Smackdown." This show portrays "wrestlers" who bombard each other with an assortment of items such as chairs and tables and have steel cage matches.

Although in real life the wrestlers are in actuality acting; what is seen on TV by viewers seems like real fighting. A 15 year study done by the American Psychological Association stated that children's perceptions that TV violence is realistic are all linked to later aggression as young adults in both males and females. It also stated that as the children grow older, they act more violent towards others.

Second, not only are the shows we watch getting more violent, so are the computer and system games we play. Many video games are coming out where the player must kill so many people to win and must bomb so many cities in order to gain a level. An example of this is *Halo 2*, a shooting game where the goal is to kill extra terrestrials. These games have dramatically changed from the past games such as Tetris.

In an article on Mediascope.org it said that in fact, recent studies show that after playing a violent video game children can become desensitized to violenceor act hostile to others.

As time passes, this issue of violence in the media is growing i[illegible] larger problem. As children view th[illegible] become more indifferent to the fa[illegible]ence. As they grow older, this indifferen[illegible]rows. Students now are growing passive[illegible]iolence. They don't see what the big dea[illegible]hen a person strikes another.

1

In order to solve [illegible]problem, the media and public must do m[illegible] things. Ratings must be strictly followed. *H[illegible]2* is rated "M" for mature, yet many children are playing this game. Parents need know what their child is playing and if it is appropriate for their age. Parents need more awareness of what their child is watching or playing.

Also, students who watch these shows and play these games must understand what they are playing or watching. They have to realize that the violence portrayed is not real. They must understand that these are not real life situations.

In addition, these new shows and games must change. They are just too violent. Creators need to think of different ways to entertain the youth. Instead of having more violence, games could be created to have more thinking involved in order to get past a challenge.

Also, shows such as "Smackdown" need to change. Other shows such as "Friends" and "The Apprentice" have high ratings without the violence. It is possible. If these shows decide not to change, then they should have warning messages before the show airs in order to warn the public.

In conclusion, there is just too much media violence. This all has to change. Yet, in reality it is up to the students to decide whether or not to play a certain game or watch a certain show. Students are old enough to understand the violence that is portrayed and that it is not an excuse to use violence in real life. This problem with media violence will not go away and in the future will probably develop into a greater problem. Student[illegible]e for themselves if they want to s[illegible] problem or the solution. *Find a related [illegible]n Page 2 of this issue.*

3

Overcoming perfection through a simple phot[illegible]graph

Quips and Qualms
by Sarah Hughes

Currently Playing: "I Shall Believe" by Sheryl Crow

As any rite of passage, someday everyone will understand they're flawed, but I just so happened to reach my point of self actualization by simply viewing a photograph in the Snite Museum of Art at the University of Notre Dame.

And it's not easy to digest, it took me 17 years to realize and come to terms with the fact that I'm not perfect. And of course, I'll relapse over and over again. As any rite of passage, someday everyone will understand they're flawed, but I just so happened to reach my point of self-actualization by simply viewing a photograph in the Snite Museum of Art at the University of Notre Dame.

I breezed through the photos, observing a mountain here, sand dune there, until I came to crashing halt. There on the walls of the gallery, among his famous landscape photographs, hung some of Ansel Adams' still lifes. It is one thing to capture the beauty of landscapes, but it is another to photograph objects in everyday life and leave the viewer with piqued curiosity and interest. Oblivious that Adams dappled into the medium of still lifes, I discovered one still life titled: "Still Life (Egg Slicer), San Francisco, California, 1942," that caught my attention, and later my heart.

At first glance, it's a simple picture of a metal egg slicer with two bottles and another egg in the background. But a secret to looking at any piece of work is to ignore the signs asking you to stay a certain distance away and try to get as close as humanly possible.

As I looked to see if a[illegible]ere nearby who would cause a commotion wh[illegible] too close to the photograph for their com[illegible]ed on the print a hair, poorly disguised by a[illegible] job. For those who have yet to experience [illegible] eye of a photography teacher, when [illegible] on the negative during the print making [illegible]or dot is noticeable on the print. And [illegible] Adam's print worth $18,500, I found [illegible] I rejoiced!

4

Adams, who some argued [illegible] photographs to display the proof of God through [illegible]distinctly perfectly represented humanity with his [illegible] If Adams could accept this flaw in his still-life arrangement, then so should I learn to accept my own blemishes and flaws, while relishing the beautiful arrangement of the people and pieces in my life.

There is a fine line [illegible]ping perfection and selling your soul to o[illegible] disorder. While I can understand the need to attempt perfection in a product, it's completely normal to rewrap a gift four or five times until you can feel the beam of happiness from Martha Stewart, even through all that concrete.

Here, in this community, we're lucky to have some of the best standards of living, facilities, houses, athletics, performing arts, teachers, students and it's easy for the whirlwind to continue. But, in a local community that stresses perfection to its youth, success over creativity, self-acceptance and enjoyment of daily life, we send dangerous signals on what's important in life: perfection over personality. We could learn from Adams.

I have a plentitude of flaws, I have no real musical talent, I have a hard time admitting I'm wrong (see, desire for perfection) and I never could skate during those wretched backward skating songs at skating rinks. But I realize, love and overcome all of my flaws by composing myself with beautiful people and pieces of my life. Then, and only then, do I create a perfect photograph of myself.

Don't worry Type A people who refuse to give up their dream of self perfection, if you're not ready to accept your self portrait, yes even with flaws, all you have to do is line up the bottoms of the newspapers, fold, shut the paper and crease three times, just in case. ***Sarah Hughes is the editor in chief of the HiLite. Contact her at shughes@hilite.org.***

Taking our democratic freedoms for granted while others suffer

Work In Progress
by Cheryl Steiman

Currently Playing: "Freedom" by Rage Against the Machine

A burst of remarks explodes during an oral argument court case, and the subject is murder. The story tells of a drunken couple's night leading up to a dead husband found on the bathroom floor and a wife charged with his death. It's a storyline found out of an afternoon soap opera, and I was a witness to this dramatic event.

On Nov. 17, I participated in a field trip to the Indiana State House along with my English class to witness an appellate court case. The wife, who is currently convicted and imprisoned for the murder of her husband, has finally managed to appeal her conviction in front of the Indiana Supreme Court. It was an eye-opening experience to the U.S. legal system, which I, like many others, have taken for granted.

Let's see if I can put this statement into perspective. A student wakes up early in the morning and throws on his favorite T-shirt. He then arrives at school and locates his locker by walking through a crowded hallway filled with students of all races. He stands and recites the pledge of allegiance during SRT and overhears a heated discussion among his fellow classmates concerning the formation of President Bush's new cabinet until, finally, just as you are now, he scans through the latest edition of the HiLite for a quick read. Believe it or not, this student has just had a very law influenced morning.

Without a thought in his mind, the early hours of this student's day were surrounded by three landmark Supreme Court cases. The second he placed his arms through his most beloved T-shirt's sleeves, his rights were protected by the 1969 decision of *Tinker v. Des Moines*, a case which ruled it legal for a student's freedom of expression in a school environment as long as it does not infringe on the rights of others. The 1954 *Brown v. Board of Education* decision made it possible for students of all races to collectively attend one school. His recitation of the pledge of allegiance in a public school was legalized this year by the U.S. Supreme Court. And, even the debate over Bush's presidency was possible due to the 2000 Supreme Court decision stating that Bush was the 43rd president of the United States in the *Bush v. Gore* case. Finally, the student's ability to read a student newspaper publication, identical to this HiLite issue, is protected by the 1969 *Tinker v. Des Moines* case.

To me, it is absolutely amazing how our own lives are influenced each day or perhaps every hour by such powerful rulings. We live in a country where a man has the right to a trial before a conviction, a much envied procedure by citizens of countries such as Iran whose punishment for stealing is the cutting of one's hands.

However, I am saddened by my overlooking of my rights, including my ability to counteract in court for a violation or to have a trial by jury.

Concerning the murder case which I witnessed in appellate court, the final judgment has yet to be announced. What really matters most is the actual judicial system that maintains our lawful rights. ***Cheryl Steiman is a managing editor for the HiLite. Contact her at csteiman@hilite.org***

Whoa, this is *so* just like that episode of "The O.C."

Stupid Freshman
by Marc Fichman

Currently Playing: "California" by Rufus Wainwright

There is a sub-culture of people here who watch the California TV drama "The O.C." and take it way too seriously.

It's kind of scary. I wouldn't really call these people just serious fans of the show, though, because they don't really do those fanatic-y kinds of things. These people just want to live in California and have never been to California. They want to live in California just because a fiction TV show depicts its exciting drama-first-then-school lifestyle.

I have only seen one episode of "The O.C.," whether that's a nerdy thing to say or not. Regardless, it's true, and the overall point of the show came well across to me that there is a whole lot of drama in Orange County's teenage lifestyle. While that makes for an interesting TV show, I really don't understand why intense drama is something people actually desire running away to.

I shouldn't be blaming just "The O.C." for this California obsession within our school, though, because there are really plenty of other important factors. There are other TV shows like "Laguna Beach," and there are endless, countless and infinite amounts of songs in the whole entire realm of the musical world that are about California. Musicians write songs about California because "all the leaves are brown" where they live. They write songs about California because they feel the need to add to the collection, like it isn't big enough yet.

But I guess a place like California has to be pretty soup'-wurtin. I've never been there, but everyone knows it's next to the Pacific Ocean, and everyone knows that people can surf there, etc. It's just that I would think people would get it by now, that California is a cool place.

For the current high school demographic, I've come to the conclusion that the recent California obsession started a few years ago with "Orange County," a really great and substantial movie about an aspiring writer in Orange County who tries to get into Stanford University.

The fact that the town of Orange County was portrayed as a place with a bunch of idiots who do drugs and surf instead of go to school, and adults who only care about money makes me wonder why people here feel so passionate about running away to a place like that. They must have totally missed the message of the movie.

After "Orange County," TV shows like "The O.C." and "Laguna Beach" popped up, and they're huge and popular, and they're *all* about California — like it's brand new to us.

Sure, people in California get to "hang out" by the Pacific Ocean while we in Carmel get to "hang out" at the outdoor mall, and sure, there may be a lot more scenery in California, and sure, the weather isn't as extreme. But deep down, just Carmel alone has more in common with the entire state of California than most people might think.

Maybe we're forgetting the fact that Carmel is in California, just with the accent on the other vowel. Also, remember those extremely annoying local TV commercials that used to come up all the time about a Carmel air conditioning business by the name of *Apple*, and they always made a big deal about how there happened to be another business called *Apple* in *Carmel* and it was hilarious? Yes, we have so much in common with California! We might as well be twin cities — even if California isn't a city. Who cares?

It's true that "The O.C." is just a drama, and it's also true that a lot of what goes on deep inside our student body — both in and out of school — is good 'ole drama. So stop complaining that this place isn't as exciting as a TV show's portrayal of Orange County because it's basically the exact same kind of life, but in a different setting.

Musician Rufus Wainwright wrote a song about California, but he totally contradicted the whole idea of the generic California song by writing lyrics that are somewhat against California. Little did he know that his lyrics were going to sum up the main point of this column: "California. It's such a wonder that I think I'll stay in bed." ***Marc Fichman is a news reporter for the HiLite. He is the first freshman to be published as a columnist. Contact him at mfichman@hilite.org.***

Potpourri
The Rest of the Story

The popular television game show "Jeopardy" often includes a section on the board that defies definition and categorization. The creators of the show call this column "Potpourri," a combination of incongruous things. This book is no different. Up to this point, you've learned how to write objective stories, how to tell those stories in alternative ways and how to package those stories in appealing ways for your visual readers.

And now comes the rest.

This final section of the book will discuss the remaining basics of journalism, from law and ethics to opinion writing to staff planning and organization. In addition, we'll spend some time discussing the future of scholastic journalism. After all, storytelling will never die (just ask Carl the Caveman), but, as you have seen, it does change in form. Who knows what tomorrow will bring, but it sure will be exciting to find out.

CHAPTER 13

The Law

Legal Rights
of Student Journalists

"Congress shall make no law respecting an establishment of religion, or prohibiting the free exercise thereof; or abridging the freedom of speech, or of the press; or the right of the people peaceably to assemble, and to petition the Government for a redress of grievances."

Recognize it? You should. It's only just about the most important freedom that our Constitution guarantees to its citizens. And from a journalistic standpoint, it's just about the most important right we have.

In case you didn't know, it's the First Amendment to the U.S. Constitution, part of the original 10 Amendments, the Bill of Rights, outlined by our forefathers, men who earned the ability to outline those rights after years of violent struggle that killed thousands of young Americans.

I say "in case you didn't know" because a recent study by the John S. and James L. Knight Foundation showed that, in terms of First Amendment rights, 97 percent of teachers and 99 percent of school principals said that, yes, people should be allowed to express unpopular views. But only 83 percent of students said yes.

Eighty-three percent. That's it.

And that's pathetic. The study goes on to say that students often think that the media goes too far in its ability to challenge the established political group in power and express unpopular views and that the media should, in many cases, be curtailed in its ability to wield that power.

But what about you? Does the above assessment apply to you? If you're like the students in the survey who were involved in media activities (i.e. newspaper, yearbook, TV production, etc.) then, no, it does not. Students involved in these kinds of activities buck the current trend and are, in fact, more likely to support expression of unpopular views—the same views, by the way, outlined by the First Amendment.

I hope you are part of the latter group.

One of the qualities that makes living in the United States such a privilege is that we do have the broad abilities outlined by the First Amendment and, in somewhat of a more specific sense, the remaining amendments. We can share unpopular views if we want to. We can bemoan the "system" without fear of imprisonment or worse. We can "rage against the machine" and gnash our teeth and demonstrate

WHAT CAN BE CENSORED

*The 1988 Hazelwood v. Kuhlmeier case gave school officials
some pretty broad parameters on what they could censor.
But that power isn't absolute. Here's what the Supreme Court
says in terms of how administrators must justify their censorship.*

Material in student publications that may be censored:

1. Material that is ungrammatical, poorly written, inadequately researched, biased or prejudiced, vulgar or profane, or unsuitable for immature audiences.

2. Topics such as "the existence of Santa Claus in an elementary school setting, the particulars of teenage sexual activity in a high school setting, speech that might reasonably be perceived to advocate drug or alcohol use, irresponsible sex, or conduct otherwise inconsistent with the shared values of a civilized social order."

3. Material that would "associate the school with anything other than the neutrality on matters of political controversy."

Note: The Supreme Court also said that school officials may review non-forum, school-sponsored publications before they are sent to print. This is a process known as prior review. If the school official opts to withhold information, this is known as prior restraint.

(within reason) to allow our views to be heard. And, once we're old enough, we can elect officials who can vote with our best interests in mind and, if they don't, we can vote other people in to take their jobs. And even if some of the people don't share our views and want to argue an opposite viewpoint, we can take solace in the understanding that it is the First Amendment that allows that discourse. Ultimately, the result is a free and democratic society. It's not a perfect system, but it's worked remarkably well for the past two centuries and, I expect, it will continue to work for centuries more ... unless...

Eighty-three percent. If that number scares you, it should. It means that 17 percent of your peers think that the First Amendment gives too much freedom and that those freedoms should be curtailed. It means that in a typical classroom, say your classroom, of 30 students, roughly five students think that the Constitution gives too much freedom to its citizens.

And that's five students too many.

One possible reason behind the survey's results may quite simply be that students don't understand their rights and how those rights apply to them; it is this opposition to the unknown, therefore, that may cause the problem. And believe it or not, the First Amendment does apply to students. Granted, there are some limitations that will disappear once you graduate from high school and become, from a legal standpoint, a full-fledged adult, but students still enjoy, within reason, most of the same rights as their parents and their parents parents.

But knowledge is power. Simply, when students understand their rights, as the students involved in media classes in the Knight survey did, then they will be more likely to give credence to those rights and ensure them for generations to come.

This chapter will outline three key categories within the First Amendment right to free speech. First, it will discuss some of the legal First Amendment limitations for student journalists—limitations that you won't really have to worry about once you graduate. Second, we will discuss free speech limitations that all citizens must keep in mind. The right to free speech is not absolute, after all, but it is broad. And rather than simply discard what may seem vague, we must understand the rules and work within them. Finally, we'll take some time to discuss ethics—what you should and shouldn't do—because even though something may be technically legal, it doesn't necessarily make it right.

The road to define the rights of student journalists—and all journalists, for that matter—is fraught with many court cases and battles, some more prominent than others. This chapter will in no way provide an exhaustive list of those cases. Rather, we will hit the high points (and the low points, depending on how you look at the matter), and use those battles to provide an accurate, albeit rough, outline of student press law. But as with the rest of the chapters in this book, use this information as a starting point and then find out more on your own.

As for our starting point, we must begin in the 1960s in Des Moines, Iowa, with a student named John Tinker and his sister, Mary Beth, and their friend, Chris Ekhardt, who made a quiet decision one day that was soon heard around the country.

Tinker v. Des Moines, 1969

Until the 1960s, it was widely believed that students didn't have any rights when they came to school. They couldn't vote. They couldn't fight for the country. In many ways, they were simply taking up space until they graduated and became valuable, productive parts of society.

But the 1960s were a particularly tumultuous time. Civil rights had come to a head, led by the charismatic Martin Luther King, Jr., among others. And the United States had been involved in a particularly lengthy and largely unpopular military campaign in Vietnam.

In December of 1965, John and Mary Beth Tinker and Chris Eckhardt decided that they'd had enough. They wanted to express their displeasure with the Vietnam War by wearing to school black armbands around their sleeves. When they arrived, the trio was quickly ushered to the principal's office where they were told, in no uncertain terms, that they needed to remove the armbands if they wanted to return to class. The students did not comply, and as a result, they were suspended.

The students' families on behalf of their children filed a petition against the school district, saying that the school had interfered with their children's right to free speech under the First Amendment. The case went through several appeals before it reached the highest court in the land — the U.S. Supreme Court — whose job it is to define and interpret the Constitution as it applies to individual cases. The decisions that the Supreme Court makes, in most instances, become law for the rest of the country.

Keep in mind that the Supreme Court didn't rule on the Tinker v. Des Moines case until 1969, four years after the incident had occurred. In fact, John Tinker and Chris Eckhardt had since graduated. But this is typical of Supreme Court cases, where lawyers and special interest groups tend to take over the case and the names associated with the case become merely figureheads.

It was Supreme Court Justice Abe Fortas who delivered the majority opinion in the court's 7–2 decision. "It can hardly be argued," Fortas wrote, "that either students or teachers shed their constitutional rights to freedom of speech or expression at the schoolhouse gate.... In our system, state-operated schools may not be enclaves of totalitarianism. School officials do not possess absolute authority over their students. Students in school as well as out of school are 'persons' under our Constitution. They are possessed of fundamental rights, which the State must respect, just as they themselves must respect their obligations to the State. In our system, students may not be regarded as closed-circuit recipients of only that which the State chooses to communicate. They may not be confined to the expression of those sentiments that are officially approved."

And that was it. With that landmark decision, the Supreme Court — the highest court in the land — had ruled on students' enjoyment of First Amendment rights, and it had ruled favorably. In other words, with the Tinker decision, students around the country could legally say that they, too, enjoyed the right to free speech and expression.

The ruling was broad and, from a student standpoint, well received. But it wasn't

A SAMPLE POLICY STATEMENT

The 1988 Hazelwood v. Kuhlmeier case applies to "school-sponsored" publications.
But many schools have gotten around the ruling by having their school
boards establish their publications as "public forums," which follow
the much looser restrictions of the 1969 Tinker v. Des Moines case.
Here's a sample policy statement to get you started.

STATEMENT OF POLICY

Freedom of expression and press freedom are fundamental values in a democratic society. The mission of any institution committed to preparing productive citizens must include teaching students these values, both by lesson and by example.

As determined by the courts, both state and federal law, especially the First Amendment to the United States Constitution, protect student exercise of freedom of expression and press freedom. Accordingly, school officials are responsible for encouraging and ensuring freedom of expression and press freedom for all students.

It is the policy of the _____ Board of Education that (newspaper), (yearbook), (literary magazine) and (electronic or on-line media), the official, school-sponsored student media of _____ High School have been established as forums for student expression and as voices in the uninhibited, robust, free and open discussion of issues. Each medium should provide a full opportunity for students to inquire, question and exchange ideas. Content should reflect all areas of student interest, including topics about which there may be dissent or controversy.

It is the policy of the _____ Board of Education that student journalists shall have the right to determine the content of student media. Accordingly, the following guidelines relate only to establishing grounds for disciplinary actions subsequent to publication.

Information from the Student Press Law Center. More information can be found at www.splc.org.

without limitations. The Supreme Court did say that free speech was acceptable as long as that speech wasn't "disruptive" to the learning environment. That meant that as long as students expressing their views didn't interfere with the learning of others, then that speech was fine by the law.

And the disruption couldn't just be "speculative" either. In other words, a principal or administrator couldn't stop a student's free speech just because he thought the speech might be disruptive; he had to have some evidence that the speech would, in fact, be disruptive. If an earlier demonstration in the year, for example, had led to a fight on school grounds and the administration had evidence of that, then it could curtail the speech.

From a student-journalist standpoint, the Tinker decision was a huge boost. While it did not directly apply to student publications, the freedoms outlined in the case did indirectly influence school newspapers, yearbooks and the like. Students enjoyed a newfound freedom to cover what they wanted when they wanted, as long as what they printed wasn't "disruptive" in the eyes of the law. Some even called the Tinker decision the Magna Carta for students (the Magna Carta is an English document that is often thought of as the cornerstone of liberty and the chief defense against arbitrary and unjust rule in that country).

For almost two decades, students enjoyed their newfound First Amendment rights. Until...

Bethel v. Fraser, 1986

In April of 1983, Matthew Fraser delivered a speech in front of a school assembly nominating a fellow student to a student-elected office. The speech was full of sexual innuendo and vulgar gestures. As a result, Fraser was suspended from school and then, subsequently, he and his family sued, citing, interestingly enough, the Tinker v. Des Moines case that supposedly allowed him the right to free speech.

The Supreme Court disagreed. In a 5–4 decision in 1986, the court supported what the Bethel High School's disciplinary rule said. "Conduct which materially and substantially interferes with the educational process is prohibited, including the use of obscene, profane language or gestures."

So why was this important? Because it somewhat limited the freedom of speech guaranteed students under the Tinker v. Des Moines decision. In a sense, it took a little of the power away from students and put it back into the hands of administrators and school districts.

But from a student publication standpoint, the Bethel decision wasn't too big of a blow. Most responsible publications didn't include vulgar or profane language anyway. However, what the Bethel decision did was set the stage for a court case that set the world of scholastic journalism on its head, a case that would hit the Supreme Court just two years later.

Hazelwood v. Kuhlmeier, 1988

Up until this point, no Supreme Court cases dealt specifically with student publications and the content found within them. As a result, students involved in those publications and their advisers used the other student free speech cases to apply to their work in the journalism classroom. If students have the right to free speech under Tinker, they argued, then that applied to free speech in their publications as well.

THE INVERTED PYRAMID OF STUDENT RIGHTS

Since the 1969 Tinker v. Des Moines case, students have seen their rights slowly diminish. Here's a quick visual rundown.

1969 Tinker v. Des Moines
Students do enjoy First Amendment rights as long as the speech is not "disruptive" to the learning environment.

1986 Bethel v. Fraser
School officials may censor speech that is vulgar or profane.

1988 Hazelwood v. Kuhlmeier
Scool officials may censor publications that are deemed "school-sponsored."

Hazelwood East High School's Journalism II class produced a publication called the *Spectrum*. At that time, it was the policy of the staff and its adviser, Cathy Kuhlmeier, to submit proofs of their publication to the school's principal. The issue in question involved, in the eyes of the principal, two objectionable articles — one describing school students' experiences with pregnancy and another discussing the impact of divorce on students at the school. The principal reasoned that there wasn't enough time to make changes in the articles in order for the paper to be delivered before the end of the school year, so he ended up withholding those stories from the paper while allowed other stories to remain.

By now, you know the drill. Cathy Kuhlmeier sued, saying her students' First Amendment rights were being violated, and in January of 1988, the Supreme Court delivered its ruling — the school was within its rights to censor the content of, what they called, a "school-sponsored" publication. In other words, the court said, a school publication should not be considered a forum for student expression.

Justice Byron White, in speaking for the majority of justices in the 5–3 decision, wrote that "educators do not offend the First Amendment by exercising editorial control over the style and content of student speech in school-sponsored expressive activities so long as their actions are reasonably related to legitimate pedagogi-

---

FREEDOM OF INFORMATION AND WHAT'S STILL OFF LIMITS

*In a democratic society, citizens are able to keep tabs on
what the government and governmental officials are doing.
Freedom of Information (FOI) laws, or "sunshine laws," as they
are often called, give journalists broad rights in finding information
for stories. You should know what you can and can't find out.*

What you can find out:

All records generated or meetings conducted by a public body are open to the public unless law specifically exempts them. This applies to school board meetings, for example.

Matters of public record, including police arrest records, salaries of people paid for by public tax dollars (i.e., teachers and administrators).

What is restricted (the Family Educational Rights and Privacy Act [FERPA], also known as the "Buckley Amendment"):

Student records. This includes transcripts, medical and disciplinary records. For example, you would have a hard time getting a school nurse to tell you who at your school suffers from seasonal allergies because of FERPA.

However, under the FERPA guidelines, students do have a right to request their own records and they also have a right to ask that the school correct or delete any information contained in their records that the student believes to be inaccurate, misleading or an invasion of his or her privacy.

Note: The guidelines listed here are pretty general and may vary from state to state. You should familiarize yourself with your own state and local information laws.

cal concerns." In other words, the court said that if the publication is geared toward student learning, then its content can, in fact, be censored.

The court went on to outline what constituted a "school-sponsored" publication (see next page), saying that if a publication met any one of three requirements it could be censored by administrators. Most school publications found that they met not just one, but all three of the requirements, which put them squarely in the middle of the parameters outlined by the Hazelwood decision.

Of course, an administrator couldn't just censor with free rein. There were some limitations to what a school official could censor, but these criteria were so broad that many administrators did enjoy almost unlimited freedom in controlling the content of their schools' publications.

The Hazelwood decision caused a tidal wave in the world of scholastic journalism. Suddenly, students involved in school publications and their advisers were on the defensive, and it took many years to sort out the problems. To this day, the Hazelwood case remains the preeminent case involving scholastic journalism, and its legacy still permeates the culture of publications.

Life After Hazelwood

Thankfully, the world of scholastic journalism didn't fall apart after the Hazelwood decision. And in a weird sort of way, it actually made parts of school publications stronger. While many administrators did and still continue to use Hazelwood to justify their blatant censorship of school publications, the case certainly made both students and administrators question what material they included in their publications, and for students and their advisers,

it made them more accountable for the information they provided. Just as with the professional press, student journalists should be responsible for the stories they produce. Hopefully, they do a good job finding credible, relevant sources to answer tough questions that are in the best interest of their student readers. And hopefully they are able to justify why they are telling readers the stories they produce — giving their student readers something to think about. And hopefully, they are doing their best to be as objective as they can, constantly searching for as many sides to the stories as they can and presenting those sides to their readers.

In fact, many strong publications have metaphorically "risen from the ashes" of Hazelwood. These publications have managed to get their local school boards to approve official policy statements, which, in a sense, overturn the Supreme Court's designation of the publications as "school-sponsored" and make them official "public forums" instead. Public forums are designed to allow the public discourse of ideas for their specific and important student audience. It is these strong, responsible publications that should be the role model for other struggling ones. And it all starts with being responsible young journalists. Because to learn to be a journalist means more than just learning how to gather information and how to place design elements on a page. It means learning how to gather that information responsibly and accurately, and it means learning how to take occasional controversy and share it in a productive manner, a manner that promotes structured discourse of those ideas.

Many journalism advisers and their forward-thinking administrators will agree that school publications, if done correctly and responsibly, provide a valuable element to the school's culture. A school publication isn't just a public relations piece that merely trumpets the school's successes, they would say, but it is a sample of how students are allowed to express their views—both good and bad—in a structured, responsible way.

Ethics

What we've discussed up to this point is the law—what you legally can and can't do. What we'll touch on now is the gray area within the context of the law—ethics. **Ethics are what you should or shouldn't do within the context of the law,** because while something may be legal, it doesn't necessarily make it right.

Let's say, for the sake of argument, that you're faced with this scenario on your newspaper staff:

A student reporter with the school paper proposes a story regarding a popular, single, male, middle-aged teacher at the school who has become very ill. The teacher has lost much weight and has missed many days of school, and word has spread among the students and staff that he may have AIDS. The teacher has been in and out of the hospital but will not see either students or colleagues who would like to visit, and the school's administration has made no official statement as to the teacher's condition.

The student reporter says to the faculty adviser and student editorial board that AIDS is not something anyone need to be ashamed of and that the teacher's story is one that should be told because it puts a face on the very real condition of living with AIDS and how that condition affects everyone.

What do you do? The first step is to look at the law, of course. You must ask yourself, "Can I write this story?" Are you within your rights to run a story like this? Maybe. You'd have to check to see, for example, if you would be invading the teacher's privacy. Granted, the teacher is a public figure, paid for by public tax dollars, so the rules are a bit more lax than if he were private citizen.

But once you're beyond the law, the next step is to ask yourself the question, "Should I write this story?" And that's a tougher question to answer, and one that,

---

SCHOOL SPONSORED OR NOT?

The 1988 Hazelwood v. Kuhlmeier case said that school officials could censor "school-sponsored" publications. But what constitutes "school sponsored"? Read below to find out.

To be considered "school sponsored," and, thus, held under the Hazelwood ruling, a publication must meet any one of the following three criteria:

1. The work is supervised by a faculty member.
2. The publication is designed to impart particular skills or knowledge to student participants or audiences.
3. The publication uses the school's name or resources.

Note: After the Hazelwood decision, most publications found that they met, not just one, but all three of the criteria.

unfortunately, has no definitive answer. You see, every person is different, and every publication is different. What may work in the *National Enquirer* may not play in the *St. Petersburg Times*. Ethical questions are never easy, and they never go away.

Summary

A solid understanding of the law is a starting point to producing responsible publications. Knowing what you can and can't do will certainly give you firmer ground to stand on when you ultimately make your decisions. And, truthfully, people may not always agree with the decisions you make. Journalists often have to develop a thick skin to deflect the ire of their readers. And that can be frustrating, especially to someone just starting out. Know that you won't always make good decisions, and you won't always make everyone happy.

And also keep this little pearl of wisdom with you whenever you're faced with conflict — if people are stirred by what you've written, then at least they're reading. In addition, if you participate in a public forum for student expression, then those readers have the ability to share their own viewpoints with readers through letters to the editor.

In the end, it is this discourse of ideas that makes scholastic journalism — and professional journalism, for that matter — so unique. When they wrote the First Amendment, our forefathers must have known that when they composed it.

Unprotected Speech for All

Now we've arrived at the next category in our discussion of journalism law — speech not protected for any journalist (or person, for that matter), regardless of age. You see, in a few years you'll be leaving the hallowed halls of your high school (we hope) and moving on to bigger and better things. And with that move, of course, means more responsibility. Granted, you'll no longer have to worry about some of the restrictions that held you back during your stint in scholastic journalism — Tinker and Hazelwood will become things of the past — but you're not off scot-free. No one is. After all, the freedom of speech guaranteed in the First Amendment is not absolute. It protects speech, yes, but it does not protect that speech if it causes harm to others. In fact, most laws in this country are designed to protect the country's citizens. And words, believe it or not, can sometimes cause harm. In this segment, we'll discuss three different types of speech not protected by the First Amendment for any person, journalist or not.

Obscenity

I mention this unprotected speech for one reason — it's one of the most widely misused words in the English language. "Did you hear what he said?" your friend might say. "That was obscene." Or "That halftime show with Janet Jackson was obscene."

No, it wasn't.

Obscenity, at least by the courts' definition, is "hardcore pornography." In fact, the 1973 case of Miller v. State of California outlined three criteria to define obscenity (see graphic at right), all of which must be met in order for a work to be considered legally obscene. The most important of these criteria is that the work must be "taken as a whole" in order for it to meet the definition. That means you can't take a small part of a larger production — a chapter in a book, for example, or one part of a halftime show — and immediately call the whole thing "obscene." It may be profane or distasteful. It might be shocking or vulgar. But my guess is, it's not obscene.

The thing is, you'll probably never have to worry about producing information that, by the legal standard at least, is "obscene." But you need to understand the definition so that others don't throw it back at you or your publication incorrectly.

OBSCENE OR JUST DISTASTEFUL?

The 1973 case of Miller v. State of California outlined the criteria for a work to be considered legally obscene.

For a work to be considered legally obscene, it must meet all three of the following criteria:

1. Whether the average person applying contemporary community standards would find that the work, taken as a whole, appeals to the prurient interest.
2. Whether the work depicts or describes in a potentially offensive way sexual conduct as defined by state law.
3. Whether the work, taken as a whole, lacks serious literary, artistic, political or scientific value.

Note: A quick, two-word definition of obscenity is "hardcore pornography."

Invasion
of Privacy

Like freedom of speech,
the right to be left alone
is not absolute. In fact,
many public figures have
a limited right to privacy.
But the courts have still
outlined four different
types of privacy invasion
that journalists must be
aware of.

THE TYPES OF
PRIVACY INVASION

The courts have outlined four specific types of invasion of privacy. Note that public figures have a limited right to privacy because of their stature.

Intrusion

Invading into a person's solitude or his or her private-area activities. This can be through the use of tape recorders, cameras and any other news-gathering devices.

Publication of private facts

This is especially true if those facts would be offensive to a reasonable person and are of no legitimate concern of the public.

False light

Publication of information that would be regarded incorrectly by the public. Like the publication of private facts, this information must be highly offensive to a reasonable person and published with malice (forethought) or a reckless disregard for the truth of whether the facts are false.

Misappropriation

Using a person's name, likeness or endorsement without the person's consent, often to sell a product. This type of invasion of privacy happens most often when advertisers want students to be in their ads. If you use this practice in your own publication, you should be sure to have those students (and their parents) sign a release form, acknowledging that they give permission to be in the ad.

Libel

Journalists do their best to write stories that are as accurate as possible. But sometimes journalists fall short in that goal. And sometimes, albeit rarely, they downright lie.

Libel laws are in place to protect citizens from those outright lies. At its core, libel is a written falsehood about someone. And libel (and its spoken partner, slander) is illegal.

Understand that the press wields tremendous power to influence policy makers and shape society. But with that power comes equally tremendous responsibility. The media (often called the "fourth estate" of government by some) is, in many ways, a watchdog of society, making sure that people do what they say they are going to do and then making sure that news is made public when they don't. Which all means that, over time, the media have earned a sort of credibility of their own, a type of trust from those who access those media.

But what happens when the media prints something that isn't true? What if that news is about someone you know or, worse, what if it's about you or one of your relatives? What then? After all, people trust the media, and when they see your name written down in the paper along with some false accusation, they'll tend to believe it. And then what happens to you and your reputation?

It seems the courts had this in mind when they created libel laws. On the one hand, the laws have to allow the media some leeway in sharing the news; if the laws were too strict, the government could do pretty much whatever it wants. But on the other hand, the laws have to establish some definitive line between what is acceptable and what is not. If the laws are too broad, then the media could do whatever it wants.

Libel laws do make the distinction between private and public figures. And if you fall into the "public figure" category, proving libel is more difficult. The courts are the final designators of who is considered public and private, but in general, public figures tend to be those who have either placed themselves into prominent positions or those who have been thrust there by other circumstances. And in some states, there is no distinction between public and private figures. In the eyes of these courts, all citizens are considered public figures.

It's difficult to win a libel suit, and that's by design. The courts know that the media need the ability to comment on public figures, even if those comments are negative, in order to keep a free and open forum for the country's citizens. But sometimes the media crosses the line. In those cases, libel laws are in place to provide protection.

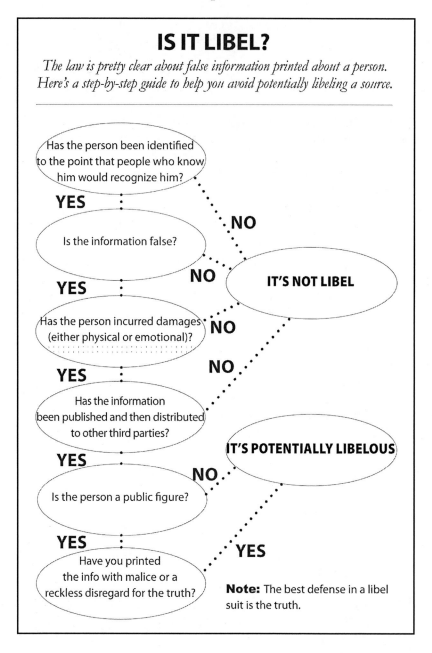

IS IT LIBEL?

The law is pretty clear about false information printed about a person. Here's a step-by-step guide to help you avoid potentially libeling a source.

Has the person been identified to the point that people who know him would recognize him?

YES / **NO**

Is the information false?

YES / **NO**

IT'S NOT LIBEL

Has the person incurred damages (either physical or emotional)?

YES / **NO**

Has the information been published and then distributed to other third parties?

YES / **NO**

IT'S POTENTIALLY LIBELOUS

Is the person a public figure?

YES / **NO**

Have you printed the info with malice or a reckless disregard for the truth?

YES / **YES**

Note: The best defense in a libel suit is the truth.

STUDY GUIDE

Terms and Concepts

Ethics — What one should or shouldn't do within the context of the law.

First Amendment to the U.S. Constitution — "Congress shall make no law respecting an establishment of religion, or prohibiting the free exercise thereof; or abridging the freedom of speech, or of the press; or the right of the people peaceably to assemble, and to petition the Government for a redress of grievances."

Invasion of privacy—The right to be left alone. Consists of four types—intrusion, publication of private facts, false light and misappropriation.

Libel—A written falsehood about someone that causes damages.

Obscenity—Work, taken as a whole, that appeals to the prurient (sexual) interest; hardcore pornography.

Policy statement—An official document approved by a school district's school board that establishes a publication as a "public forum."

Public figure—A person who thrusts himself or who has been thrust into the public spotlight. Public figures usually find it more difficult to win libel or invasion of privacy suits because of stricter guidelines that protect the public's right to know.

Public forums—Publications that are designed to allow the public discourse of ideas for their specific audience.

School sponsored—Established after the 1988 Hazelwood v. Kuhlmeier case, a designation that allows school officials to censor a publication if it meets any one of three criteria.

Find Out More About Law and Ethics

More Cases

Each of these court cases deals with press freedoms in some way. Try looking up each case to find out the details. How would these cases' outcomes relate to your own role on a publication staff?

New York Times v. Sullivan

Associated Press v. Walker

Rosenbloom v. Metromedia

More Ethical Questions

Try this ethical situation on for size:

One of the reporters on your newspaper staff is also a member of the school's drama department. The drama director has offered to pay her $100 if she will "just cover all theater activities in the paper" as part of her news beat.

1. Is this legal?
2. If so, what would you do in this situation? Why?
3. What would you do to try to prevent this situation in the future?

Here's another one:

One of your reporters has written an in-depth story about hate groups and has interviewed several students who say they believe in and practice white supremacy. Both of the students are 18-year-old seniors and have said that the reporter could use their names in the story. Just before the issue goes to press, the mother of one of the students calls you and begs you not to use her child's name in the story.

1. What do you do (i.e., should you run an anonymous source)?
2. What legal concerns should you have?
3. How could you prevent this problem in the future?

CHAPTER 14

Everybody's Got One

When and Where to State Your Opinion

OK. So up to this point in the book we've discussed how to tell objective news and feature stories. Granted, we also talked about how true objectivity is a myth. After all, journalists make subjective decisions all the time — what sources to include in a story, who gets included first, second, third, where the story appears on the page, etc. But those types of subjectivity are incidental. For the most part, the stories that we write follow the basic rules of objectivity, from having credible sources answer questions to always using "said" — the most objective word we have — as the appropriate verb of attribution.

This chapter will explore another field of journalistic writing entirely: the world of opinion writing.

Some argue that the pages that include the subjective articles in a paper are the most important pages in that publication. Certainly those articles can be the cornerstone of a paper's role as a true public forum (see previous chapter), and often it is these pages that are held to the most scrutiny from readers and administrators alike. It also means that these subjective pieces can give your paper a distinct personality which makes it different from other school publications in your area. When people refer to a professional publication as being either conservative or liberal, it is most often because of the types of opinions expressed within the context of the subjective articles that they publish.

And that's a lot of responsibility to take on. This chapter will describe the different types of opinion writing and, further, describe how to write each type properly and responsibly.

The Staff Editorial

Perhaps the most important of all the types of opinion writing is the staff editorial. This piece of writing encompasses the general consensus of your newspaper or magazine staff and, arguably, holds the most sway with student readers and adult teachers and administrators alike. Staff editorials are unbylined, so even though one staff member may be assigned to write the editorial, his name is not used. It is the staff's opinion. In fact, it sometimes occurs that the person who writes the editorial may not even agree with the opinion that he is writing about.

TYPES OF EDITORIALS

*Try to keep the staff editorials you write within
the guidelines of these five different styles.*

Explanation

Explains the basics (who, what, when, where) of a news event. Particularly useful if readers may be confused about a certain issue or if the matter is complicated (new dress code policy, what status as a Blue Ribbon School means, etc.).

Argumentation

Supports or refutes an action or proposal by an individual or a group. If the administration wants to create a new attendance policy, for example, and your staff disagrees, then you could write this type of editorial.

Criticism

Points to a problem or issue in or out of school. A great way to localize a national or even regional event to relate directly to readers.

Commendation

Publicly acknowledges a person or group that has positively affected the school or community.

Commemoration

Encourages readers to support and participate in either a traditional or newly organized event (i.e., encouraging readers to give to the poor during the holidays).

And that may not be too uncommon. After all, the staff editorial should be decided by a group of people who represent the best interests of the readership. In a professional publication, where the staffs are large, those interests are usually represented by an editorial board, which consists of some of the top editors in a publication. But for a scholastic publication, staffs are smaller and you may be able to get your entire staff involved in the discussion. And that's important. The more opinions you can get from your staff members, the more accurately your editorials will be in representing the staff's feelings toward a particular issue or event.

Like the objective story, the most important part of the staff editorial is the lead. If you don't capture your readers' atten-
tion there, again like the objective story, they won't read any further. **And that editorial lead needs to include some important information — namely, the topic of the message, the audience to whom that message is intended and what you want that audience to do.**

The first decision you must make as a staff is the topic — what you want to write about. Because several weeks (or even months) may pass between publications, it's not a bad idea for scholastic publications to write an editorial that is related in some way to an objective story that appears earlier in the paper. Have you written a news story about the school's new dress code policy? Then comment on it in your editorial.

Next, you have to decide to whom

A SAMPLE EDITORIAL

Here's an example of an editorial of argumentation. Notice how the editorial uses specific examples and research to illustrate its point. In addition, notice the clear lead and the behavioral call to action at the end.

Faculty Should Censor Consistently

From the HiLite *(Carmel, IN, H.S.)*

The First Amendment may possibly create the most confusion of all the provisions in the Constitution. It lulls many students into thinking that they have the right to say whatever they wish and that censorship violates the right to express themselves.

However, the question has never been whether or not school administrators have the authority to censor material they consider amoral or offensive; they do. The issue is that they should censor with due necessity and with consistency. This school is no exception. In light of recent events, administrators should be more consistent in meting out disciplinary action.

While critics of censorship in schools argue that it violates the right of free speech outlined in the First Amendment, the courts have continually ruled in favor of schools on this subject. In Bethel School District No. 403 v. Fraser, the Supreme Court held that schools retain the right to refuse to sponsor speech that is "inconsistent with the 'fundamental values of public school education.'" In other words, the First Amendment does not protect types of speech that the school deems inappropriate. Censorship provides a means for protecting students, many of whom are minors, from types of speech and expression administrators have decided are inconsistent with their educational mission or just plain inappropriate.

But times have changed. What society considered inappropriate decades ago has become part of mainstream culture today. For example, cursing used to earn the offender a severe punishment (the classic washing the mouth out with soap). In today's world, students learn cuss words early and use them often. One rarely passes a day without hearing strings of words that would embarrass the average baby boomer.

The trend has been particularly evident at this school. For one reason or another, clubs bearing names with innuendoes or curse word modifications have proliferated this year. Case in point: Wild Buck. Whether or not the club founders had the innuendo in mind while formulating a name is irrelevant. The important part is that the majority of the high school family picked up on an innuendo, and the administrators felt it was inappropriate. Similarly, the phrase "feather plucking," which was said once on the video announcements, earned its offender disciplinary action as well.

Though administrators have the right to penalize students who use types of speech they have deemed inappropriate, they still have an obligation to censor or restrict fairly. If the administration plans to create a hullabaloo over possible obscenities in names like "Wild Buck" or phrases such as "feather plucking," it must penalize all students who invent forms of speech which may be offensive. If "We Funk" (another club here at the high school) and "Wild Buck" possibly reference inappropriate sexual themes, then surely "Pound it," the slogan of the clarinet section in the marching band, is inappropriate for its violent context if not its blatantly sexual one.

If the above scenario sounds ridiculous, that's probably because it is. In our generation, cuss words have become as mundane as computers in the life of the average teenager. The administration needs to acknowledge that the definition of profanity has changed and spend its time censoring forms of speech that truly corrupt our minds rather than searching for every possible innuendo that solely entertains. However, if the administration chooses to look for these supposed inappropriate references, it must fairly censor all the displays of speech which may be "inconsistent with 'the fundamental values of public school instruction.'"

you're addressing your editorial. Every staff editorial should have an intended audience, and that audience should be made clear from the outset. Are you speaking to the administration? The senior class? The English department? The principal? The more specific you are, the stronger your message will be.

Once you've decided on the topic and the audience, then your next task is to determine what kind of message you want to send. There are many different types of editorials (see "Types of Editorials"), and each one serves an important purpose. Do you want to criticize the administration for passing what you consider to be an unjust rule? Or do you want to commend the upperclassmen for helping to ease the transition to high school for the new freshmen? Whatever you decide, you must make that message clear in your editorial's lead.

After that, the majority of the editorial should be spent supporting your opinion. You can take a lesson from folks on your local debate team for this one. In debate, competitors spend much of their time researching information that will help to support their case, and that often means gaining an understanding of what the opposition to that case will say so that they can refute it. Editorials are no different. Like an objective news story, you need concrete evidence to give credibility and relevance to your argument. If you say, for example, that the new dress code is unjust and that other schools have no such poli-

cies, then you'd better have the research to support that claim. In fact, it could even be to your benefit to use research and even quotes from expert sources from the objective story to help support your opinion. Also, like good debaters, you should acknowledge the other side's opinions in a given matter. Often, the secret to a solid argument is to acknowledge what the other side (or sides) will say and then, systematically, blow those opposing arguments out of the water.

The final step to a good staff editorial is to end with a clear call to action. In other words, you've spent the last 400 words telling the administration why its cell phone ban is a terrible idea, but now what do you want them to do about it? Without a clear call to action, your editorial will fall flat. You will become one of the many who complain but then offer no solutions. And keep in mind that your call to action should be behavioral, not just emotional. You should give your intended audience a clear course of action to follow in order to rectify the situation. Don't just tell the senior class, for example, that they should "think twice" before they cross the line between conducting a harmless senior prank and an act of vandalism. Rather, instruct the seniors to redirect their energy from completing senior pranks to doing a specific community service, something that, inevitably, will help them to leave their mark more indelibly than any prank could ever do.

The Review

Another common type of opinion writing that appears in many student publications is the review, and rightly so. Students have quite a bit of disposable income, after all, income that they often use for products and services like music, movies and food. But teens are also notoriously fickle with their money, and they often look to the advice of others for ideas on where or how they should spend their cash.

A SAMPLE MOVIE REVIEW

This review does a good job of giving only the barest of plot summaries and then spending the rest of the time actually reviewing. Notice the use of specific examples to illustrate and the fact that the reviewer has obviously seen the prequel, which is helpful when readers want to know how the sequel stacks up to the original.

SEQUELS DON'T ALWAYS LIVE UP TO EXPECTATIONS OF THEIR AUDIENCE
By Anisha Vichare, Carmel (IN) H.S.

There is a common adage that states that movie sequels hardly ever match their predecessors in quality. "Meet the Fockers" is an example of this in that it is even less entertaining than the kind-of-funny "Meet the Parents."

The basic storyline consists of the recently engaged couple Greg (Ben Stiller) and Pam (Teri Polo) visiting Greg's parents Roz (Barbra Streisand) and Bernie Focker (Dustin Hoffman) with Pam's parents, Jack (Robert De Niro) and Dina Byrnes (Blythe Danner) and their grandson, Little Jack (Spencer and Bradley Pickren) along for the ride. As the ultra-conservative and uptight Byrnes meet the overly affectionate and unconventional Fockers, highjinks ensue.

"Meet the Fockers" comes across as sometimes funny, always embarrassing and predictable. In the same vein as the first, the majority of the film is one humiliation after another and jokes get driven into the ground. Though the sequel is more endearing than the first, most likely because of the addition of Hoffman and Streisand as the eccentric Fockers, there seem to be too many subplots and running jokes that are, in fact, not nearly as humorous as they are intended to be.

The "Focker" jokes get milked dry, a dog that humps anything that moves is still not funny and a baby cursing loses its novelty after the first three times it happens.

"Meet the Fockers" does have its funny moments, most of which occur in the first 30 minutes, such as an incident involving a brick thrown by Greg that destroys the windshield of an uninsured rental car. But it's as if there's a kind of building anticipation for something genuinely funny to happen, but it never does. The movie runs for nearly two long hours, leading to a non-specific feeling of boredom, especially toward the last fourth of the film where whatever semblance of a storyline is left just gets tiresome. With such a stellar ensemble of actors, it's a shame they didn't have better material to work with.

Though unremarkable and mediocre at best, "Meet the Fockers" succeeds in being generally amusing to fans of the original and those who think the name "Pamela Martha Focker" is funny.

A SAMPLE MUSIC REVIEW

Music reviews should be specific. Notice how this one gives detailed information about some of the tracks. In addition, it's a good idea to compare new music to a group's previous releases. If it's a new group, how does it compare to other similar, but more well known, groups?

PAPA ROACH BRINGS MUSIC LOVERS FRESH OUTLOOK ON NEW ALBUM

By Neil Ahrendt, Carmel (IN) H.S.

Anyone who listens to Papa Roach's new CD, "Getting Away with Murder," can tell that the band has matured significantly from its first big single, "Last Resort." Apparently, when a band reaches major label status, songs about suicide are somewhat frowned upon.

The lyrical content is not the only thing that has changed with the band, though. Papa Roach's first release shared the genre of "rap rock" with such bands as Linkin Park or Limp Bizkit. With Papa Roach's second CD, "Lovehatetragedy," the band evolved into a more alternative sound with the singles "She Loves Me Not" and "Time and Time Again." And with "Getting Away with Murder," Papa Roach continues that process of growth and development, expanding upon the group's previous success. In a time period of oxymoronic titles like Creed's "Greatest Hits" CD, progression isn't always a bad thing.

The two singles on the CD are the title track and the emotional "Scars," which boasts the chorus "My scars remind me that the past is real, I tear my heart open just to feel." Though they each strive to have a distinctive sound, the songs more or less sound the same. This makes Papa Roach a fairly "love or hate" band, where if you like one song you'll probably like the next. The only other song that stood out was "Do or Die," which says, "It's never to late to live your life."

The most detracting trait of the CD is its length. Even with 12 tracks, it lasts only 38 minutes, which by most standards is sub-par for a group's third major CD release. The songs average around three minutes each, except for "Do or Die," which is around six minutes long. The CD retails at Best Buy for $12.99 and $9.99 at Circuit City.

Enter the review. You can review anything, really — movies, books, music, restaurants, video game systems. If students use it, you can review it. But you must make your review clear and specific.

In any review, regardless of topic, you want to make your opinion clear from the outset. Without a clear opinion, your article falls into the realm of objective writing or, even worse, boring, pointless prose. If I had a nickel for every restaurant review that I've seen that reads like a long-running, play-by-play of the person's evening without ever getting to the most important part — the food — I'd be a wealthy man. ("First, we walked into the restaurant and were greeted by the hostess who then showed us to our table. And then our waiter, Steve, showed up and took our drink orders. And then he brought napkins ... AAAARGH!). When you review, you've got to get to the heart of the matter at the beginning. Did you like it? Did you hate it? Were you somewhere in the middle? Make it clear.

And then, for the rest of the review, tell me why. Be specific here. If you liked the CD, what did you like about it? What

A SAMPLE COLUMN

Here, this columnist has credibility — she has recently visited the country she discusses. Notice how she takes an international issue and localizes it in words that her readers can understand. Notice, too, how she attempts to provide some perspective for readers by moving away from her personal experience and "globalizing" her opinions.

VIOLENCE IS NOT THE ONLY VIABLE OPTION; TRY PEACE

By Cheryl Steiman, Carmel (IN) H.S.

I believe it is my mother's inherent inclination to read the newspaper daily and regularly watch the evening news that has sketched my adolescence with pictures of "live video" depicting the aftermath of suicide bombings in Israel. I have grown disturbingly accustomed to the act of eating my breakfast and hearing my mother say, "Well, there was another attack in Israel."

The repeated newsbreaks have slowly gnawed away my ability to feel complete remorse. Lately, I have responded to my mother's breakfast announcements with a simple nod and second of silence. Sadly, it took the personal experience of another suicide bomb to turn my emotions toward these horrific attacks.

I recently spent my summer traveling Israel in one of seven buses filled with teenagers from all over the United States and Canada. Our particular program for July 11 included touring the streets of Tel Aviv. On this ominous day, handfuls of participants suddenly received phone calls from anxious parents back at home sharing their personal "breakfast announcements" with their children. (They sheltered us from the news on the trip.) According to reports, on that day, while my group toured and gazed about the busy streets of Tel Aviv, an individual planted a bomb outside the city's central bus station. The explosion murdered a woman and wounded at least 20 other people. The motive of the bombing: to strike against Israel's construction of a security barrier around the West Bank.

Still under construction, Israel's separation barrier will divide the West Bank from the surrounding Israeli cities, which are often victims of violent attacks from terrorists residing in the West Bank. According to the Israeli government, the purpose of the separation barrier will be to prevent terrorists from entering Israeli cities and assaulting their innocent citizens.

However, Israel receives relentless criticism internationally. On July 9, the United Nations passed a resolution condemning the barrier and demanding Israel to cease its construction. Furthermore, the International Court of Justice judged the separation barrier as an infringement on international law. Yet Israel refuses to end the construction of the barrier.

Why is Israel condemned for creating a barrier in times of conflict? As human beings, we create our own personal walls every day. Even children create barriers in response to conflict. If a playmate harms a toy or game belonging to another, separation will ensue because of instinct. No one can call the creation of walls right or wrong because all humans build their own walls.

Even though, as people, we create metaphorical barriers, some conflicts need physical blockades because of their intensity. Building a wall won't solve the everlasting Israeli and Palestinian conflict. It merely creates a political "time out," thus reducing the tension in the Middle East.

Worldwide complaint argues that the separation barrier inconveniences Palestinian people by distancing them from the rest of country. After experiencing a summer in Israel, it's difficult to express the fear for personal safety. Therefore, after more than 50 years of terrorist violence in Israel, I support the barrier's reduction of the countless deaths of innocent Israeli citizens by suicide bombers. Who knows? Maybe one day I'll sit down to breakfast and hear my mother say, "Well, the news says that the weather is supposed to be warm today."

songs? What lyrics? If the movie sucked a raw egg, what about it sucked most specifically? Was it the actors' performances? The bad costumes? The stilted dialogue? And, better yet, give details. (For example, if I heard the young Anakin Skywalker say "Yippee!" one more time in "Star Wars Episode 1," I think I would have punched the guy sitting next to me.) It's also not a bad idea to compare your impressions to other things that readers can relate to. If it's a musical group's new release, how does it compare to the previous one(s)? If it's a new restaurant, how does the food compare to other restaurants that offer similar fare?

The bottom line on reviews is that, unless they're specific and clear, they'll just take up valuable space. But if they're well written, they can be a great way to lend personality to your publication. In fact, sometimes well written reviews can be even more entertaining than the "entertainment" they discuss.

The Column

I almost hesitate to include a section on column writing in this book. Ask most young journalists why they took journalism in the first place, and, nine times out of 10, they say, "I want to be a columnist."

The thing is, while there is no limit to the number of people who want to write columns, there is a limit to the number of people who can write them well. Many aspiring columnists think they are the funniest thing this side of the Mason-Dixon line, but it's hard to write funny. That's why there aren't a whole lot of syndicated funny columnists. So let's avoid talking about funny columns for the time being and spend our time discussing the rest of the columns—the ones you'll more likely be writing.

What good columns should do is to give readers a certain perspective on some issue or event. And this is where many young columnists go astray. They are so egocentric that they never look beyond their own little world. For some reason, these "columnists" think that their readers even care that they went to Grandma's house over the weekend or that they took a vacation to Hawaii for spring break. I mean, good for them, but, as a reader, so what? The best columnists take those personal experiences and lend a more global perspective to those events. They are able to relate what may be a very intimate memory and share it for the greater good of the readers. Good columns often read like good narrative stories. They have a face and gold coins, but they also include elements like research and expert sources to lend credibility and relevance to what they're saying. The only difference is that objective narratives tell readers what to think about, while subjective columns, like editorials and reviews, try to tell readers what to think.

The Editorial Cartoon

Consider cartoons to be illustrated columns. Oh, and, by the way, they don't have to be funny.

Nothing can cheapen the quality of your opinion pages more than a badly rendered editorial cartoon simply because it tends to be the dominant visual image on those pages. And if they aren't insightful, your readers will simply move on. So if you want to make editorial cartoons something special in your publications, here's the lowdown:

1. Being artistic certainly does help, but if your message isn't strong then it won't matter if you're Leonardo da Vinci.

2. Consider your editorial cartoon to be a column told in pictures rather than words. Your artwork should stand alone.

3. Cartoons should be insightful, not necessarily funny. If readers laugh, it should be because they recognize the truth of what you write about.

4. Don't clutter your cartoons with too many words. You should be able to share your message in a few concise phrases. If you're writing a lot, maybe you should be writing a column instead of drawing a cartoon.

Editorial cartoon at bottom by Lydia Comer (Carmel, IN, H.S.). All other cartoons by Mustafa Hameed (Carmel, IN, H.S.).

Some of the best columnists in the professional press are sports writers Mitch Albom (from the *Detroit Free Press*) and Rick Reilly (from *Sports Illustrated*). What those two men realized a long time ago is that not everyone is a sports fan, so articles that merely rehash the foibles of a particular team at the free throw line or a player's inability to tackle late in the fourth quarter don't really enjoy a more global appeal. So Albom and Reilly write about the human side of those sports, and those stories, which happen to focus on athletes, speak to a more general audience, even those who don't particularly like sports.

Where to Find Opinions

There is a contingent of readers who will immediately go to a publication's opinion pages before they read anything else, so placing those pages in a consistent location is important. First, it allows readers, like those mentioned, the ability to find opinion articles quickly and efficiently. Second, from a content standpoint, it creates a visual division between subjective writing and the objective content in the rest of the paper. And that's an important distinction. After all, you don't want readers mixing up the two types of writing. That would only lead to confusion and, ultimately, your readers' distrust.

Most opinion writing appears in a newspaper or magazine's opinion and op/ed pages. Some think that "op/ed" stands for "opinion and editorial" pages, but, in fact, it stands for "opposite the editorial" page. The staff editorial, editorial cartoon and staff columns usually appear on the left "editorial" page, and additional columns (including guest columns) and letters to the editor appear on the "op/ed" page. Often, these pages appear at or near the end of a section in a paper, in a location that follows the paper's news content.

SOURCES OF OPINION WRITING

Most subjective writing in a school publication comes from its staff members, but not always. Part of being a responsible public forum (see Chapter 13) is allowing the readers that you serve to share their opinion as well.

TYPE OF OPINION WRITING	INTERNAL	EXTERNAL
Staff editorial	X	
Review	X	
Column	X	
Editorial cartoon	X	
Guest column		X
Letter to the editor		X

These pages should be clearly labeled and also should contain no advertisements. Inclusion of ads on editorial pages presents two problems—first, it might give readers the impression that a certain company or organization has encouraged a certain opinion in the paper and, second, it might wrongly associate a business with an opinion that it does not support. Imagine, for example, that ad for a local church appears on the same page as a column or editorial that discusses teen pregnancy. For these reasons, it's usually best to leave ad content to your remaining objective pages.

But not all opinion writing appears on editorial or op/ed pages. Columns, for example, may show up on sports pages and reviews usually get published on entertainment pages. These opinion pieces on non-opinion pages, though, should be clearly labeled as opinion pieces. In the case of columns, you can often identify them as columns because of the column logo that accompanies it — a stylized byline that usually includes a picture of the person who wrote the column.

Writing from Outside

While most opinion writing is done internally, occasionally publications include information from outside sources. And it is this ability to include the opinions of others that can make your publication a true public forum.

The first type of external writing is the guest column. Occasionally you'll want to include some sort of expert opinion on an issue or event, but you'll have no one on staff who is qualified to write it. Case in point: a reporter of mine wrote a draft of a column on the history of the Black Panthers and that group's significance on the civil rights movement. The problems with

the column were that the student wasn't even alive when the Black Panthers rose to prominence and the student wasn't even black. In that case, we didn't run the column, but if the editors had felt strongly enough about it, I would have suggested that they find a local teacher or community member who had some ties to the Black Panthers and ask that person to write the column. Contrast that to a separate occasion when a student on staff wrote a column to accompany a story about gender equity and women's role in today's society. In that case, though, the student also happened to be the president of our local student group Student Advocates of Gender Equity (SAGE); so, unlike the student who wrote about the Black Panthers, she was qualified to write the piece.

Finally, no discussion of opinion writing would be complete without acknowledging letters to the editor. You can often tell the mark of a well-read publication by the number and quality of letters to the editor in it, particularly if those letters respond to the content of the stories you write. If the goal of presenting objective news is to give readers something to think about, then letters from those readers actually advancing those themes is exactly what you want. Those types of letters show that readers are actually reading the stories that you print, and they feel strongly enough about those stories that they've taken the time to respond.

But keep in mind that any good journalist needs to develop a thick skin in terms of audience. It is rare when a reader tells you that you've done something well. But it is far more common for those readers to tell you when you've done something objectionable. Sometimes readers can even be downright mean. But don't fall into the trap of trying to get into some sort of dialogue with those writers. In other words, don't try to publish a rebuttal to a letter that someone has written against your first article. You're job is to present the issue, not to get in the last word. You are a newspaper, not a message board. In general, it's best to drop the issue after one exchange — you have your opportunity to write the story and the reader has the opportunity to respond. Period.

Summary

Opinion writing is some of the most important writing that you can include in your publication. Some even argue that the most important pieces in any publication are the opinion pieces because they allow publications to exercise their First Amendment rights as public forums. Opinion writing can lend your publication personality and, even more important, can help you to exercise your ability to be a responsible public forum — a true voice of the student readership. But with that power comes responsibility. Remember that what you write reflects on the entire publication. It's easy to lose credibility and trust with a few misguided attempts, but it is far more difficult to gain back that credibility.

STUDY GUIDE

Terms and Concepts

Column — Type of opinion writing where a reporter shares his views on a specific issue or event.

Editorial cartoon — A visual column where a cartoonist shares his opinion through illustrations.

Letter to the editor — A piece of opinion writing that comes from someone not on staff.

Staff editorial — An unbylined article that shares the opinion of the publication staff.

Op/ed — The page "opposite" the editorial page. Note that "op/ed" does not stand for "opinion/editorial."

Review — Type of opinion writing where a reporter shares his views on a particular product, performance or service.

Practice Your Editorial Writing Skills

Using the information you've learned from this chapter, write an editorial about one of the following topics or you may choose your own topic:

> *Lengthening the school year*
> *Weighted grades*
> *Cell phones in school*
> *Dress code*

Conduct relevant research and complete any relevant interviews before you begin. Then determine what opinion you have about that topic and to what audience you want to gear your message. Also, remember to have a clear, behavioral call to action in your editorial.

CHAPTER 15

Yadda, Yadda, Yadda
Staff Planning, Organization, the Web and Beyond

The popular sitcom *Seinfeld* featured an episode where the characters used the phrase "yadda, yadda, yadda" extensively to replace the details in the middle of their stories. The joke was that people kept using "yadda, yadda, yadda" to replace the most important parts of the stories. Like if I told you, "Well, I went to go meet the president at the airport and I got stuck in traffic and — yadda, yadda, yadda — the next thing I know I'm waking up in a Turkish prison in a pool of strawberry Jell-O." Get the idea?

This chapter kind of fits into that "yadda, yadda, yadda" category. The information in here defies categorization in the rest of the book, yet it's too important to be left out. Since this section is titled "Potpourri," this chapter is sort of the "potpourri of potpourri." Here we'll start with a quick look at the basic organizational workings of a scholastic publication — basic ways to plan content and how to build the trust of your readers — and then we'll move beyond, to speculate about scholastic journalism's future and what the media may have in store for you.

Staff Planning and Organization

Henry Ford was well known as one of the pioneers of the manufacturing assembly line. As the founder and president of Ford Motor Co., he created a method of producing cars (mostly Model T's) that was quick and efficient and, more importantly, kept costs down.

For years, journalists used to use this same method when producing papers. First, a reporter would write a story. Then, a photographer would be assigned to take some photos to accompany that story that may or may not be related to the point of the article. Finally, the reporter and photographer would submit their work to a waiting designer who would then attempt to combine their work — like a puzzle with no solution — onto a blank page in some semblance of order. Usually, in this method, the designers were under the most deadline pressure, since they were the last people in the assembly line and they had to wait until material was submitted before they could actually do their work.

We don't use this method anymore — or, at least, we shouldn't. See, Henry Ford is pretty well known for telling consumers that they could have a Model T in "any color they want, as long as it's black," meaning that the cars he produced, while efficient and cost effective, were also all the same. But the news is not the same. And it shouldn't be treated in the planning stage as if it is.

Nearly two decades ago, publications started a new, radical form of staff planning and organization called the "maestro" method. Like a maestro in front of an orchestra who coordinates the different musicians so that they can all play a cohesive piece of music, **the maestro method is an organizational method that coordinates all of the different stakeholders in a story or page or section of the publication.** Those stakeholders include reporters, photographers, designers and editors.

The concept behind the maestro is simple — everyone who is part of a particular story or package should have an equal say in that package's creation. Even better, the maestro method ensures that everyone who is creating something for that story — from the reporter who's writing it to the photographer who's shooting pictures for it to the designer who is creating some alternative coverage to accompany it — understands the basic point of the piece — what they want readers to think about — and can use their particular skill to enhance that point. What the maestro prevents is that last-minute, assembly-line process where the poor designer is left in the lurch at the end. In addition, the maestro method reinforces good communication among staff members with different skill sets. In the old days, photographers, for example, seemed to be alienated from the rest of staff. They would receive assignment sheets in their mailboxes and they would submit those photos in some other impersonal way. It's no wonder that many staffs had (or still have) several bitter looking photographers on their rosters.

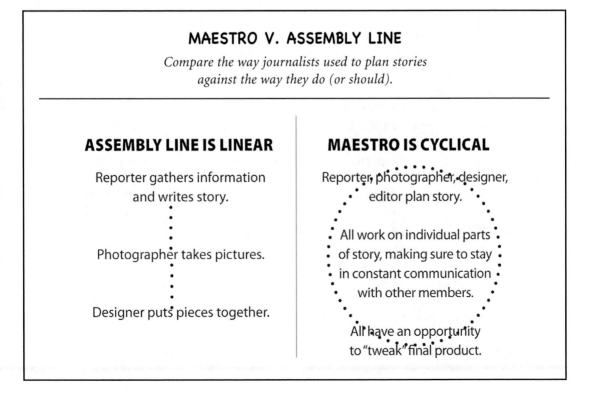

MAESTRO V. ASSEMBLY LINE

Compare the way journalists used to plan stories against the way they do (or should).

ASSEMBLY LINE IS LINEAR

Reporter gathers information and writes story.

Photographer takes pictures.

Designer puts pieces together.

MAESTRO IS CYCLICAL

Reporter, photographer, designer, editor plan story.

All work on individual parts of story, making sure to stay in constant communication with other members.

All have an opportunity to "tweak" final product.

THE FOUR C'S OF MAESTRO

*One way to remember the planning method
is with this handy mnemonic device.*

Conception

The initial planning phase when a reporter, photographer, designer and editor sit down to come up with packaging ideas.

Collection

The process of gathering data for the various parts of the package. This includes getting observations, interviews and research, taking photos and completing preliminary designs.

Construction

The act of placing the individual parts of the process (the photos, the story, the alternative coverage) on the page.

Correction

Happens before a publication goes to press. Everyone involved in the maestro should have an opportunity to complete final edits and to tweak the final design.

The key to a successful maestro is communication, and the first stage in that communication process is the initial meeting. In a maestro meeting, those who will be working directly with the story should sit down together before any story has been written and before any photos have been taken to plan out the story. And that discussion should begin with the following question: What do we want our readers to think about? Once you have determined that point, the rest of the maestro should go more smoothly. The reporter can discuss who he plans to talk to and why. The photographer, hearing what the reporter has said, can offer some photographic suggestions that will further enhance the story that the reporter is writing. The designer, meanwhile, can take those ideas and complete some rough sketches of designs to show how those elements might all work together. The designer might also suggest some alternative coverage ideas that would make the page more visually appealing.

When this process—which can take anywhere from five minutes to an hour—is complete, all of the different staff members can go off and start completing their assignments—get this—at the same time. The reporter (who may now even be accompanied by the photographer) can start compiling information for the story. He knows, too, how long the story should be to fit the design. The photographer can go off and start taking photos, and he knows what types of photos to get. From the reporter he has learned what "faces" are in the story. And from the designer he has learned about the photos he plans to use on the page—whether they're horizontal or vertical and what direction they should face. The designer, even with no photos or story, can actually sit down at the computer and begin designing the page, knowing that, soon, the reporter and photographer will submit their material to fill in the blanks.

Sounds easy, right? Well, it is—or, at least, it can be. As I've said, the key to a successful maestro is communication. And

MAESTRO IN ACTION

Like the leader of a group of musicians, the maestro in journalism works to ensure that the elements on a page are closely related to the angle of the stories on it; the elements (and those who create them) work together to make a unified, coherent package that readers will appreciate.

This is a pretty typical example of a maestro sheet. The key component is not the format but the fact that all of the people involved with creating this story are involved in the process.

Notice how the sheet allows separate places for story ideas, photo ideas, alternative coverage ideas and design ideas. Also look at how the point of the story (the angle) is clearly labeled for all to see.

During the information gathering process, it's important that the different members of this team stay in close contact to make sure elements don't change. If they do, then the maestro team will need to reassemble to make sure everyone knows how to proceed.

White: Reporter Yellow: Photog Pink: File Gold: Editor   Editor *Jane*

Assignment Sheet

Issue Date _3/31_
Maestro Date _3/3_

	Name	Deadlines
Writer	*Peter*	
Photog	*Evan*	
Artist		

Story

Number of words: _800_

Story idea with angle _What are students' First Amendment rights to free speech + expression?_

Important questions to answer for readers _What rights do kids have? Who determines what is/is not acceptable here?_

Info needed for alt. coverage _Impt. court cases involving students' First Amendment rights_

Sources

Names / Phone number, etc.

Alex Liederbach (blue hair spikes)
David Day – school attorney
Liederbach's teacher – the one who sent him down

Photo placement/direction on page

Nameplate

Photo/Art

Dominate description _Profile of Liederbach's head w/ blue spikes in his hair_

Secondary description _Liederbach in class w/ other students (put on jump page)_

A SAMPLE SOURCE QUESTIONNAIRE

Use this form as a guideline for your own staff as a way to ensure that the information included in your stories is accurate and keep your credibility high. Note that the story the questionnaire refers to should be attached to the form.

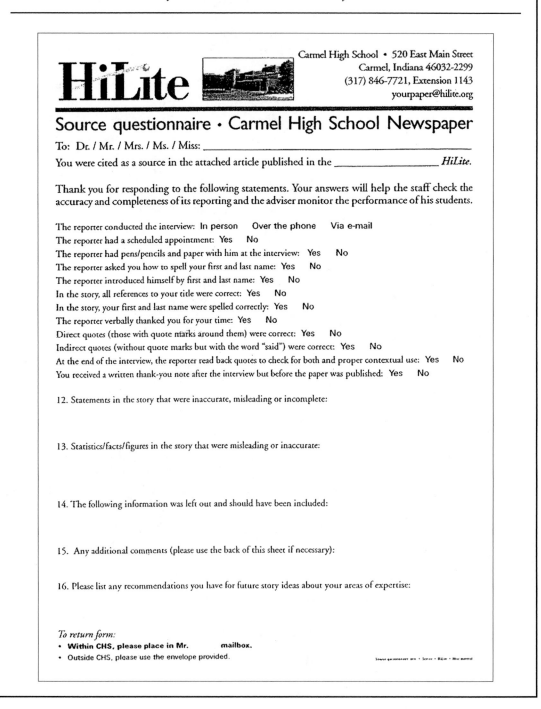

HiLite

Carmel High School • 520 East Main Street
Carmel, Indiana 46032-2299
(317) 846-7721, Extension 1143
yourpaper@hilite.org

Source questionnaire · Carmel High School Newspaper

To: Dr. / Mr. / Mrs. / Ms. / Miss: _____

You were cited as a source in the attached article published in the _____ *HiLite.*

Thank you for responding to the following statements. Your answers will help the staff check the accuracy and completeness of its reporting and the adviser monitor the performance of his students.

The reporter conducted the interview: In person   Over the phone   Via e-mail

The reporter had a scheduled appointment: Yes   No

The reporter had pens/pencils and paper with him at the interview: Yes   No

The reporter asked you how to spell your first and last name: Yes   No

The reporter introduced himself by first and last name: Yes   No

In the story, all references to your title were correct: Yes   No

In the story, your first and last name were spelled correctly: Yes   No

The reporter verbally thanked you for your time: Yes   No

Direct quotes (those with quote marks around them) were correct: Yes   No

Indirect quotes (without quote marks but with the word "said") were correct: Yes   No

At the end of the interview, the reporter read back quotes to check for both and proper contextual use: Yes   No

You received a written thank-you note after the interview but before the paper was published: Yes   No

12. Statements in the story that were inaccurate, misleading or incomplete:

13. Statistics/facts/figures in the story that were misleading or inaccurate:

14. The following information was left out and should have been included:

15. Any additional comments (please use the back of this sheet if necessary):

16. Please list any recommendations you have for future story ideas about your areas of expertise:

To return form:
• **Within CHS, please place in Mr.**   **mailbox.**
• Outside CHS, please use the envelope provided.

this is where some maestro teams fall a bit short. See, the news sometimes changes. Maybe a source wasn't available. Or maybe the light wasn't right for a particular photo. Or maybe a better photo presented itself. Hey, that's life in the world of journalism. What you need to do, though, is stay in close contact with your maestro team. As things change, as they often do, the rest of the maestro team should be kept in the loop so that they can make adjustments accordingly. But that flexibility is both necessary and important. If done well, staffs that use the maestro method have readers that consistently and effectively enjoy much better publications, publications that, ultimately, meet those readers' needs much better than publications that do not utilize the planning method.

Building Credibility and Trust

Before we move away from the publication itself, we have one more thing to discuss—credibility and, more importantly, how to keep it. In the world of journalism, credibility is all you have. If you strive to be as accurate as you can, you become more credible. Ultimately, this credibility leads to something even more important — trust. If your readers trust the information that you provide, then you're doing a tremendous service for them. And if you lose that trust? It's difficult, if not impossible, to get it back.

We've already discussed ways to establish credibility within the publication itself. Using consistent style, for example, builds credibility. If you can't spell correctly, why should your readers trust that the information you've presented is credible? Attributing information to relevant, credible sources also establishes credibility. But what about other, less visible methods

of building credibility and, eventually, trust?

Certainly the way you conduct yourself on a day-to-day basis is a start. Members of a school publication should always remember that they are representatives of that publication. The way they dress and act outside of the newspaper room should comply with the standards you set in the classroom. But outside of that, there are other methods of building credibility and trust.

The first of these methods is the source questionnaire. **A source questionnaire is a survey that you can send to the people that are given attribution in your stories.** It doesn't have to be long but it should ask a few pertinent questions. First, it should ask if all of the information attributed to the source is accurate. In addition, it should ask for corrections to any inaccurate information.

The source questionnaire serves two purposes. First, it keeps your staff members honest. If reporters and editors know that source questionnaires will be sent out after every issue of the paper, it gives those people added incentive to be as thorough and accurate as possible. It's no surprise that the work you do on a publication is meant for and read by a wide audience. The source questionnaire serves as a tangible reminder of that audience each time you publish an issue.

The second purpose of the source questionnaire is perhaps even more important — it lets sources know that you care about accuracy. Of course you should try to be as accurate as you can be, but even the best publications make mistakes sometimes. By submitting source questionnaires, you take a proactive (as opposed to reactive) approach to correcting any errors in your stories. This attention to your product gives the tangible impression to your sources that you are doing your best to be as accurate as possible. It gives them an opportunity to respond, and, even when their responses are favorable (which, you should hope, is most of the time), you will have built your publication's credibility.

In addition to source questionnaires, a second method to establish credibility and trust is the use of thank-you cards. Every source you interview for stories should receive a professionally written thank-you (see "Saying Thank You"). Most staffs even have these cards and envelopes preprinted and ready to use, but if yours doesn't, you can still write your own thank-yous. Use of the thank-you card shouldn't be too much of a surprise. After all, you're probably used to writing them if your mom, like mine did, makes you sit down after Christmas every year to write them for your Aunt Diane who sent you those wonderful purple socks and your Grandma Ruth who got you that T-shirt that's three sizes too small.

It's amazing how far a simple "thank you" can go. While most people don't keep them, they will remember that they received them, and that kind of positive attitude will do wonders in terms of your readers' perceptions of your publication and its professionalism.

Finally, while you hope it never happens, occasionally your paper may make some mistakes. Perhaps you misspelled a name in a story. Or maybe you misidentified someone. Possibly you got your facts a little mixed up. When this happens (and it will happen), you should have a place in your publication to print corrections and apologies. This should appear in the same place each issue so readers can find it easily. While you may catch some of these errors yourself, chances are you'll get more of them from the source questionnaires mentioned above.

It seems a bit like an oxymoron, but a good way to maintain credibility is to fully disclose your errors to your readers. Believe it or not, it is this honesty that will

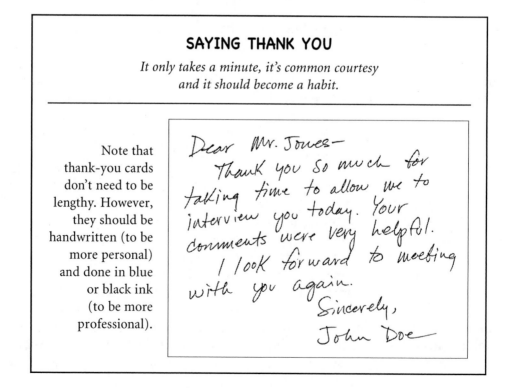

SAYING THANK YOU

It only takes a minute, it's common courtesy and it should become a habit.

Note that thank-you cards don't need to be lengthy. However, they should be handwritten (to be more personal) and done in blue or black ink (to be more professional).

> Dear Mr. Jones—
> Thank you so much for taking time to allow me to interview you today. Your comments were very helpful. I look forward to meeting with you again.
> Sincerely,
> John Doe

speak volumes to them. By printing these corrections, you publicly acknowledge your errors and correct them, and, in the interim, you let your readers know through your actions that you continue to strive to be as accurate as possible.

Printing timely corrections and apologies can help in the event of legal problems, too. For example, if someone claims he has been libeled by a story that you've written (see Chapter 13) and you have already printed a correction and an apology, that person can only sue for compensatory damages. Compensatory damages (also called "actual damages") consist of actual money that the person has lost due to the story's printing. A correction and apology prevents the person for suing for punitive damages—money awarded to punish the publication. And since punitive damages can be far larger than compensatory damages, it's a good idea to catch mistakes and share them with readers before more problems arise.

The Future of Journalism

OK. I'm no Nostradamus, but in this section we can speculate as to what may be the future of storytelling. And one thing we can say with almost absolute certainty—the newspaper will not completely disappear.

Since the advent of the computer, people have said that the print version of the newspaper would go the way of the dinosaur and people would, instead, receive their news electronically via the Internet. But while online news has become more commonplace, print publications still exist. And I think there are a couple of reasons for this.

First, there's still the portability issue. Newspapers, like books, are "a uniquely portable magic," as Stephen King says in his book *On Writing: A Memoir of the Craft*. They're easy to fold up and put in a bag to be looked at later, at your desk or in your easy chair or on the subway. Of course, some publications, like the *Chicago Tribune*, are working on new technologies that would enable readers to purchase a sort of electronic news page—about as big as a regular sheet of paper—that would receive electronic signals and would have access to both audio and video feeds. Those ideas are still in the works, though, and have yet to be released into the mainstream.

Second, I think readers will continue to purchase and use newspapers because those newspapers do a good job of prioritizing the news. As we have already discussed in this book, most of your readers are pressed for time anyway. They don't have much time in the first place to read the paper, let alone decide which stories are more important than others. Newspapers, by the simple fact that they present information using a definite hierarchy, essentially do the hard work for readers. In their content, not only do newspapers provide a blend of local, national and international news and features, they also prioritize that information by putting some of it on the top of Page 1 and some of it on the bottom of Page 17.

And the byproduct of that prioritization and the fact that readers don't have a lot of time raises the third reason why newspapers will still exist—they have a definite ending point. The online universe never ends. If you're a prolific surfer, you know that you can be on a site which has a link to another site which has another link and another and so on and so on to infinity. You could spend your entire life surfing the Internet and never reach the end of it. But newspapers do have an end. In roughly 20 or 30 minutes, you can read the content of a daily or weekly publication and, when you're finished, feel pretty confident that you've gotten all of the information that you need to know. And for a time-pressed society, that's a pretty important feeling to have.

But the assumption that print publications won't disappear (at least not in the near future) does not mean that those publications aren't changing. Much of this book, in fact, has discussed how readers are becoming more visual and how print publications are changing to meet the "reads of their needers." But outside of those obvious physical changes, some exciting changes are happening behind the scenes, too.

One new concept is called "convergence." Convergence is a cooperative blending of print and broadcast media to tell stories. In the past, print publications and broadcast media (TV and radio) were in competition with one another, each trying to "outscoop" the others. But today, professional storytellers have realized that, rather than compete, these media should work together to better tell stories. Television, for example, does a wonderful job of getting information out quickly, but it falls short in terms of providing background and details that are equally important to the story. That's where print publications come in.

Some professional media outlets are even using convergence today. Perhaps you've seen a newscast on CNN where the host will go live to the newsroom where a reporter from, say, *The Washington Post* is standing by, reporting on the latest developments from the White House. Or maybe you've seen an editor from your local newspaper on the evening news telling folks that they can get more information about a particular story in the next day's issue of the paper.

In fact, some newsrooms are even being set up differently to facilitate con-

vergence. Some major journalism colleges now feature "convergence classrooms" that have banks of computers on one side of the room to write and design print pages while a mini "studio" sits at the other side of the room with a camera and microphone for those same reporters to use to go on air.

The point is, certain types of media tell certain types of stories better than others. What we're seeing now (and will see in the future) is further definition among these different media as they carve out their specific niches in the market.

In fact, while the Web will not fully replace print publications, more and more media outlets (including scholastic publications) are discovering how the Internet can provide a valuable extension of the products that they already provide. In the case of newspapers, web sites can serve a very specific role.

First, web sites can be updated on demand. This works great in the event of breaking news. As we discussed in Chapter 6, the inverted pyramid is dead in the world of print scholastic journalism, where publications come out every two weeks, every month or even less. Not so with the Internet, which can be updated every minute, if need be.

Second, Web sites working in conjunction with print publications can provide wonderful extensions of the material that is included in the paper itself. This could be additional coverage, more photos or links to gain more information, because, while the pages you have available in print are finite, the possibilities on the Web are much more limitless.

Finally, Web sites give readers a better opportunity to interact with your publication. Perhaps there's a link online that allows readers to respond in a safe public forum. Or perhaps your site includes video of the upcoming school play or audio of the student council candidate speeches.

And what about surveys and polls? The list goes on and on.

Summary

The bottom line is that, while journalism is changing, some things will never change. People will always have a need to hear and tell stories, and they will need someone — a professional storyteller, a journalist — to record those stories and share them with the masses. Since the dawn of time, man has shared stories, and that desire to share has never wavered. Carl the Caveman was the first storyteller, and certainly the methods of storytelling have changed as technology and audiences have changed. But the basic premise or storytelling has never wavered.

Who knows what the future of journalism will bring? Only time will tell. Maybe someday you'll be a professional storyteller — the Carl the Caveman of your day.

And perhaps someday, someone will be telling your story.

Only time will tell.

STUDY GUIDE

Terms and Concepts

Maestro — An organizational method that coordinates all of the different stakeholders in a story or page or section of the publication. Stakeholders include writers, photographers, designers and editors.

Source questionnaire — A survey that journalists can send to sources after a story is published to ensure that information is accurate.

Check Out the Future of Journalism Today

Get onto the Internet and spend some time perusing various newspapers' web sites. See how they're incorporating additional elements to make their site true extensions of their print publications rather than just mirrors of them.

You may also look at the different design problems that arise when designing for the Web as opposed to designing for print. What considerations should you keep in mind when designing in these different modes?

Finally, spend a bit of time looking at "popular" web sites — sites that a majority of your student population find interesting. What is it about these sites that is so intriguing? Is it the way they're designed? The content? The way that content is presented? How could you incorporate those ideas to your own publication?

Index

224 Index